ON APPEAL

ON APPEAL

Courts, Lawyering, and Judging

FRANK M. COFFIN

Illustrations by Douglas M. Coffin

W · W · NORTON & COMPANY
New York   London

Printed in the United States of America

First Edition

The text of this book is composed in Trump Mediaeval,
with the display set in Trump Mediaeval.
Composition by Crane Typesetting Service, Inc.
Manufacturing by The Courier Companies, Inc.
Book design by Jacques Chazaud.

Library of Congress Cataloging-in-Publication Data

Coffin, Frank Morey.
    On appeal : courts, lawyering, and judging / Frank M. Coffin.
        p.   cm.
    Includes index.
    1. Appellate courts—United States.   2. Appellate procedure—
United States.   3. Judicial process—United States.   4. Lawyers—
United States.   I. Title.
KF8750.C625   1994
347.73′8—dc20
[347.3078]   93-14459

ISBN 0-393-03582-4

W. W. Norton & Company, Inc., 500 Fifth Avenue, New York, N.Y. 10110
W. W. Norton & Company Ltd., 10 Coptic Street, London WC1A 1PU

1   2   3   4   5   6   7   8   9   0

To

those who have contributed so much
to my life and work as a judge—
my secretaries, my law clerks,
and my colleagues.

Contents

11. Opinions III:
The Workings of Collegiality   213

Prologue

Before the play begins, a few words may help to set the stage. The reader ought to know something about where this book is coming from, what it seeks to cover, and how various kinds of readers can be served by it.

I. The Author's Lenses

The pages of this book contain the reflections of the author about the institution of the appellate court, those who people it—lawyers and judges—and those whom it serves. The reflections are filtered through two lenses. The first, the lens of experience on the appellate bench, focuses on what goes on during the arguing and deciding of appeals. It is process-oriented. This is a summing-up of the thoughts and insights of nearly three decades of observing lawyers and working with judges.

A second lens is the author's total service in the three branches of the federal government—as a member of Congress, as a deputy administrator of the Agency for International Development, and as a circuit judge. The focus through this lens is a broad one, institution-oriented. It looks at our system of appellate justice—at its basic values and its place among competing systems, at the original concept of state and federal courts as coequal parts of a whole, and at the threats to the continued health and independence of these courts. This is a summing-up of thoughts and concepts of concern to all citizens—students, lawyers, judges, journalists, and laymen.

II. A Word to the Audiences

The two lenses provide a sharp image of interdependence among all participants in and beneficiaries of our appellate justice system. The practitioner needs an understanding and conscientious judge; the judge needs a competent and cooperative lawyer; both need the support of knowledgeable and concerned citizens; and such a citizenry in sufficient numbers will not likely emerge unless the colleges and universities instill in their students—and journalists instill in their readers and viewers—the basis for a critical evaluation, appreciation, and support.

Having said all this, I still have a separate message for each of the reader groups.

A. To the Lay Citizen—in and out of College

Here I address both undergraduate students majoring in pre-law studies and political science and citizens of all ages. Citizens should have not only a general understanding of our system but also some deeper insight into what lawyers and judges do in presenting and deciding cases on appeal. In the long run the citizenry's perception of what lawyers and judges should and should not be expected to do will shape the course of the institution. It is of critical importance that the perception be an informed one.

Wholly apart from this observation, a more fundamental point should be made, even at the risk of saying the obvious. It took the gentle reminder of a friend to make me realize that everything I shall say between these covers is based on the assumption that appeals are a vital part of a civilized justice system. This assumption is not shared by everyone. Today there is widespread unhappiness over the costs and delays of litigation, ever-expanding caseloads, and particularly perhaps over the occasional granting of a new trial to a convicted criminal because of a "technicality"—which usually means extending a constitutional right to someone who we think does not deserve it. So it would not be surprising if the idea of doing away with, or at least cutting back on, appeals had for many a seductive attraction.

Is the right of appeal merely a luxury afforded by an affluent, postindustrial society? In the Appendix I have sketched "The Appellate Idea in History," an outline of the efforts of the world's civilizations from ancient times to respond to the urge to take one's case to "a higher court" for a second chance at obtaining justice. Most civilizations have found a mechanism for some kind of appeal. But even in recent times some countries have done without it. Appeal in the former Soviet Union was often tainted and made meaningless by a phone call from the all-powerful prosecutor to the judge ("telephone justice"). The citizen was completely at the mercy of one judge, who could be pressured, biased, incompetent, lazy, or tyrannical.

Even in a more "civilized" society, the absence of any right to appeal would make a mockery of justice. The non-lawyer reader will sense the infinite possibilities of unfairness latent in a trial conducted by, before, and between human beings—a judge getting a critical fact wrong, or drawing an improper inference; a judge cutting off a party too quickly in her pre-trial discovery or cross-examination; an incompetent or ill lawyer; a judge failing to read the most relevant case law; or a jury inflamed by passion or prejudice. If a losing party had no right of appeal, a judge or jury would be free from any restraint. This is why the right to appeal can be called the linchpin of justice. Just as a linchpin keeps a wheel from slipping off a shaft, the opportunity to appeal keeps decision-making by agencies, judges, and juries within reasonable bounds.

B. To the Law Student and Practitioner

I have not tried to be encyclopedic in giving my reflections on what is good and bad written and oral argument, but I have tried to point out some of the potholes awaiting the unwary and to assemble as useful a collection of insights from my own experience as I could. Beyond this I have tried to probe and reveal my own behavior as a judge, because I believe that the more lawyers understand how judges think and react, the better advocates they will become—just as the thoughts of a fish might be of interest to a fisherman. And I have devoted some space to the institution of the judiciary, state and federal, because of my feeling that its continuing independence and vitality must have a higher priority for the coming generations of lawyers.

But there is a separate question lawyers and law students might ask: why should a lawyer or law student who does not expect to do much or any appellate litigation be interested in this subject?

There are several good reasons why "the compleat attorney" should develop a feel for the appellate process. It supports a lawyer in many ways—in advising a client on a course of action or in evaluating a possible lawsuit or defense to one; in evaluating a case for settlement; in preparing for and engaging in trial; in arriving at a sound decision on taking an appeal; and in counseling colleagues on appellate matters.

Finally, as one lawyer friend once confessed to me, the opportunity to brief and argue an appeal is a "luxury." It is functioning at the summit to practice one's craft and continue a rich tradition challenging the intellect, and testing preparation, insight, and performance before an audience of informed and attentive judges—and peers—whose favorable evaluation is a pearl of great price.

C. To Judges

I recognize full well that all appellate judges have their own approaches to and burnished wisdom about reading briefs, hearing oral argument, conferencing, doing research, working with law clerks, writing opinions, and dealing with their colleagues. My hope is that what I say in this book will stimulate my fellow judges to contribute their own thoughts to the profession at large. For I am a great believer in the efficacy of judges helping one another by narrating their own experience and revealing their own insights. I also think that judges should look at the problems and restraints of time and space affecting appellate advocates. Judges should never forget that once they were lawyers.

Beyond these thoughts, I have a special aspiration—that this book will prompt judges to think about what is essential to the kind of appellate review we cherish. For we live in a time when many changes are being proposed for both federal and state appellate courts. We shall do well to distinguish those changes which reinforce the essence and those which threaten to dilute or eviscerate it. My conviction is that judges must, consistent with the dignity and independence of their office, firmly take the lead in thinking about our state-federal court system and the steps to be taken to preserve and strengthen it.

D. To Journalists

I save a final word for those who, through the media of printed and spoken words, have so much to do with the levels of understanding and commitment of the people of this land. If journalists can see beneath the surface of appellate decision-making, can develop a feeling for the basic values, roles, and standards of the appellate system, and can acquire a discriminating capacity to assess the quality of courts and judges, their readers' appraisal and support will be more informed and effective. There is a profound relationship between a free press and a healthy system of justice. Well-informed journalists can do much to resensitize the nation to the essential needs of state and federal courts.

Acknowledgments

Like one filing a petition in bankruptcy, but with a much cheerier attitude, I gratefully acknowledge my debts.

First come my colleagues on the United States Court of Appeals for the First Circuit. They have taught—and are still teaching—me most of what I think I know.

More immediately involved have been my day-to-day collaborators. My computer-wise secretary, Gail Rice, has graciously given her healing touch to the open-ended task of amending my manuscript. My invaluable career law clerk, Barbara Riegelhaupt, has been a steady source of sage judgment. My Governance Institute colleague Robert Katzmann has been a fount of fruitful insights. And my graphic artist-designer son Douglas has made this solemn book smile with his pertinent (or impertinent) drawings.

Providing expert advice on special chapters were Professor L. Kinvin Wroth of the University of Maine Law School (Chapter 2), Justice John M. Greaney, Associate Justice of the Supreme Judicial Court of Massachusetts (Chapter 3), and my former law clerk Laura Kaster, Esq., partner of the Chicago law firm Jenner and Block (Chapter 5).

I also wish to express my appreciation to our First Circuit Court Librarian, Karen Moss, and her staff for bird-dogging hard-to-find books and articles.

Finally, my editor, Donald W. Fusting, has provided just the right combination of support and critical nudging.

ON APPEAL

1

A Day in Court

Before we begin our tracing of the justice subsystem we call the appellate process, I invite the reader for a quick preview, a visit to an appellate courtroom, in this instance that of a federal court of appeal. Here, viewing a day's worth of oral arguments, you will see only a small segment of the process, but that segment contains clues to almost everything we later encounter.

Perhaps the most difficult problem in visiting an appellate courtroom is finding it. It is not the court frequented by most people. Not the bustling, noisy, chaotic big-city municipal court, whose corridors are overflowing with alleged felons or misdemeanants, unhappy couples, creditors, debtors, police, bondsmen, lawyers, social workers, clerks, and an occasional harried judge. Nor is it the more measured and stately court of general jurisdiction where jury trials are held—the state superior courts and the federal district courts. Here the crush is not so visibly pressing; trials are held with order and dignity. These are the courts that most often make headline news.

Pass these by. Your destination may be a separate building, far removed from the throng of litigants and the press. Or you may merely have to ascend the elevator to what looks like an ivory tower loftily looking down on human frailty. Here the corridors are dim and quiet. A few clerks carry files and papers with decorous tread. Their steps echo.

A swinging door gives entry into a chamber as high as it is wide and deep, paneled in rich walnut or gleaming mahogany. On the walls are portraits of the worthies who have served this court for a century or more. Those dating from the last century seem terribly important, striking ponderous Roman poses, standing by elaborate Corinthian columns, or enthroned in large chairs and fingering volumes of threatening proportions. The portraits from midcentury on, though still featuring black robes, have more lightness, informality, color, and even occasional smiles. You spend several minutes trying to penetrate their psyches and wondering whether, when, and why they laughed, cried, cursed, and showed other human emotion.

The centerpiece of the chamber, the judges' bench, looms well above the floor and spans most of the width of the room. Its facade boasting elegant carving, it awaits its occupants expectantly. Below it is the desk of the clerk of courts where mysterious entries are made in a huge docket book. And in front of that is the lawyers' lectern, soon to hide advocates' nervous hands from the stern scrutiny of the judges. Attached are a clock, warning lights, and a microphone connected with a tape recorder.

Clusters of chairs to the right and left of the clerk's desk and the lectern are reserved for law clerks. Beyond the lectern, proceeding toward the rear of the courtroom, are two tables for counsel, and beyond them a row of chairs "inside the bar" for other lawyers. Behind the barrier are seats for the audience. Not many, for this kind of courtroom is seldom the object of much attention. On a typical day there might be twenty-five to thirty people, including a dozen lawyers to argue six cases, a few of their clients, a scattering of students, and some perennial "court watchers," to whom an appellate argument is better than a B movie.

On occasion the pulse quickens. If an important insurance, antitrust, or environmental case is to be argued, or a First

Amendment case affecting the press or a civil rights case involving a highly charged issue such as abortion or prayer in public schools, or if a renowned gladiator or local law professor is to argue, the advocate's admirers, interested attorneys, representatives of industry, and the media can fill the courtroom to standing room only.

Today, however, is routine. There is a choice of seats. As the witching hour approaches, clerks bring in boxes of files. Young men and women with notebooks, the judges' law clerks, take their seats. The bailiff–court crier pours water into glasses on the bench. A group of new lawyers who are to be admitted to practice exchange small talk. The lawyers who are scheduled to argue gossip and speculate about what judges will hear their cases. Then the court crier gives the traditional "cry": "All rise, please. The Honorable United States Court of Appeals for the First Circuit is now in session. All persons having anything to do before this Honorable Court may draw near, give their attendance, and they shall be heard. God save the United States and this Honorable Court. The Court is in session. You may be seated."

You are then treated to an unusual spectacle—the picture of some seven judges filing in. This would not be unusual in a state supreme court, which usually sits in plenary session with five, seven, or more justices present. But a federal court of appeals sits in panels of three judges, excepting only when it sits *en banc*, that is, the entire bench—when a panel's decision is deemed so important or controversial that all of its judges participate in rehearing the case. The first case today is such a case. In most federal courts of appeal the sight would be even more spectacular; *en banc* sessions of fifteen or more judges resemble a small legislature more than a court.

You listen intently, straining a bit to hear, as the first lawyer begins. He represents a dyslexic medical student who is complaining that he has been dismissed from medical school in violation of a federal law giving certain protection to the handicapped. The school's action was prompted by the student's poor showing in taking written multiple-choice examinations. The student, who now is called "appellant," claims that the school, under the Rehabilitation Act of 1973, was obligated to make a good-faith effort to see whether other means of testing him would be feasible. The school counters with statements of its dean that its judgment is that there is no such alternative. The trial judge ruled on the basis of the pleadings and the school's affidavit that appellant could not make out a case and entered what is called a "summary judgment" for the school. This meant a quick end to the plaintiff's case, with no chance to present it to a jury. A panel of three appellate judges has reversed, holding that the dean's statements were conclusory and did not establish that there were no other reasonable testing methods. But enough other judges have questioned this decision to obtain this rehearing.

It is easy to see why the court has called for this full-scale *en banc* argument. Some judges are clearly in sympathy with the gutsy dyslexic student, who worked hard to reach this point in his medical education, and they feel that the federal statute puts on the school an obligation to explore other alternatives. Some judges feel that the school has already gone beyond the call of duty in extending scholarship aid and tutorial assistance. Some stress the technical legal point that whatever the final result might be, the trial judge should not have foreclosed the student at this early stage of the case. And some judges feel that a basic issue of academic freedom is involved. In fact, the judges have thought so much about the case and are so primed for argument with one another that the lawyers have a difficult time making their arguments.

The *en banc* case takes about forty minutes. The courtroom clears and a panel of three judges returns to hear the rest of the morning's cases. A towering stack of briefs and court records is at each judge's place. The remaining five cases are allowed only fifteen minutes a side. The pressure of time is obvious. The lawyers somehow have to distill all their research and argument into the short time allotted . . . and share it with frequently voluble and inquisitive judges.

The next case is an appeal arising from a criminal conviction for possessing cocaine with the intent to distribute it.

At first, the defendant-appellant's lawyer seems to make a strong argument that the trial judge made a serious legal mistake in instructing, or charging, the jury. Later, the young assistant United States attorney first reminds the judges that they are confined to the record of the testimony, objections, arguments, and rulings at trial. Then she ticks off her litany of responses: during the original trial, there was no request by the defendant's attorney that the judge charge any differently and no objection to the charge; even if there had been an objection, the charge was correct; even if it had been erroneous, the charge as a whole was fair and any error was harmless. When appellant's counsel begins a rebuttal, the judges ask only one question: "Did you object after the judge gave his charge?" The answer, "Your Honor, I was appointed to represent the defendant on appeal; I didn't try the case below," does not seem to impress the court.

The next case takes on interest. You have noticed a number of fairly senior-looking lawyers file in and take seats, and soon understand why. They represent insurance companies, and this case is important to them. They consider the district judge's ruling below a red warning flag for their industry. A small New England factory had been discharging toxic wastes into a river over many years. Both the state and federal governments had prosecuted the polluter and recovered very substantial damages. Now the company sought to cash in on its liability insurance policy. It faced an obvious hurdle: the policy excluded pollution from coverage. But the company felt it could surmount the hurdle because there was an exception to the exclusion: there would be coverage if the pollution was both "sudden" and "accidental." And it convinced the trial court that flooding from a violent rainstorm of rare intensity fifteen years earlier was just such an event. Now the insurance company, and many of its competitors, are protesting that such a reading of the policy would in effect allow a very small tail to wag a very big dog.

But why is this case in federal court? Although the earlier prosecution by the state and federal governments was largely based on federal environmental law, this case is solely based on state law as it guides interpretation of an insurance policy.

This is a "diversity" case, a case between companies that are citizens of different states, a kind of lawsuit that has been permitted to be heard in a federal court ever since the first Congress passed the Judiciary Act of 1789. So even though the manufacturing company brought its suit in a state court, the defendant insurance company, having been incorporated in a different state, is entitled to remove the case to federal court.

The lawyers have a great deal of ground to cover, for many state courts have interpreted similar insurance clauses in somewhat analogous situations. One can sense anxiety after the warning light comes on, flashing the news that time is running out. The court allows each lawyer two additional minutes. Though the lawyers speak with intensity, the subject matter is so technical that the argument is hard to follow.

Your interest picks up as you observe the cast of characters in the next case. For the person at the rostrum is not a lawyer. He is a black former policeman, who is arguing his own case of wrongful discharge *pro se*, "for himself." He is assisted by his more poised and articulate wife. The judges on the bench seem resigned to wasting the next half hour. But as the appellant reads his argument, with dignity, being occasionally prompted by his wife, they begin to lean forward and take interest. The city police department's attorney points to a number of instances where the appellant's performance on the job was criticized. But one of the judges is not satisfied that the evidence was so clear that the district judge should have thrown out the case on summary judgment (as had happened in the dyslexic's case). As he speaks, the other judges, who have been monumentally indifferent, prick up their ears and lean forward. You sense that the judge making the comments is really talking to his fellow judges. Maybe today Goliath is encountering David.

The forenoon is getting along, and you are beginning to feel pangs of hunger. But there are still two cases to be heard. The irreverent thought enters your mind that the judges have taken no break from their sitting for several hours, except for their brief exit after the *en banc* case. You wonder whether one of the less heralded requirements for appellate judges, even elderly ones, is superior bladder control.

The next case is a labor-management case. Unlike the other cases, this is not an appeal from a trial court. It is a petition from a federal agency, the National Labor Relations Board, to enforce its order that a drugstore chain resume collective bargaining with the union which has long represented its employees. The case has arisen out of efforts of some disaffected union members to decertify their union and have an election in which they might choose another union, or none at all. The Labor Board found that the company had made improper statements in the course of efforts to gather signatories to a petition for an election. The company's lawyer makes a powerful argument that her client has a good labor relations record and has done nothing egregious to prejudice the union in this case, and that in any event the evidence that the union no longer commands a majority of the employees is impressive. But the Labor Board attorney reminds the judges of the high degree of deference courts must give Labor Board decisions. You already know something about the deference owed juries and trial judges; deference to an administrative agency is new to you.

Finally, at 12:30 P.M., the court reaches the last case. There is a new twist to this. It is a criminal case, but the government is represented not by an assistant United States attorney but by an assistant attorney general of a state. It is a case from a state court. You soon hear the words "habeas corpus" and gradually understand that when state prisoners seek their liberty because of an alleged violation of the federal Constitution in connection with their state court prosecution, they can apply to a federal district judge to set them free. This he can do by issuing to the institution of incarceration an order bearing this ancient Latin phrase meaning "you have the body," with the implicit command to deliver it to court.

But you quickly learn that before one can open the door to a federal courthouse, one must try all available doors to the state courthouse. While a person convicted of a crime in a federal court may, indeed must, press all issues on appeal, a state prisoner who seeks habeas corpus relief in federal court must not only have raised all issues in state court but have pursued them to the state's court of last resort. In legal parlance, the prisoner must "exhaust" all state remedies before filing a petition for a writ of habeas corpus in federal court. But in this case the prisoner and his attorney have not done that. Moreover, only four of the thirteen issues he argues in his federal brief have been preserved in his original trial. The judges are distinctly unhappy to be dealing with a legally meritless case, and they are further discomfited by the presence in the courtroom, in a semihysterical condition, of the appellant's wife. The appellant has compounded his bad fortune by hiring an incompetent lawyer. With difficulty, the judges restrain themselves from adding insult to injury.

You are somewhat surprised that even this frivolous case is given its half hour of argument time. Still, most of the cases have some merit. And some have been both important and fascinating. The court adjourns until tomorrow morning.

In these few hours an appellate court brought its judges together and was both visible and audible—the only time this happens in public during the entire appellate process. Whether you then sensed it or not, almost all of the basic ingredients of that process were revealed.

To start, the six cases were a fair sample of a federal court of appeals caseload. The morning began with the federal statutory claim under the Rehabilitation Act. Then followed a routine appeal from a federal drug prosecution—a genre which has come to dominate criminal litigation. Later came two staples in the federal appellate diet—a civil rights case and a federal agency enforcement petition. Two cases arose out of our unique federal-state dual court system—the diversity case involving a state's common law interpretation of an insurance policy and a federal habeas corpus review of a state criminal conviction. There was variety in the kinds of attorneys who argued: attorneys from large firms and solo practitioners, federal and state prosecutors, and even one non-lawyer arguing his own case.

Beyond the variety of cases and counsel, you have become aware of the quintessential elements of the appellate process. One is that nothing that is not in the record of the original trial is to be considered. You gradually grasped the idea that when someone is unhappy with a first decision, the target has to stop moving if a reviewing decision is to be fair.

You were also conscious of the fact that there had been a heat-tested decision below by a district judge and/or jury or a federal agency. An impressive amount of time and talent had already been poured into the decision. Such a decision was not lightly to be overruled. This factor explained the solemn meaning given by the judges to the word "deference." But this did not mean abandonment to either trial court or agency; there was still room for discerning abuse of discretion or error of law, and even the possibility of making new law.

While you were not privy to the process, you somehow knew that the judges and their clerks had done something to prepare for oral argument. Otherwise, there would not have been so much questioning, life, and spontaneity on the bench. You realized, in some cases more than others, that some of the questions of the judges and some of the answers of the lawyers seemed to open up new issues, to put the controversy in a light quite different from that at the beginning of the argument. Although you didn't know it at the time, you were given a look at two stages in a prolonged process of decision—the first being the judges' impressions after reading briefs and the second their impressions after hearing oral argument. If the case was simple, perhaps the final decision has already been made. But in a case of any substance and complexity, it is likely that the judges will continue to change their views in some significant respect as they probe the facts and peel off layers of analysis.

Then you saw, at first hand, the play of other forces. This was, obviously, a collegial court. Several distinct and diverging personalities would have to be, eventually, corralled into a consensus. This collective consensus is, after all, the only justification for reviewing another judge's decision. The engine that drove the court was the confrontation of adversaries. Judges relied on the opposing briefs and oral arguments of wily contestants to sense the merits of a case. The written and the spoken words served somewhat different purposes. Each domain is a spacious one, as we shall see.

Perhaps you were not conscious of the extent to which certain conventions and disciplines came into play, but you could not have avoided noticing a few. For example, even though evidence, such as answers of witnesses to questions, is in the record, fairness requires that only if objections to the questions were raised before the trial court—that is, "preserved"—can the appellate court take note of them. In several of the morning's cases, a key question on appeal was whether summary judgment, bringing a case to a sudden end, had been properly granted. The test, a tough one, is whether the party asking for judgment has shown that there was no real issue concerning any significant fact. Another basic ground rule or convention is the depth of deference an appellate court has toward a trial court or an agency. Still another, all too clearly revealed in the last case argued, is the absolute necessity for a state prisoner to exhaust his state remedies before knocking on the federal courthouse door. These, and many more, are reminders that despite an attorney's, judge's, or clerk's own feelings about a litigant or hopes to develop pathfinding law, the game is played by specific rules.

Finally, there is the scene as yet unrevealed, what is yet to come. First of all, a conference takes place that very afternoon in which the judges exchange their views and often decide the case. Then, after they separate and go back to their individual chambers, come the solemn tasks of research, working with their clerks, writing, and circulating opinion drafts to colleagues. Writing is the distinguishing characteristic of an appellate opinion. The very discipline of putting thoughts, value judgments, and reasoning into writing is perhaps one of the most effective guarantees of rationality. Beyond the writing is the collegial exercise of circulation and response. As the draft of an opinion is considered by the other chambers, the authorities checked, the language refined, and questions asked and answered, there emerges a precious final product—a collegial opinion.

In short, the essential elements of this distinctively American appellate process are:

> Reliance on a closed lower court record
> Deferential review of a prior heat-tested decision
> Graduated, sequential decision-making
> Collegial decisions
> Substantial (though not complete) reliance on the oral and written presentations of adversaries
> The restraint of professional conventions and rules
> The discipline of justifying a decision in writing

Your day at appellate court has given you a snapshot of many aspects of appellate practice as it is carried on today in the United States. Although this particular court was a federal one, the basic pattern would apply to a state supreme court, except that a full bench of five, seven, or more justices would be sitting on all the cases, rather than a panel of three. But a solitary snapshot of our present system is not enough for any serious lawyer or judge practitioner within the appellate process. A look at the large album—and other snapshots—is well advised if one is to appreciate our appellate institutions and the values served, and to develop the skills to maneuver within them.

We turn now to a very large snapshot—a panoramic view of the three major appellate systems in the western world today.

2

The Appellate World Today

In this chapter, we look around us to see how contemporary traditions in the modern world determine the nature of appeals. In doing so, we see our own system in perspective. The perspective of the past tells us that ours is not the only way, nor is our system fully "ours." As we shall see, we have borrowed from other traditions in the past, and we continue to borrow—and lend.

Professor Arthur T. von Mehren has identified the uses of the comparative study of legal systems. They are relevant to the readers of this book:

> Comparative study . . . helps us to see our legal system's forest; providing perspective, comparative study helps jurists to understand better law's constraints and law's potentials. Insight into how other legal systems have dealt with particular problems not only stimulates the jurist's imagination but reveals the strengths and weaknesses of particular solutions. Comparative study thus assists legal reforms as well as lawyers' efforts to find creative solutions for problems that arise in legal practice.[1]

We live in an era of unprecedented change in legal systems. The years since World War II have seen new or radically rewritten constitutions in the Third World, Canada, and Western Europe.[2] And since the collapse of communism in Eastern Europe in 1989, what Professor Herman Schwartz calls a "wave of constitution writing" has swept the Balkans and Central Europe.[3] The process of cataclysmic constitutional change continues in the republics that have emerged from the former Soviet Union. At the heart of the new constitutions is the creation of institutions to enforce a rule of law respecting specified human rights, a real separation of powers, an independent judiciary—and a right of appeal.

Change in the United States appeal process is far less dramatic. Even so, just as Eastern Europe and the nations of the former Soviet Union will look to us and to Western Europe for guidance and inspiration in fashioning their appeals processes, our own system's evolution feeds in part on a continuing interaction among competing traditions.

The two major appellate traditions we shall examine and contrast with ours are the civil law and the English common law. The civil law tradition is the most venerable, its first embodiment being the Digest of Justinian, adopted in 533. English common law traces its roots from the Norman Conquest in 1066. And our state-federal system can claim at most some three centuries. The civil law tradition is also the most widespread, dominating Western Europe, Latin America, and much of Africa and Asia. English common law was the model for our own country, as well as for Canada, Australia, New Zealand, and significant parts of Africa, South Asia, and the Far East. And our own system, as it has evolved, has had influence in civil law countries in Latin America, Europe, and Africa and in Japan.

Our survey does not pretend to cover the world. We leave aside the contemporary realm of Islam and the present and former domains of socialist law (including China), now in flux. Although we shall note sharp distinctions among our three models, we must take them with more than a grain of salt; the folklore and the reality are often quite different. We shall also see a powerful new tradition emerging in Europe from the international juridical institutions of the European

Community. This promises basic changes not only in the civil law and English traditions, but in all of the Eastern European nations, which seek to join the European Community and the Council of Europe.

I. The Civil Law Appellate Tradition

A. Underlying Values

As we have just noted, the Digest of Justinian was the intellectual beginning and foundation of civil law.[4] A compilation of the best thinking on the law of persons, things, and obligations, it was intended by Justinian to supplant all prior law and to be immune to future tinkering. Relegated to the shadows during the Dark Ages, Justinian's Digest was rediscovered in 1137, at almost the same time as the gathering and collation in 1140 of six centuries of opinions of the Catholic Church's supreme tribunal, the Sacra Romana Rota. Both sources, Roman and canon law, formed the backbone of the *jus commune*, the common law of Europe.

So it happened on the continent of Europe that, without any emergence of a dominant centralizing secular power, the spirit, style, and content of the Roman-canon legal tradition became widely disseminated. The chief agents of this revolutionary movement were the universities, starting with Bologna but penetrating even Scandinavia and the British Isles. In concept, organization, and subject matter, these contributions, together with the accreting pragmatic law of the merchants of Europe, fed directly into the vastly influential Code Napoléon of 1804, and thus down to the civil law systems of today.

To this intellectual fabric of comprehensive and coherent rules designed to cover all legal problems the revolutions of the late eighteenth and nineteenth centuries added a distinctive prescription of roles and articulation of aspiration. In the first place, the French Revolution was in significant part targeted at judges, "the aristocracy of the robe."[5] For judges had not only sided with the landed aristocracy, but had frustrated royal efforts at reform, had misinterpreted laws, and in general had thrown sand in the gears of administrative machinery. When the smoke of revolution cleared, several propositions had been durably established. One was that to curb the judges, powers of governance would be sharply separated. Only legislators were to have law-making power. A decision of a court in a case was not to be "law" and would have no status as precedent for the future. A separate system of administrative courts was created, quite apart from the judicial establishment.

A corollary of this separation-of-powers-with-a-vengeance was a diminished role for judges. Judges were merely to apply the law. They could not review legislation, and they could not interpret statutes. Judges themselves became civil servants; they entered a judicial career after passing examinations and worked their way up the hierarchy of courts. They enjoyed the respect accorded the civil service in general, but nothing more.

These two principles, a rigorous separation of powers locating all lawmaking in the legislature and a deep fear of a *gouvernement des juges*,[6] fueled by postrevolutionary national zeal, led to the seminal Napoleonic Code. Professor John H. Wigmore describes this historic effort:

> The composition of these codes [Civil, Criminal, Commercial, and Civil and Criminal Procedure] was the most rational and thorough proceeding of its kind in all history up to that time. Justinian's undertaking had been in comparison a superficial and mechanical task. This one was a model of representative political method. The entire bench and bar of France took part; scores of professional meetings were held; hundreds of reports were filed; the drafts were debated in successive stages in various legislative bodies. The printed proceedings on the codes fill forty volumes.
>
> Napoleon himself presided officially at many of the debates, and his will shaped more or less of the code.[7]

The Code Napoléon was soon widely translated and emulated by most of Europe. Its goal, like that of Justinian, almost thirteen hundred years earlier, was to repeal all earlier laws and to set forth a self-contained, self-sufficient repository of the law of the land, making lawyers unnecessary. What Professor John Henry Merryman calls the "rampant rationalism of the time" led to a code purporting to be complete, coherent, and clear "to such a degree that the function of the judge would be limited to selecting the applicable provision of the code and giving it its obvious significance in the context of the case."[8] The principal hallmark, then, of the civil law tradition is a reliance by lawyers and judges on a specific codified system of laws. In practice, it should be acknowledged, civil law judges do look to decisions applying code provisions, not as binding precedent but as "accumulated examples of wisdom in action."[9] Nevertheless, the traditional image of the judicial function is that it is "narrow, mechanical, and uncreative."[10]

B. Trials and Appeals: A Paper Trail

It is this set of values and attitudes, widely spread and deeply entrenched in civil law jurisdictions, that governs the appellate process. The threshold determinant is the trial process itself. Both civil and criminal cases are processed in stages which cannot be equated with a single, concentrated, oral event like a "trial" as we understand the term. In civil cases, pleadings are first filed and a hearing judge appointed; then, over time, the hearing judge gathers evidence and prepares a written summary record; this record then goes to other judges, who decide the case on the basis of the record. When the case goes on to the court of appeals, the whole record goes, and indeed the "trial" is not viewed as ended until the last appellate authority has reviewed the entire record.[11] Criminal cases proceed through similar stages: an investigative phase under direction of the prosecutor, the critical examining phase in which the examining judge prepares a complete written record of the evidence, and the decision stage involving other judges or a jury. If a jury is to decide, the record is presented to it as well as arguments of counsel.

The role of counsel is in any event a limited one. Here is

an extract from my journal. I had been visiting in the Palais de Justice in Paris and dropped in at a *tribunal d'instance*, where a single judge was presiding over a petty criminal case.

> The judge, a smartly coiffed woman, gray hair bouffant, and half glasses, thoroughly dressed down a young female lawyer for attempting to bring in facts outside of the "dossier." This courtroom, though of the lowest rank, was elegant, with paneling and, behind the judge, a martial painting representing the French Republic. The French, I take it, accouter their courts, even the lowest (at least in Paris), with greater dignity than we do.

It can readily be seen that many issues facing appellate courts under our system either do not arise or, if they do, must arise only infrequently. There is little occasion for evidentiary rulings, rulings on discovery or qualification of witnesses, or scope of cross-examination. Rules of proof have become irrebuttable presumptions. The emphasis on a written record diminishes the scope of discretion on the part of a judge or jury in assessing the demeanor of witnesses. At least in principle, judges are not to invoke principles of equity, since doing so would introduce uncertainty.

These limitations on the scope of decision-making at the trial level are complemented by an absence of deference at the appellate level. Appellate courts not only are to review issues of law but may reconsider evidence and may even receive additional evidence. They are expected not only to issue a fully reasoned opinion, but to do so with unanimity, since separate dissenting or concurring opinions would derogate from the goal of certainty. Even so, however, the opinion is not precedent for other cases; *stare decisis* (the influence of earlier decisions upon later ones) is not recognized. This is another hallmark of the civil law tradition.

Here is another snapshot from my journal of a criminal appeal before the traditional number of three judges:

> The three judges would have made marvelous fodder for a modern Daumier. The defendant, charged with being an accom-

plice in an attempt to commit a burglary, had tried to run away
when accosted by gendarmes. His counsel was a young woman
with long blond hair who talked and walked easily, speaking
rapidly with many gestures. My guide said that it was his opinion
that the lawyers in criminal cases, having very little to do with
developing the facts, usually contented themselves with pleading
extenuating circumstances. So this *avocat* did.

   And, just as in the United States, the prosecutor chose the role
of the dry, logical, remorseless commentator. The judges will
announce their judgment later today. I think defendant's goose
is cooked, though not for lack of ability or energy of his counsel.

A dissatisfied litigant has the right to seek further review
limited to questions of law. The mode of such review is
called recourse in cassation, which brings the case before a
Supreme Court of Cassation. As implied by the terminology
(*casser* means "to quash"), this court was originally limited
to setting aside the judgment below; further proceedings
would be necessary to resolve the matter. Today the court
may perform the added function of saying what the law
should be. But deciding the actual case still remains the
prerogative of the lower court.[12] The German model, called
revision, allows a supreme court not only to quash an incor-
rect decision and to give the correct interpretation, but to
"revise" the decision below without further proceedings.[13]
Professor Martin Shapiro describes the "basic civil law style"
of appellate opinion as "a single impersonal opinion that
does not cite previous cases, present extended explanations
or analyses, or suggest the alternatives or explain why one
was chosen over others."[14]

What we have been reviewing is the appellate process for
the ordinary court system in the civil law tradition. Wholly
separate tracks are maintained in two other important appellate areas. One is the review of administrative agency decisions. Early on, it was recognized that there was need for
coherence in administrative processes and decisions, even
though ordinary judges were not to be entrusted with lawmaking power. The solution was to establish, outside the
judiciary, a separate tribunal (in France, the Conseil d'Etat

or Council of State) or system of administrative courts that could make administrative law that would have general applicability.

A similar approach, establishing a separate track and court beyond the realm of the ordinary judiciary, governs constitutional review. Such review was formerly almost nonexistent in a civil law jurisdiction. But after World War II, such tribunals came into vogue: a nonjudicial, political Constitutional Council in France, and judicial constitutional courts in Germany, Italy, Spain, and other countries. These courts are vested with the exclusive prerogative to deal with the constitutionality of statutes. When such an issue surfaces in ordinary litigation, all proceedings are suspended while the constitutional issue is referred to the constitutional court. This is the "incidental" procedure, involving a specific "case or controversy." "Direct" attacks or tests of constitutionality may also be initiated by government agencies and individuals, even in the absence of a case or controversy. In this respect, a broader review exists under a civil law regime than under our American system.[15]

Although, as we note later, reality today is at some odds with the classic civil law model, the folklore persists. And that traditional model, writes Professor Merryman, "glorifies the scholar, flatters the legislator, and demeans the judge."[16]

II. The English Tradition

A. Underlying Values

If the late eighteenth and nineteenth centuries gave to civil law its dominant characteristics—its principled and detailed codes, lack of *stare decisis,* scholars' dominance, parliamentary supremacy, distrust of judges—the seventeenth century provided the creative mold for English law.[17]

Of course, a foundation had been building through the centuries. It was a structure that had not so much been built as had sprouted from fortuitous struggles over rules of procedure and the jurisdictions of the several courts of the monarch. The intellectual tradition of the common law, emerging from the twelfth and thirteenth centuries, rests, in Professor von Mehren's words, "on the political fact that an effective, centralized administration of justice was established in England long before Western societies had come to look upon law as a rational system of rules and principles. . . ."[18] The teaching of lawyering was left to the Inns of Court rather than the scholars. The common law was law made by judges in case after case, and had as its essence the solving of problems rather than the proclamation of a rational catalogue of principles.

Topping off this foundation, itself a monument to evolutionary pragmatism, is that unique English invention—the unwritten constitution. As one English barrister has noted, there is no one document. "The provisions of our constitution must be gleaned from [a] vast mass of source material," including custom, cases, statutes, and even writings of jurists.[19] Determining what comes within it "remains largely a matter of personal opinion."[20] The "personal opinion," we should note, is the highly disciplined opinion of a small group of elite citizens occupying a revered position in the judicial structure.

On this foundation, the English Revolution of 1688–89 firmly established the supremacy of Parliament vis-à-vis the Crown. And in 1701 the Act of Settlement jettisoned the idea that judges were dismissible at pleasure. It established the principle that they had life tenure, forfeitable only for breach of good behavior. Thus were created "the twin pillars [of English law] . . . an omnicompetent Parliament and an independent judiciary for common law," neither interfering with the other.[21]

If these are twins, they are not identical, indeed hardly fraternal, for the supremacy of Parliament dominates in all spheres that implicate "constitutional" issues such as separation of powers, validity of legislation, and individual rights. Supremacy means that there is theoretically no legal limitation on the power of any Parliament to pass any law, that an Act of Parliament may indeed change the constitution, and that no Parliament can bind or be bound by another Parliament. The enduring power of the doctrine is attributed to an influential scholar of a century ago, A. V. Dicey, who, according to one scholar, had an abiding faith "that English gentlemen would only pass morally acceptable laws."[22]

Parliamentary supremacy affects the judiciary in several ways. In the first place, as Patrick Atiyah notes, "There is no such thing as an unconstitutional statute in English law. . . ."[23] Secondly, English courts are not activist; they are apolitical, and deem themselves bound by precedent. Gaps in the law where they might consider "making law" are "relatively few and far between."[24] Part of the reason for this is the extent to which the Office of Parliamentary Counsel drafts technically proficient legislation in accordance with a tradition and technique known to and highly respected by the judiciary.[25]

Despite parliamentary supremacy, however, the role of judge is accorded a respect far beyond that customary in civil law countries and probably, because of the small numbers involved, beyond that generally accorded in the United States. The English judiciary consists of some four hundred circuit judges, who handle most civil and criminal trials; some eighty-five high court judges, who try the most serious cases; some twenty-eight Lord Justices of Appeal (constituting the Court of Appeal); and, at the apex, the Master of the Rolls and ten Lords of Appeal in Ordinary (the Appeal Committee of the House of Lords, the equivalent of the Supreme Court in the United States). All are chosen by the Crown on the recommendation of the Chancellor. High court and appellate judges are a homogeneous group, described by one scholar as follows:

> They are all male and all white; all have come to their position from the High Court below, all have been career barristers, and virtually all went to Oxford or Cambridge. In addition, most went to exclusive private schools, and all were professionally socialized by attendance at one of the four Inns of Court. . . .[26]

As this catalogue of the English judiciary already suggests, the appellate universe is dramatically smaller than that in the United States. A much smaller population, a geographically small and compact area—the size of the state of New York—and an absence of the complexities of federalism are a large part of the explanation.

The twenty-eight Lord Justices of Appeal on the Court of Appeal are to be contrasted with some 179 federal circuit judges, 356 state supreme court justices, and 833 judges on state intermediate courts of appeal.[27] The immensity of this difference came home to me on a visit to the English Court of Appeal in 1986, when I learned that all Lord Justices of Appeal had their chambers under one cluster of roofs and came together "for a chat" on administrative and policy matters once a month. Another measure of disparate size is simply the number of cases heard on appeal. In 1986, Lord Justice Roger Parker told me that, fighting to whittle down the remorseless backlog, the Court of Appeal heard eight hundred cases a year, with only seventy-five going on to the House of Lords. This contrasts with 47,013 cases filed in the thirteen federal circuit courts of appeal in 1992[28] and 238,007 appeals filed in the state appellate courts in 1990.[29]

These differences of size of the appellate universe are not wholly explained by the difference in population size of England and Wales on the one hand and the United States on the other. In 1963, after an interesting exchange had taken place, with American lawyers and judges visiting the English courts in London and English lawyers and judges observing appeals in both state and federal courts in the United States, Professor Delmar Karlen, then director of the Institute of Judicial Administration, attributed the disproportionately small number of appeals in England to "a smaller volume of litigation at the trial level . . . greater satisfaction with the trial courts . . . [and] the discouragement of frivolous appeals by costs sanctions [the loser pays both his own costs and those of the winner] and a highly responsible bar."[30]

An additional factor was observed a quarter century later by Professor Robert Martineau, who spent three months "n site" in London, studying the appellate system. He described, as a "major variance" between American and English appellate practice, a trend in England deliberately to constrict the right of appeal. He cites four new provisions of law: the County Courts Act of 1959, which allows a rules committee to define the classes of orders for which permission to appeal would be required; the absence of criteria for granting or denying such permission; the granting of authority to give or deny that permission to the trial judge or a single appellate judge; and the absence of any right of review of the decision of the single appellate judge.[31]

Leaving aside all comparisons of scale, the very nature of appeal is strikingly different in England from its common law cousin in the United States. If the essence of civil law trials and appeals is the assembling over time of the written word, the essence of the English appellate tradition is the single event in open court of almost exclusively oral discourse between judges and counsel. "Comprehensive orality" is the label ascribed to the tradition by one scholar.[32]

B. In the Court of Appeal: An Oral Experience

Here are my observations and impressions of a civil appeal in the Court of Appeal in the Royal Courts of Justice in London a few years ago. I am quoting from a detailed entry in my journal. I think that these proceedings illustrate the major facets of the English system.

At 10:30 A.M., we were shown to a favored seat in the press box in Lord Justice A's courtroom. It was a small, windowless, intricately paneled, rich, dark-wooded box of a room, with a few sloping rows for spectators, a barrier to set off barristers' space, and counterslopes for clerk's desk and judges' bench, over which was a swooping wooden canopy.

Lord Justice A and a much older colleague, Sir David B, around eighty-three (retired, without chambers, but serving whenever asked), entered. The barristers were a slick young man, early-fortyish, and a stolid, (to me), more confidence-inspiring fellow a few years older.

The case was this. Plaintiffs-appellants had sued the *London Observer* for libeling their business group as one associating with a Mr. X, who, in turn, knowingly associated with "figures in organized crime." The newspaper had managed to introduce into evidence a thick book of newspaper "cuttings" to show that X was acquainted with people widely reported to be Mafia "capos." The defendant submitted proof that the "figures" had indeed been convicted of several crimes of an "organized" nature. But the cuttings (or clippings) covered many other crimes, as to which no other proof was submitted.

The appellant's argument that the cuttings swept too broadly obviously appealed to Lord Justice A. Appellant's attorney talked from 10:30 A.M. to 11:40 A.M., leading the court through the pleadings and the contested book of cuttings. After what appeared to me an unconscionable time, Lord Justice A, after whispering to his brother, said, "We're disposed to think the proffer below [i.e., the submission into evidence of the whole book of clippings] was much too broad. This being the case, we suggest you sit down and hold your fire unless your adversary succeeds in changing our view."

Whereupon appellee set up his lectern in front of him. He clearly had an uphill row. The justices had obviously bought appellant's argument that the proof of X's awareness of the crime figures' reported criminal associations should be limited to the crimes that had been proved by other evidence.

After the appellee's barrister had spent perhaps a half hour in repeating over and over again his contention that the notoriety issue was separate from the issue of proof of actual convictions, he gallantly said, "Your Lordships, there comes a time when one sees that there is no more that one can say. I have perhaps already said too much. I shall desist."

Lord Justice A then proceeded with a brilliant, extemporaneous summary of the case, the issue, the arguments, and his personal conclusion that the collection of cuttings was too broad and should be pared to contain only newspaper references to crimes that had been proved. Retired Lord Justice B made a short speech seconding these remarks.

The time occupied by this appeal, from start to finish, was about two and a half hours, much shorter than the median time of slightly over one day. A day of argument begins at 10:30, winds up at 4:15, and spares an hour for lunch; elapsed time is four hours and forty-five minutes, compared to a half hour for an argument in the United States.[33]

This process carries with it inherently a number of implications which further differentiate it from the American tradition. In the first place, the judge has no staff support, other than a non-lawyer attendant, who has no legal, university, or secretarial training. His duties are personal, similar to those of a batman to a British military officer.[34] Since the judge is on the bench almost all of the time, he has no time for discourse with a law clerk. And since the opinion is delivered orally, there is no function for a secretary. Even Law Lords, who lack even the above-described clerk, must apply to a secretarial pool for assistance in their correspondence.

In addition, a congeries of circumstances conspires to forestall advance thinking, although steps have recently been taken to effect some remedy. First, there is little acceptance of the American concept of a brief. Second, there is little time made available to read a brief, if there were one, in advance of argument. Third, there is little time for consultation among judges, reflection, and writing after an argument has concluded.

In the case we have just discussed, for example, I was uneasy about the result. I suspect that in the United States the existence of the First Amendment would have dictated a different result. Under the authority rooted in *New York Times* v. *Sullivan*, 376 U.S. 254 (1964), the newspaper would have been protected if, whether or not the published comments were accurate, it had not acted out of malice. Even without considering the First Amendment, I would have wanted to ponder over the case, read other cases, talk with my law clerks, have a wholly private conversation with my colleagues, and work over and polish an opinion before announcing our decision to the world. In my journal I entered this final reflection: "My feeling is that our system, relying more on average journeymen like me than the elegant products of the higher reaches of British education, has the estimable virtue of being, if not foolproof, at least fool-minimizing."

Some changes have been made—at glacial pace. After the Anglo-American exchange in the early 1960s, English judges engaged in a short-lived experiment in reading relevant materials in advance of hearing. This was not thought a good idea; advance reading was too likely to prevent judges from having an open mind at argument.[35] But since 1982, several changes have been instituted. Since 1989 a "skeleton argument" has been required. It is not quite a brief, in the American sense. Its purpose is "to identify not to argue the points." It should be succinct, stating a principal authority or authorities and the relevant pages, and, as to issues of fact, relevant transcript pages.[36] The "brief" given the barrister by the solicitor includes pleadings, key documents, fact summaries, witness statements, and other useful material.[37] A written chronology is also required. And since 1982, an appellate judge does not sit five days a week for a judicial year, but has the fifth day reserved for reading, thinking, and writing.[38]

This hardly implies a life of leisure. In a 1985 report to Parliament, the Review Body on Top Salaries noted the provision for "reading time" and added, "The Lords Justices themselves argue, however, that any benefit flowing from such provision is far outweighed by the effect of changes in procedure which have added to their burdens."[39] My own distinct impression is that the English appellate judges I have met belie the glamour with which they are viewed; they work extremely hard, take home work at night, and put in a six-day week.

A final feature worth noting is the way in which precedent is created. We have noted that there may be several opinions delivered from the bench in a given case. What finally emerges in the law books depends upon not merely the editorial but substantive judgment of a small group of barristers who have turned their talents to reporting cases. Indeed, theirs is the decision in the first instance to report the case at all. Two thirds of all Court of Appeal decisions are not reported at all.[40] Only a small fraction of argued cases find their way into the permanent volumes of the *Law Reports*. For example, in 1986 only 5.2 percent of opinions were published in the prestigious *Law Reports* and 13.8 percent in the more widely distributed general series.[41]

Partly compensating for this restraint, specialized reports, of interest to a specialty bar, constitute "unwritten" common law. Not only may these occasionally be relied on, but barristers (and judges) have some freedom to choose among the several published opinions issued in a case. And sometimes when a court confronts a decision issued in ignorance of a line of authority which ought to have controlled, it relegates it to oblivion by denominating it *per incuriam* ("through lack of care")[42]—a device I would on occasion love to have available. In sum, English courts, while professedly strictly bound by the concept of *stare decisis*, have considerable flexibility in dealing with precedent.

III. The United States Tradition

In the development of legal tradition in the United States, there has been, as might be expected, some borrowing from both civil law and English models. Although the dominant one has been the English tradition, civil law has left its imprint in several areas. Moreover, considering the length of our association with England, it is surprising that our tradition differs in so many vital respects from that of the mother country. We turn first to our English inheritance and our divergence from it.

A. Our English Inheritance—and Divergence

We begin with the fact that both because of the professional competence of the higher English courts and the widespread participation of ordinary freemen in the business of the plethora of local courts, the English judiciary occupied a position of unmatched preeminence.[43] Not only did colonists bring with them this ingrained attitude of respect, but judges came to be looked on as a progressive force on the side of the individual. There was no fear of judicial interference in administration. Their power to shape common law was familiar. And, as Professor Merryman put it, "The judiciary was not a target of the American Revolution in the way that it was in France."[44]

True, in Massachusetts the judiciary was a major target of the Sons of Liberty—but only because of an accretion of events: the perverse decision of Lord North and the British government to "reform" the Massachusetts courts by substituting payment of superior court judges by the Crown, not the provincial treasury; the publication of inflammatory letters written by Governor Thomas Hutchinson, a former chief justice; the solitary acceptance with pleasure of the king's grant of salary (the four other judges had refused) by Chief Justice Peter Oliver; the subsequent rump impeachment of the chief justice by the Massachusetts House of Representatives; and the resulting refusal of jurors to take the oath from the chief justice.[45] Once revolutionary government was established a year later, the prior court system, with judges appointed by the people, was continued and traditional practice was resumed.[46]

While this pro-judge value was shared with the English, the new nation differed from its mother country in three other fundamental respects. One was its insistence on a written constitution. This, of course, was an inevitable consequence of our own history on the new continent as colonies operating under a royal charter. Professor Julius Goebel, in tracing the antecedents of our judicial system, wrote, "Because [we] and [our] forebears had lived for generations according to the terms of our written instruments establishing or regulating the structure of [our] governments, the conviction had been bred that only through matter of record could the metes and bounds of the fundamental law be secured."[47] So we set about to marshal the relevant wisdom and put it on paper. The extent of our insistence on a writing was dramatically demonstrated by our belated but widespread recognition that a catalogue of individual rights should also be reduced to writing, as a condition of ratification of the Constitution itself.

Our second difference with the mother country lay in the power we gave our judges, beginning in colonial days, to pass on the validity, even the constitutionality, of legislation— something unthinkable in a polity where Parliament was always "supreme." In 1771, William Blackstone had published his *Commentaries on the Laws of England*, in which he had expansively delineated the doctrine of Parliamentary Supremacy. The colonists came to know this doctrine all too well as the British Privy Council rode roughshod over colonial acts it deemed inconsistent with Acts of Parliament. But while colonial reaction to these vetoes serving Parliamentary Supremacy fed the fires of revolution, the idea that courts could strike down invalid legislation in this country took root. It empowered colonial judges to disregard any local legislation not in conformity with English law, and, later, judges of newly independent states to invalidate laws contrary to the new state constitutions.[48] This experience with the Privy Council and with early instances of judicial review of legislation was not forgotten in the tortuous process leading to our constitutional provision for an independent judiciary exercising common law powers within a clearly defined framework of separation of powers. From this it was but a short step to Chief Justice John Marshall's formal articulation of judicial review in *Marbury* v *Madison*, 1 Cranch 137 (1803).

A third difference was practical and psychological rather than doctrinal. It was the readier access to the appellate process and the increased propensity to appeal that had developed during colonial times. The colonists had borrowed the English example of setting up a myriad of local courts and had provided for appeal from the county courts to the Court of Assistants, with further appeal to the General Court. But in so doing, they could be more rational than the feudal inheritance of England permitted. Not only could they avoid such antique lumber as manorial courts, but, under an early ordinance of colonial governor Edmund Andros of Massachusetts Bay, all of the powers of King's Bench, Common Pleas, and Exchequer were combined in one centralized "superior" court to which litigants could appeal decisions of lower courts all through the colony and which was charged not only with seeing justice done between the parties but also with seeing that "the right rule" was applied.[49] Although this ordinance had a short life, it became a model for other colonies.[50]

In addition to simplifying structure, the colonists also greatly simplified procedure by borrowing and adapting the right of appeal from a justice of the peace to a full bench of such justices sitting in General Quarter Sessions—far less technical and wider-ranging than the traditional writs of error and certiorari.[51] Add to this a litigious spirit and reluctance to accept defeat, born of the independence rising from the possibility of acquiring ownership of land, and a likely dissatisfaction with judgments of the largely lay bench of the rural inferior courts,[52] and we can see how the view became entrenched that wide-ranging, easily accessible appeal was a right for all to enjoy.

B. Influences of Civil Law

If the colonists succeeded in placing their unique stamp on the English tradition, it is easy to understand that civil law had little chance of exerting a wide or permanent influence. Professor Lawrence Friedman, in *A History of American Law*, points out that early in our nationhood, civil law domain had us pretty well surrounded. French and Spanish law governed along the Mississippi and its tributaries, on the northern edge, and in Florida, Louisiana, and Texas. But, excepting some surviving civil law remnants in Texas, he concludes, "A massive invasion of settlers doomed the civil law everywhere, except in Louisiana. The new judges and lawyers were trained in the common-law tradition. They supplanted judges of French and Spanish background."[53]

This is not the end of the story. In the mid-nineteenth century, David Dudley Field's Code of Civil Procedure, first adopted in New York, won a wide following among some twenty states in the West. Professor Friedman reports: "Stylistically, no greater affront to the common-law tradition can be imagined than the 1848 code. It was couched in brief, gnomic, Napoleonic sections. . . . It was, in short, a code in the French sense, not a statute."[54] Although this code suffered various fates, code pleading did result in "procedure [becoming], on the whole, much less technical."[55] Indeed, it can be said that Field's procedural code was the ancestor of the Federal Rules of Civil Procedure and thus of most state rules of procedure.

More ambitious were the efforts of Field and others to create and disseminate a general civil code, following the French model. California provided the signal victory, with its 1872 civil code, followed by a penal and a political code.[56] And, of course, the Louisiana Code germinated and is alive and well today. So are code principles, provisions, and precedents in the Commonwealth of Puerto Rico. Generally, however, the codes failed to take root. Professor Friedman comments: "It is hard to resist the conclusion that the codes had almost no impact on behavior, either in court or out."[57] But they were "the spiritual parents" of this century's Restatements of the Law. Produced under the aegis of the American Law Institute, they are "black-letter codes . . . meant for persuasion of judges, rather than enactment into law."[58]

So the United States legal tradition does not exclude codes. But a code has a different meaning from codes in a civil law country. Even the California Civil Code and the Uniform Commercial Code, though resembling a French or German code, "are not based on the same ideology . . . make no pretense of completeness . . . are not rejections of the past . . . do not purport to abolish all prior law in their field, but rather to perfect it and . . . to supplement it. A code provision will be interpreted in such a way as to avoid conflict with a common law precedent."[59]

As we shall later note, one cannot write "finis" to the story of civil law influence on American law or tradition. But we can probably expect interactions between these systems at the margins rather than near the center.

IV. Major Differences Among the Three Models

It remains for us to note some of the major differences in the appellate tradition of the three models.

—The appellate stage is a far grander one in the United

States than in England or civil law countries. Not only does the country span a continent with a dual federal-state system in fifty states, but there is a right of appeal in every civil and criminal case. It may also be that there is more litigation, trial and appellate, per citizen in the United States.

—Judges as objects of respect occupy a position between that of their colleagues in civil law countries and that in England. Unlike judges who are career civil servants, American judges are usually looked up to as persons of considerable stature. They usually come to the bench in midlife, with an impressive career in practice, teaching, or government behind them and the confidence of the supreme executive of the state or nation. But, except in rare instances (usually postmortem), they do not rise to the pinnacle of prestige enjoyed by the very small number of top judges of England, who are uniformly selected from the top ranks of barristers. American judges, in contrast, represent a more heterogeneous background—whether measured by college and law school affiliation, geographical origins, or type of law practice or public service—and their power is far greater, embracing the power to declare statutes unconstitutional.

—Lawyers and judges rely less on documents in the United States than they do in, say, France, but substantially more than do barristers and judges in England; correspondingly, we in the United States are more "oral" than our counterparts in France, and much less so than those in England.

—Judges in the United States invest far more time in preparation for oral argument than do judges in England. In civil law countries, courts of appeal review the entire record and arguments at the initial trial and make their own findings of fact. Additional oral argument is quite limited.

—In the United States we rely extensively upon a network of supporting staff—secretaries, law clerks, and staff attorneys. Institutional support in the other systems is far less prominent. One Law Lord friend in England admitted to me his envy of the kind of support given our Supreme Court Justices.

—Appellate judges in the United States generally exercise a marked deference to the trial judge's findings of facts; in

France there is no such reluctance to take new evidence or review questions of fact, and in England, while the Court of Appeal can examine witnesses, take new evidence, consider new issues, and bring in new parties, it seldom does.[60] On the other hand, American judges are not reluctant to invalidate statutes on constitutional grounds, to revise rulings of law, or even to exercise their supervisory power. They feel more free to consult legislative history as an aid to interpreting statutes. In civil law countries and in England, judges are more likely to confine their analysis to the statutory wording. And while English and civil law judges generally focus narrowly on the case at hand, American judges are at least as interested in laying down guidelines for the future as in deciding the case before them.[61]

—There is less unanimity in the decisions of appellate courts in the United States than in France, but more collegial reflection, interchange, and reasoning than in the Court of Appeal in London, where the judges orally announce separate opinions.

—There is less subservience to the scholar on the part of United States judges than in a traditional civil law jurisdiction and far less delegation of discretion to court reporters as to the style, content, and publishability of opinions than in England. The judges are at center stage in the United States tradition.

—American judges view the appellate opinion as an important end product, contributing to the mainstream of legal development by its publication and status as precedent. In civil law countries the opinion is not, formally, precedent; in England publication is quite infrequent and, as we have noted, opinions even when published are not automatically to be considered ironclad precedent.

—Judges in the United States have recourse to a wider assortment of remedies than generally is the case in civil law jurisdictions or in England. In civil law countries, for example, there may be a lack of power exercisable against a person to compel the doing of an act, and in England there are limitations on the ordering of new trials.

V. Traditions in Flux

Notwithstanding the clear differences in values and practices among these three appellate traditions, there is a blurring around the edges as each experiments with or borrows parts from the others.

A. The United States

We in the United States have borrowed more than we like to acknowledge. Despite our historic aversion to classic civil law codes, we find ourselves in an era when Congress is tempted to micromanage through codelike detailed legislation. I had a recent occasion to report that the average statute today "occupies over nine pages of closely printed text, compared to fewer than two pages in the mid-fifties."[62] Extreme examples are the new provisions establishing a complex grid system for determining when a person is "disabled" within the meaning of the Social Security Act, and the intricate, mechanistic, step-by-step calculus required of a federal trial judge in sentencing a convicted defendant under the Sentencing Guidelines adopted in 1987.

We may also be borrowing a civil law inquisitorial feature in building the record of a case when courts utilize, in complex factual matters, the services of a special master. And, with six hundred or more federal magistrate judges and bankruptcy judges doing very important work, we may find ourselves encouraging career paths for a significant cadre of judicial officers. Moreover, some of our courts are borrowing the English focus on oral exchange; the eleventh federal judicial circuit, for example, disposes of roughly half of its total appeals by a simple order, following, however, painstaking study of briefs and an active exchange during oral argument. Finally, with unification of the European market, Europe's civil law systems, as one practitioner has noted, may well "undergo a renaissance as Europeans harmonize and unify their laws."[63] We can anticipate more borrowing.

B. Civil Law Jurisdictions

The process works both ways. Civil law also reflects the influences of other traditions. Not only have substantial bodies of statutory law developed to compete with codes, but judges have had to do a great deal of gap-filling and interpreting. Moreover, since opinions are regularly published, though they are somewhat short on factual context, there is a strong tendency for courts to respect earlier decisions. Then, too, the heyday of legislative supremacy has passed, leading to skepticism of legislative infallibility and the rise of constitutional review. With the advent of constitutional decision-making has come an enhanced respect for the judges making such decisions.

Professor Merryman has neatly capsuled the emerging effects of the adoption of "modern rigid constitutions" and the establishment of judicial review of the constitutionality of legislation. He writes, "[T]he legal center of gravity has begun to undergo what promises to be a drastic shift from civil code to constitution, from private to public law, from ordinary court to constitutional court, from legislative positivism to constitutional principle."[64]

C. England

The thrust of change is also felt across the Atlantic. Following recommendations of the English Law Commission, implemented in 1977, simplifying procedures for obtaining judicial review of administrative acts, there has been, in the words of Lord Griffiths, "an enormous increase in the use of the courts to challenge administrative action at all levels."[65] He reports Lord Diplock terming this " 'the greatest achievement of the English courts' in his judicial lifetime."[66] On the other hand, the lack of a written, unrepealable bill of rights remains a live issue after over two decades of debate. David Williams, Cambridge University vice chancellor, speaking to the American Law Institute in 1990, said, referring to a number of Royal Commission inquiries into human rights issues, "External inquiries cannot be an adequate substitute for such a Bill of Rights, and there is increasing judicial restiveness."[67]

D. European Institutions

Quite apart from internal reforms and voluntary borrowings from other traditions, both civil and common law traditions in England and Europe are feeling external forces as formidable as the movement of tectonic plates that budges continents.

1. The Council of Europe. First are the institutions of the Council of Europe—the 1950 European Convention on Human Rights and Fundamental Freedoms, the European Commission of Human Rights (1954), and the European Court of Human Rights (1959). The European Convention, ratified by all twenty-one members of the Council of Europe, obligates all signatories to "secure to everyone within their jurisdiction" the rights described in eighteen articles, plus those in several additional protocols.

What is unique about the Council of Europe is the effective machinery it has in place to bring reality to aspiration. Its international Commission of Human Rights examines complaints of individuals against states, determines the facts, and endeavors to bring about settlements. If settlement is not forthcoming, cases may then be referred to the Court of Human Rights. As of 1987 the court had issued some two hundred rulings—all based on and implementing a written constitution, the 1950 European Convention on Human Rights and Fundamental Freedoms.

The catalogue of decisions is impressive, bearing on rights of access to courts, conditions of detention, corporal punishment, prisoners' rights, wiretapping, and restrictions on expression and the press. When one bears in mind the background of English law and the doctrine of Parliamentary Supremacy, it is no less than astonishing to learn of the extent to which English courts, Parliament, and officials have accepted and implemented decisions of the European Court of Human Rights, even when this meant repealing old laws and enacting new ones. The civil law countries on the European continent have had similar experiences.

2. The European Community. A second set of centripetal institutions are those of the European Community, created by the Treaty of Rome in 1958. Twelve nations now subscribe to the partial governance of the European Council, its Council of Ministers, the cabinetlike European Community Commission, and the largely advisory elected European Parliament. But central to the integrative pull of the European Community has been its own European Court of Justice.[68] Declaring the Treaty of Rome to be a constitutional instrument obligating member states and their citizens to abide by provisions enforceable through normal state judicial processes, the Court of Justice has exercised its influence in three major ways.

It gives "interpretations" of the Treaty of Rome to national courts, chiefly in the economics arena, liberalizing the movement of goods and services. It exercises significant administrative judicial review of the regulations issued by organs of the European Community. And it interprets fundamental human rights constraints implied by the European Community's treaties, looking to common traditions and to the European Court of Human Rights. If and as the European Community achieves further integration of its market and monetary system, the making of European Community law through the appellate decisions of the European Court of Justice will become even more significant.

The significance of the new regionalism is only beginning to be realized. Cambridge Vice Chancellor Williams has hazarded this statement: "What is clear is that Britain is rapidly acquiring a constitution, albeit European in scope. . . . [T]he broader impact of the European community could be seen as the central factor in what, for the United Kingdom, is the greatest constitutional readjustment since the seventeenth century."[69] Professor Merryman sketches an even wider impact:

[S]ome observers draw an analogy with the medieval period, when Europe was united by the Roman civil law—canon law *jus commune*. They see the law of the EEC and the European Human Rights Convention as the foundation of a new European *jus commune*, based on common culture and common interests, after centuries of exaggerated glorification of the nation-state. The fact that Great Britain, the mother country of the common law tradition, is a member of the EEC and a party to the Convention suggests to them the possibility, indeed the necessity, of a rapprochement of the civil law and common law traditions. Although there have been difficulties and disappointments, European federalism is a lively and significant force with important consequences for contemporary civil law (and common law) systems.[70]

These statements, made in a book published in 1985, proved to be startlingly prophetic. By 1991, Professor Herman Schwartz could write of the aftermath of the rejection of communism in Eastern Europe:

All the East European nations want to join the European Community (E.C.) and the Council of Europe. When they join the latter . . . they will have to agree to be bound by the European Convention on Human Rights, the institutions of which (the European Commission and the European Court of Human Rights) together constitute one of the most effective international human-rights instruments.[71]

The processes of adaptation and osmosis are accelerating. The growth of multinational corporations, the proliferation of international treaties, the emergence of great regional common markets and free trade areas, the increasing influence of regional conventions, commissions, and courts—all these forces signal to lawyers of today and especially tomorrow that they cannot safely confine their expertise to one tradition. They must be aware of the major features of other traditions not only because these may well affect their cases and clients, but also because features in other systems may have something to offer us.

3

The State-Federal Court System: "One Whole"

In Chapter 1 the reader was taken to a federal appellate court and heard oral arguments in six cases. Because the court was "federal," the impression might well have been given that the cases had nothing to do with state courts or state law. If so, closer analysis shows how misleading that impression was. For in every case, state law was either intimately implicated or could have been if the facts were slightly different or a different litigation strategy had been adopted.

One seeking state law facets, actual or potential, in the six cases would not have to look very long. In the case of the dyslexic medical student, the major claim, true enough, was brought under the federal Rehabilitation Act, but there was a second, "pendent" claim brought under a state civil rights act. The routine narcotics prosecution could equally well have been brought in state court by the state's attorney general rather than in federal court by the United States attorney. The lawsuit of the company seeking to shift to its insurance carriers the damages it incurred for its toxic discharges directly involved state law—not only as to the existence of coverage, but as to when any coverage was triggered and what constituted proper notice of a claim.

The wrongful discharge case brought by the black police-man involved, as it happened, only federal civil rights stat-utes, but could, in a number of states, have been brought under a state civil rights statute. And while the labor-management case happened to involve only federal labor relations law, even in this highly nationalized field of law cases sometimes present complex questions of preemption, asking, for example, whether a state law governing workers' or employers' conduct can be given effect, notwithstanding broad federal legislation. Finally, the state prisoner who sought federal habeas corpus relief might very well have been better advised to make a full-scale effort in state court, not just to meet the "exhaustion of remedies" requirement, but because the state court might very well have given effect to a remedy under the state's constitution that would not have been available under the federal Constitution.

Even this small cross-section of cases illustrates the inti-mate interweaving and interacting of the state and national legal systems which characterize our overall "federal" sys-tem. This is a dual concept of power sharing between a central national government—which we often designate by the word "federal" in its secondary sense—and multiple sub-ordinate state government possessing residual powers. While many countries share this concept, few, if any, have done as the United States has done in establishing parallel state and national court systems which complement each other. Each is based on the same assumptions, principles, and discipline. The analogy which comes to mind is what astronomers call a binary star—two stars revolving around a common center of gravity.

Although there has always been tension in settling upon the proper scope of the components of this dual system, there was never an intent that one be considered inferior to the other. Yet today the state component is likely to receive too little attention in the teaching of law, in scholarly research, and in bar association activities—to our incalculable prejudice. It is the purpose of this chapter to recognize the compelling importance of the state component of the binary star.

I. The Origins:
Regaining Perspective

It is well, therefore, to recall the delicate balancing act that characterized our beginnings. The first proposal concerning the structure of the judiciary was "that a national judiciary be established . . . to consist of one supreme tribunal and of one or more inferior tribunals." The language concerning the establishment of inferior tribunals was then deleted because of a strong belief by some that state courts would fully serve the purpose. After considering a more permissive congressional power to "appoint" inferior tribunals (which would have left the door open to designate state courts as such tribunals),[1] the Convention finally settled on the present "ordain and establish" language. These words, according to Professor Julius Goebel, sent the message "that federal inferior courts must be created, and further that designation of state tribunals would not do."[2] But it was not a message shouted from the rooftops.

Writing in *The Federalist*, No. 81, in an effort to defuse the virulent Anti-Federalists in the fight over ratification, Alexander Hamilton envisaged federal district judges, "with the aid of the State judges, [holding] circuits for the trial of causes in the several parts of the respective districts."[3] Abandoning this language because of the varying tenures and judicial oaths involved, he nevertheless pursued the theme in No. 82, saying, "[T]he national and State systems are to be regarded as ONE WHOLE. The courts of the latter will of course be natural auxiliaries to the execution of the laws of the Union. . . ."[4] (The capital letters are Hamilton's.)

The issue of state courts serving as the federal inferior courts rose again during the First Congress and was rather speedily put to rest, but not without serious recognition of the interests represented. Not only were federal districts to be coterminous with state boundaries, but, unless indicated to the contrary, state laws were to be the rules of decision in common law trials in federal courts. Goebel has termed this a "solution . . . brilliant in its conception of bonding federal jurisprudence to extant American law in all its diversity."[5]

We should also remember that at the beginning the federal courts were given jurisdiction over only a few matters—admiralty, treaty rights, diversity, and crimes against the United States. Not until the 1875 Judiciary Act[6] did federal courts receive a broad federal-question jurisdiction ("all suits of a civil nature, at common law or in equity . . . arising under the Constitution or laws of the United States, or treaties made . . ."). It is only those without a sense of history and, I would add, without a resulting informed intuition about the future who would look upon state courts as second-class or upon federal courts as the intended elite.

Why is it important to regain this perspective of ONE WHOLE? There are at least five basic reasons:

—The first is that the two realms of our dual court system are not entirely separate and independent; they intersect and overlap in a number of important ways—ways which require of the skilled practitioner a knowledge of the workings of both state and federal courts.

—A second reason is that it is in state courts that by far most of the nation's litigation is decided; the huge size of the state court component of our dual system is seldom appreciated.

—Thirdly, students and practitioners ignore at their peril the practices and procedures in place not merely in the courts of last resort of the fifty states but, perhaps even more important, in the forty-six intermediate courts of appeal. Increased access to quality decision-making, in both procedural and substantive terms, is afforded by this relatively new level of appellate courts.

—Fourthly, state court jurisprudence is often at the cutting edge of constitutional law and increasingly sets the standards of conduct expected of officials and institutions. The two networks are roughly parallel. Over a decade ago, Hans Linde, then a justice of the Supreme Court of Oregon, urged that state courts turn first to their state constitutions because they are "first in time and first in logic."[7] And Justice Brennan heartily endorsed California Supreme Court Justice Mosk's observation: "I detect a phoenix-like resurrection of federalism, or, if you prefer, states' rights, evidenced by state courts' reliance upon provisions of state constitutions."[8]

—Finally, all of these factors underscore the compelling national importance of confronting certain systemic problems relating to rationalizing the roles of state and federal courts and to securing a truly independent state judiciary.

II. Comparisons and Interrelationships

A. A Bird's-eye View

To begin, we take a bird's-eye view of the two systems, side by side. In Chart 1, we can see what first appears as a baffling maze of institutions. At the very top, embracing both state and federal court systems and providing the final unifying link between them, is the Supreme Court of the United States. On the right is the state court system with four levels of decision-making: agencies and local or specialized courts, state trial courts of general jurisdiction, intermediate appellate courts, and courts of last resort. On the left is the federal court system with only three levels (excluding the Supreme Court) but a more complex feeder system. Magistrates' and bankruptcy judges' decisions may be appealed to the district courts, with further review by the courts of appeal. But another track leads from administrative agencies (which have reviewed decisions of administrative law judges) directly to courts of appeal. Both the state courts of last resort and the federal circuit courts of appeal are the final arbiters for almost all cases. For although the Supreme Court of the United States annually receives some four to five thousand requests for review of both state and federal decisions, only a minuscule 150 to 170 cases are accepted for oral argument each year, with perhaps a few more than a hundred argued, and full opinions issuing in perhaps two thirds of those argued.

The Federal Courts

CHART 1 FEDERAL-STAT

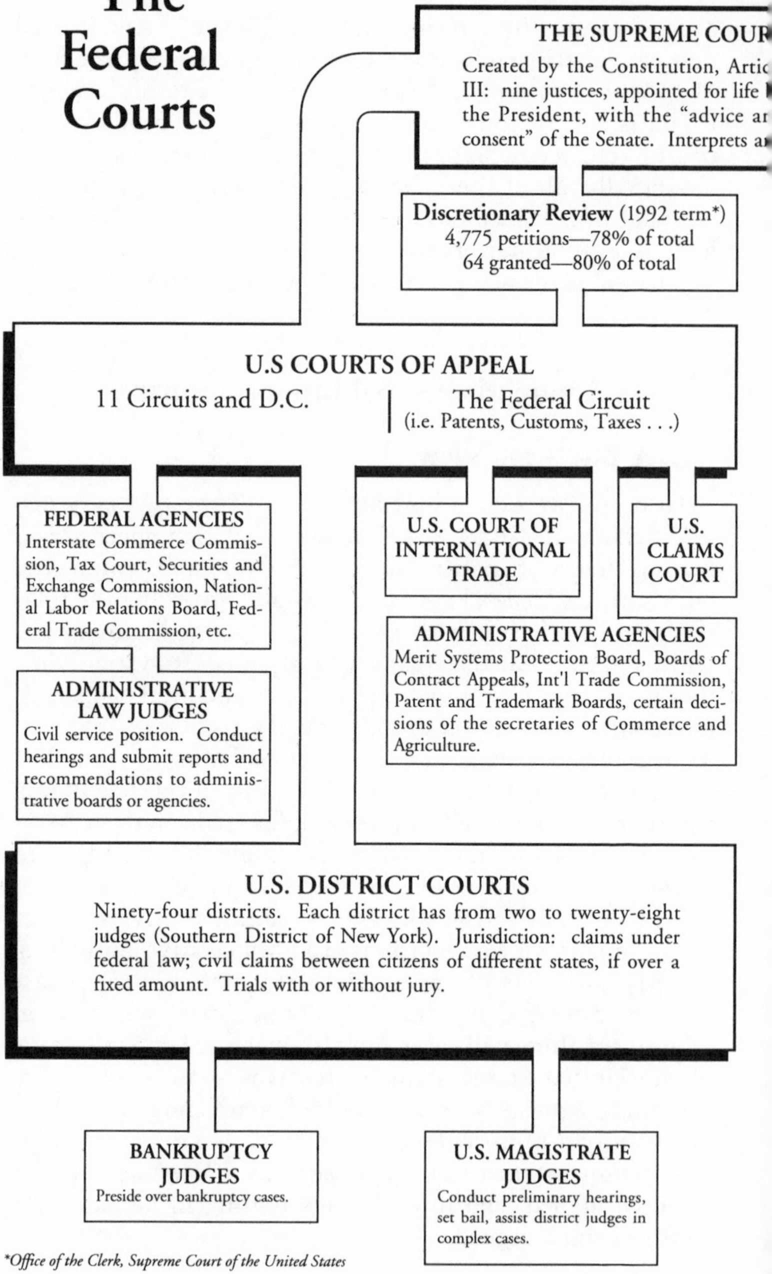

THE SUPREME COUR

Created by the Constitution, Artic
III: nine justices, appointed for life
the President, with the "advice ar
consent" of the Senate. Interprets a

Discretionary Review (1992 term*)
4,775 petitions—78% of total
64 granted—80% of total

U.S COURTS OF APPEAL

11 Circuits and D.C.

The Federal Circuit
(i.e. Patents, Customs, Taxes . . .)

FEDERAL AGENCIES
Interstate Commerce Commission, Tax Court, Securities and
Exchange Commission, National Labor Relations Board, Federal Trade Commission, etc.

**U.S. COURT OF
INTERNATIONAL
TRADE**

**U.S.
CLAIMS
COURT**

**ADMINISTRATIVE
LAW JUDGES**
Civil service position. Conduct
hearings and submit reports and
recommendations to administrative boards or agencies.

ADMINISTRATIVE AGENCIES
Merit Systems Protection Board, Boards of
Contract Appeals, Int'l Trade Commission,
Patent and Trademark Boards, certain deci-
sions of the secretaries of Commerce and
Agriculture.

U.S. DISTRICT COURTS

Ninety-four districts. Each district has from two to twenty-eight
judges (Southern District of New York). Jurisdiction: claims under
federal law; civil claims between citizens of different states, if over a
fixed amount. Trials with or without jury.

**BANKRUPTCY
JUDGES**
Preside over bankruptcy cases.

**U.S. MAGISTRATE
JUDGES**
Conduct preliminary hearings,
set bail, assist district judges in
complex cases.

*Office of the Clerk, Supreme Court of the United States

COURT SYSTEM

OF THE UNITED STATES

applies the Constitution and all federal
statutes, after decision by federal courts
of appeals and state supreme courts.
(1992 term–116 oral arguments*)

The
State
Courts

Discretionary Review (1992 term*)
1,338 petitions—22% of total
16 granted—20% of total

STATE COURTS OF LAST RESORT

52 plus D.C. (Texas and Oklahoma have two)

LARGELY
DISCRETIONARY
REVIEW

MANDATORY
REVIEW

INTERMEDIATE COURTS
OF APPEAL (IACs)
44 in 38 states

LARGELY
MANDATORY
REVIEW

STATE SUPERIOR COURTS

All cases, criminal and civil; trials with or without jury. One in each county
or similar geographic area. Jurisdiction: state constitution; statutes, common
law; also federal Constitution (including most of Bill of Rights) and statutes.
Limited by the supremacy, commerce, full faith and credit, and equal protection and due process clauses of the Fourteenth Amendment.

STATE/LOCAL
AGENCIES
Industrial accidents,
zoning boards, licensing
boards etc.

SPECIALIZED
COURTS
Probate (wills), domestic
relations, Juvenile.

DISTRICT COURTS
Small towns, a justice of the peace; large
urban centers, a municipal or district
court. Jurisdiction: petty crimes, traffic
offenses, small claims. No jury.

This roughly parallel vertical structure of the state and federal systems reveals one asymmetry: the state system has an additional level—that of the intermediate appellate court. This institution is fairly new but widespread, now numbering some forty-six in thirty-eight states. Most of them have come into existence since 1958. And it is here, as we shall see, that a lion's share of state appellate decision-making takes place, cases that formerly had to wait in line to be heard by a court of last resort.

B. Differences in Caseloads—and Opportunities

In addition to comparing structures, it is well to note both differences and similarities in caseloads. Alan Tarr and Mary Porter, in their recent study *State Supreme Courts in State and Nation*, have compared the business in state supreme courts from 1940 to 1970 with that in the federal courts of appeal between 1960 and 1975.[9] Their study reveals that business cases and criminal cases are roughly equal in their percentage of the total caseload, that the state courts have twice as large a share of tort cases, and that the state courts have substantial segments of real property, family law, and estate cases which are almost completely absent from federal dockets. Moreover, as Professor David O'Brien observes, "Apart from criminal cases, the largest portion of state supreme court litigation involves economic issues—whether relating to state regulation of public utilities, zoning, and small businesses or labor relations and workmen's compensation, natural resources, energy, and the environment."[10]

The federal courts surge ahead in public law cases, having twice as large a share as the state courts. But we cannot make too much of this difference, for state courts have, in the years between 1959 and 1979, seen the number of federal questions involved in their decisions tripled. And a 1983 survey reported that over 25 percent of all published state supreme court opinions dealt with federal questions.[11]

The practitioner of today, and particularly tomorrow, is well advised to rethink conventional litigation strategy. To the extent that such strategy automatically dictated either bringing a case in or removing one to a federal court, it is vulnerable. A civil rights case does not always belong in federal court; indeed, some state civil rights statutes permit suit even where no state or official government action is involved. A lawyer may begin by taking pride in her acumen in suing in or removing to federal court, only to find her case on a long and slowly moving assembly line, inching ahead at a glacial pace because of an overload of priority criminal cases. Or the case may have finally reached a federal district judge or even a federal appellate court only to be derailed by the fatal question: Why shouldn't this case be certified to the state court for an answer to this novel question of state law? This, of course, means a further delay of at least fifteen months.[12]

Even if the case is not certified, the federal judge or judges involved will agonize interminably over trying to intuit what the state supreme court would say if it were faced with the issue. When the answer is finally forthcoming, it is highly likely that the federal opinion as to what state law is will be far more hidebound than a state court opinion would be. A state supreme court, after all, can change its mind, overrule or qualify precedents, and strike off in new directions with far more freedom than a federal court.

Increasingly a lawyer will be caught up in complex litigation brought in state courts against manufacturers of products such as asbestos, DES, and the Dalkon Shield. In such cases it may be almost impossible to so structure the litigation that there will be complete diversity of citizenship, i.e., that all of the parties on one side will come from different states than all of the parties on the other side. Indeed, even if this problem could be surmounted, Professor Arthur R. Miller, reporter for the Complex Litigation Project of the American Law Institute, points out, "[L]itigation in the federal courts may not always be the most desirable means of handling complex litigation." He cites as examples "single disaster" events such as the 1981 collapse of the Hyatt skywalks, area pollution cases, and insurance coverage litigation.[13]

Accordingly, a legislative proposal has long been under

consideration by the American Law Institute that would permit the transfer of some complex multiforum, multiparty cases from federal court to a state transferee court, where the best forum would be that of a particular state.[14] The proposal would also allow cases dispersed among a number of state and federal courts to be aggregated and assigned to a single state court. At its annual meeting in May, 1993, the Institute formally approved this proposal. Professor Miller characterized the purpose as ensuring that state courts "remain players" in complex litigation.[15]

Finally, Judge William W. Schwarzer, director of the Federal Judicial Center, and co-authors Nancy E. Weiss and Alan Hirsch have studied eleven complex lawsuits arising from mass torts involving air crashes, hotel catastrophes, asbestos-induced disease, and massive oil spills. They identified the existing cooperation between state and federal judges that has taken place in calendar and discovery coordination, joint settlement efforts, and joint hearings and rulings on motions, with some judges even contemplating joint state-federal trials. They conclude that extensive further coordination "can be achieved without new legislation or rules, and without subordinating one system to the other."[16]

In language resonating with overtones of Alexander Hamilton's ONE WHOLE, the study concluded, "Many judges expressed a vision of the courts as a unified system and a "national resource,' and thus regarded intersystem coordination as a national process in the effort to improve the administration of justice."[17]

C. Areas of Interconnection

Our first substantive inquiry in our tour of judicial federalism is the area of overlap and interconnection of state and federal courts. This covers relationships of tension as well as those of cooperation. These relationships are outcroppings of a rich ore that is mined intensively by law students enrolled in Federal Courts classes and by any practitioner whose practice transcends the purely parochial. On the sensitive and sophisticated application of the various doctrines governing these relationships depends in large part the effective functioning of our unique form of federalism.

To profile this area most succinctly, I present a box entitled "The Push-Pull of Judicial Federalism" to highlight the major forces tending to give dominance to federal or state law in different situations.

D. A Quantitative Look:
The Dominance of State Courts

A simple look at vertical structure, even noting the recent growth of the state intermediate appellate courts, does not begin to convey the immensity of the terrain occupied by the state courts. Chart 1 is accurate in revealing the hierarchical structure of the two court systems, but insofar as it suggests that the two parts are roughly equal in size, it is misleading.

I have, therefore, created Chart 2, which conveys some idea of the vast difference in size of the two establishments. Putting to one side the United States Supreme Court (for the reason that for most cases the federal courts of appeal and the state supreme courts are the courts of last resort), we see that the state system dominates appellate decision-making in the following dimensions:

Appellate Court Comparisons

	Federal	States	Ratio
Courts	13	100	1 to 7.5
Judges	179	1,189	1 to 6.5
Cases	47,013	238,007	1 to 5

In sum, state appellate decision-making occupies approximately 85 to 90 percent of the field.

At the trial level of courts of general jurisdiction, the disparity in magnitude of operations is even greater:

The Push-Pull of Judicial Federalism

The Push of Federal Law	The Pull of State Law
### Supreme Court Review	
The Supreme Court will review a state court's constitutional decision . . .	But not if it clearly rests on an "adequate and independent state ground."
### Federal Constitutional Interpretation	
A state court may adopt a federal constitutional interpretation for its own state constitution . . .	But it may reject the federal model and find greater protections in the state constitution.
### Federal Issues	
Federal Court precedent normally controls . . .	But a state decision is binding in the absence of a contrary federal ruling.
### Which Law Governs	
Federal law may preempt inconsistent state law . . .	But state law applies in diversity cases and is the rule of decision in any case unless federal law otherwise provides.
### Diversity	
A federal court may determine novel issues of state law in cases involving citizens of different states . . .	But it must look to state cases and its decision is not precedent. The federal court may also ask the state court to resolve the question.
### Habeas Corpus	
A federal court may free a state prisoner if federal law was violated . . .	But it will not review until state procedures and court review have taken place.
### Injunctions	
A federal court may enjoin enforcement of a state law . . .	But it may abstain from decision, pending resolution of a parallel state court proceeding.

CHART 2

MAGNITUDES: State and Federal Court Systems

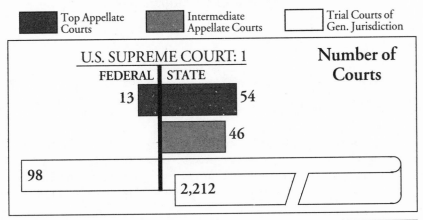

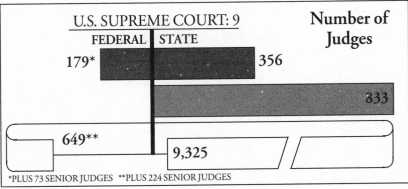

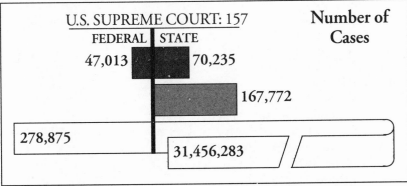

NOTE ON SOURCES: FEDERAL: *Annual Report of Director of Administrative Office of U.S. Courts, 1992.* Cases: Trial Cts.–pp. 4, 6; Appeals Cts.–p. 1; Judges–p. 20. STATE: *State Court Caseload Statistics: Annual Report 1990.* Cases: Trial Cts.–p. 4; Appellate Cts.–p. 69. Courts: Trial and Appellate–pp. 185-237. Judges: p. 275

Trial Court Comparisons

	Federal	States	Ratio
Courts	98	2,212	1 to 23
Judges	649	9,325	1 to 14
Cases Filed	278,875	31,456,283	1 to 113

In sum, state cases occupy 99 percent of the field at the trial level. The disparity would become even more pronounced if we included courts of limited jurisdiction where some 18,000 judges handle over 73,000,000 cases a year.

III. An Additional State Forum: Intermediate Appellate Courts

A relatively new and major institution on the appellate scene is the intermediate court of appeals (IAC). The most significant development in state court systems in recent years has been the proliferation of these courts. Between 1891 and 1957, the number of states with such courts increased from seven to thirteen—six in sixty-six years.[18] In the past three decades, twenty-five more states have established one or more such courts; there are now forty-six IACs in thirty-eight states, and additional states are contemplating their establishment.[19]

As can be gleaned from Chart 2, IACs in 1989 handled 60 percent of all appeals filed in federal and state courts and 70 percent of all state court appeals. A 1989 report on state court caseload statistics observed, "IACs are clearly the workhorses of state appellate systems."[20] They also are in reality the courts of last resort for most appeals. In 1987, for example, only 14.1 percent of the petitions seeking discretionary review of IAC decisions from the state supreme courts were granted.[21]

In the federal courts, appeals from agency and district

court decisions are mandatory, i.e., appeal lies as a matter of right. In most of the state systems the intermediate appellate courts handle the bulk of mandatory appeals of right and exercise the function of correcting error in the application of law and procedure, while in theory the court of last resort serves the law-developing function by selecting on a discretionary basis only those cases and issues "of overarching importance."[22]

This distinction between correcting error and developing law is often exaggerated, with the result that IACs are undervalued in writings about courts. Benjamin Kaplan, an eminent scholar-teacher, former associate justice of the Massachusetts Supreme Judicial Court, who has also served on recall on the Massachusetts IAC, the Appeals Court, has this to say about the distinction:

> [T]he intellectual process in the handling of appeals must be much the same whatever the court. Any case other than the trivial has to be located in the jurisprudence of the State and nation. It will be found perhaps at a crossroads of competing doctrines where a choice has to be made. . . . The case may appear at the limit of announced doctrine, raising the question whether that doctrine . . . should be extended or held in check. Often, all too often, there is an obscurity or a muddle where the relevant law ought to be. . . . An appeal, occasionally, but more often than one might expect in a mature jurisprudence, will be genuinely novel . . . and a judge moves toward decision by analogy, by historical or philosophic reflection, by intuition. It is by all the processes I have mentioned, and others familiar to us all, that law is "made," and more in the way of gradual unfolding than by revolutionary leaps. *An intermediate court shares in all this and inevitably is a maker of law in the same sense as the supreme court.* (Emphasis supplied.)[23]

Despite the obviously prominent role of IACs, little systematic information about them has been gathered, organized, and analyzed. Some states have IACs in from five to fourteen locations. Some are limited to civil or criminal appeals. Some may be confined almost wholly to mandatory appeals; others are given a larger component of discretionary appeals. While appeals in most states go directly to IACs, in some the courts of last resort first review the cases and make assignments to the IACs.[24]

The practitioner, therefore, must not assume that knowledge of the jurisdictional charter of one IAC will suffice for practice in another. But beyond differences in jurisdiction there are wide variations in rules and patterns of practice. For IACs provide a current and striking application of Justice Brandeis's classic observation in his dissent in *New State Ice Co.* v. *Liebmann*: "It is one of the happy incidents of the federal system that a single courageous State may, if its citizens choose, serve as a laboratory; and try novel social and economic experiments without risk to the rest of the country."[25] The traditional steps in the appellate process, which are the subject of much of this book, have been modified by IACs in different and important ways.

In their comparative study of IACs in New Jersey, Arizona, Florida, and Maryland in the late 1980s, *Intermediate Appellate Courts: Improving Case Processing*, Joy Capper and Roger Hanson have detailed some of the areas of innovation.[26] They include accelerating some appeals; limiting or dispensing with briefs or oral arguments; varying policies as to length, publication, and even the requirement of opinions; and the utilization of two-judge panels for some classes of cases.

One significant example of state court pathbreaking is, to use the words of one practitioner, "the remarkable Massachusetts judicial institution known as the 'single justice session.' "[27] This is a practice, statutorily authorized since 1974, under which appeals from interlocutory orders in civil cases may be heard by a single justice, usually a justice of the intermediate Appeals Court. As one of that court's justices, Justice Rudolph Kass, has noted, "For better or worse, review from interlocutory orders of the trial courts is much more accessible in Massachusetts than in the federal system."[28] He adds: "Single justice review is a safety valve system to adjust some major malfunction in the trial system which will severely untrack a case, produce irremediable disadvantage to one side, impose acute hardship on a party, or involves an error of law so glaring that it manifests capricious or whimsical thinking."[29]

Although the safety valve exists, it does not easily open. In one recent period, less than one fourth of the petitions filed were granted. The practitioner faces the challenge of briefing—succinctly—why the justice is not being asked merely to "second-guess" the trial court, why the trial court's action was a serious abuse of discretion, why one's client would be severely prejudiced if the interlocutory order is allowed to stand, why the trial court made an error of law, why the issue has significance for public policy beyond this case, and why granting relief now makes sense in terms of sound judicial administration.[30] Here, then, is yet another area of opportunity in appellate advocacy that exists in state systems but not in federal courts.

IV. State Constitutional Law: A Moving Frontier

Perhaps the area of greatest promise for appellate advocates in the foreseeable future is state constitutional litigation in state courts of last resort. My sense is that appellate practice is very much the same in the federal courts of appeal and in the state courts of last resort. Although in the state courts the advocate faces a bench of from five to nine judges as contrasted with a panel of three judges in federal court, I have seen nothing on my occasional visits to state courts to indicate any different approach that the advocate should take that he would not take in a federal court. My observation includes both preparation of a brief and the manner of engaging in oral argument.

There is, however, a distinct advantage for the practitioner whose mission is to try to persuade a state court of last resort to overrule, modify, or create precedent, constitutional or nonconstitutional. In the federal courts of appeal, one would seldom—very seldom—urge a departure from Supreme Court rulings, whether constitutional ones or not. Only in the rare case of a ruling remote in time, where the advent of obvious changes in conditions and a tide of critical comment have signaled a time for interment, would an inferior appellate court essay the task of burial. A federal appeals panel would even hesitate long before departing from precedent established by a number of sister courts, out of reluctance to create a split among the federal circuits. But an advocate in state court plays in a less cluttered field; the court, steward of its own law, is not insulted by hearing argument based on sense and policy indicating that a time for rethinking a past rule has come.

This atmosphere of openness is of special significance in light of the recent and remarkable development of state constitutional doctrine. Toward the end of the decade of the 1970s, Justice Brennan, putting together some thoughts for a talk to New Jersey lawyers, decided to vent his frustration with his Court's decisions, which he felt had receded from the high-water mark of constitutional protection of individual rights. He expressed the thought that such action was an invitation to state courts to step into the breach. Subsequently, the *Harvard Law Review* asked the Justice to edit and submit his talk for publication. The resulting article, "State Constitutions and the Protection of Individual Rights,"[31] proved to be something of a lightning rod for a movement which came to be variously labeled "reincarnation,"[32] "renaissance,"[33] and "phoenix-like resurrection of federalism."[34]

By 1986 there had been some three hundred state court opinions declaring federal constitutional minimum standards insufficient under more stringent state constitutional requirements.[35] By 1987 there were 350.[36] And by 1990 there were more than six hundred.[37] In 1986, civil cases outnumbered criminal cases.[38] Beyond issues of criminal procedure, the state court opinions dealt with abortion funding, church-state issues, gender discrimination, freedom of expression, funding of public education, state equal rights amendments and constitutional torts, and environmental law.[39]

A case in point, one in which I played a part, involved the question whether a murder suspect's right not to incriminate himself had been violated when the police, after misrepresenting to defense counsel that they would not be further interrogating the suspect, proceeded to obtain confessions from the suspect. After our court held that this conduct had violated defendant's Fifth Amendment right, the Supreme Court reversed.[40]

In our court's decision we drew on decisions of five state supreme courts. What intrigued me was that since the Supreme Court spoke, a number of states have continued to adopt higher standards of police conduct for their own officials than required by the Supreme Court's reading of the federal constitution in *Moran* v. *Burbine*. They include Connecticut, Florida, California, and Illinois.[41] This resurgence of state courts' interest in applying their own constitutions does not indicate a universal trend to reject or avoid Supreme Court precedent in favor of greater individual protections. One scholar has concluded, on the basis of a study restricted to criminal cases, that for every state court opinion rejecting a Supreme Court precedent, there are two opinions adopting one.[42] Indeed, he identifies twenty-two "adoptionist" states, which have embraced Supreme Court doctrine in at least five cases, and only four "rejectionist" states, which have rejected such doctrine in five cases.[43] But new decisions in both camps are continually being issued.

The point for the student and the practitioner is not whether state court constitutional rulings are "liberal" or "conservative," but that state constitutional law is now a field ripe for cultivation. Law schools must teach it. Scholars must write about it and publishers must publish. And practitioners must learn how to analyze and present state constitutional issues.

V. Flaws in the System: State Court Shackles

In discussing the concept of our binary court system as "ONE WHOLE," we have so far noted the points of intersection and overlap, the sheer quantitative dominance of state court decision-making, the variety of practices and experimentation in the state IACs, and the fruition of state constitutional law. That a top-quality, readily accessible, independent state judiciary is essential to the effective functioning of the state-federal court system is obvious. The whole thrust of this discussion has been to spotlight the often overlooked advantages for the practitioner who understands and values the opportunities afforded by state courts—particularly state appellate courts.

But the way to state appellate courts lies through state trial courts. And candor compels us to recognize several shackles that prevent state courts from realizing their full potential as coequal and corespected parties in our justice system. Although a full and fair discussion of these is beyond the scope of this book, three merit brief recognition: chronic underfunding, the election of judges, and the perpetuation of diversity jurisdiction.

A. Underfunding

In an era when most states face stubborn deficits and learn to live under conditions of extreme budgetary stringency, state court systems find themselves uniquely vulnerable. Although they constitute a separate and independent branch of state governments, charged with the basic mission of providing citizens prompt access to even-handed justice, state courts have been treated simply as ordinary agencies and departments of the executive branch.

A panoramic view of state courts in the 1990s reveals almost unrelieved crisis. Courts have been closed, and newly built courtrooms have remained unused for lack of judges, judicial vacancies not being filled. Plans for new facilities and equipment replacement have been canceled. Civil jury trials have been delayed, have been made conditional on the payment of a substantial fee, and have even been suspended for substantial periods. Criminal charges, even felony charges, have been dismissed for lack of capacity to hold prompt trials. Crime reduction programs, youth shelters, and public defender services have been eliminated or curtailed. Probation staffs have been cut in half. Prisons are overcrowded, forcing the early release of inmates. Public access to clerks' offices has been limited to allow shrunken staff to catch up with paperwork. Court employees have suffered massive reductions, payless vacation days, freezes in hiring, reductions and deferments in compensation, curtailment in travel and court security, and elimination of training programs.[44]

Recognizing that there is, indeed, a crisis in the justice system, the American Bar Association established a Special Committee on Funding the Justice System. It summarized its findings from a survey of all the state justice systems:

> The central message emerging from the survey is the unmistakable: The justice system in many parts of the United States is on the verge of collapse due to inadequate funding and unbalanced funding.[45]

B. The Election of Judges

During the heyday of populism in Jacksonian times, the popular and partisan election of judges came into vogue. Since then, unhappiness with the politicization of the judiciary has led to a number of reforms.

Today the methods of appointing state judges run the gamut from gubernatorial appointment subject to legislative confirmation, to appointment by the legislature, to partisan and nonpartisan elections, and to some form of the Missouri Plan (initial appointment by governor followed by noncompetitive retention elections). In 1990, thirty-four states and the District of Columbia followed the Missouri Plan approach for at least some level of their court systems.[46] But fifteen states still resort to partisan elections for all or some of their major courts.

The inappropriateness of choosing judges by popular election has been simply put by Norman Krivosha, former chief justice of Nebraska: "Legislators have constituents and therefore should be popularly elected. Governors have constituents and therefore should be popularly elected. Judges are prohibited by law from having constituents; therefore, subjecting them to popular election is totally without reason."[47] Or, as Justice Stevens, writing for the Supreme Court in a recent case, stated: "The fundamental tension between the ideal character of the judicial office and the real world of electoral politics cannot be resolved by crediting judges with total indifference to the popular will while simultaneously requiring them to run for elected office."[48]

In addition to this lack of fit, there is the drain of as much as a third of a court's time in campaigning for office together with the adverse impact on the appearance if not the reality of justice of raising the astronomical sums required by today's political campaigns. Candidates for a state supreme court have spent as much as $2,700,000.[49] The specter of judges being concerned over building their image, commissioning polls, engaging in mass mailing and stump speaking, and relying on the efforts of lawyer fund-raisers and single-issue interest groups would turn any dream of justice into a nightmare.

The wonder is that state courts so often perform so well in the face of these handicaps.

C. Diversity Jurisdiction

Ever since the passage of the Judiciary Act of 1789, federal courts have been empowered to hear controversies involving state law between citizens of different states. This is what is called the diversity jurisdiction of the federal courts. It originally reflected the fear that state courts would be biased against outsiders and Federalist distrust of debtor-dominated state legislatures. The principal effect today is to allow large nonresident corporations that are sued in state courts to remove their case to federal court.[50]

The results are to burden federal courts with one-fourth of their caseload and one-half of their jury trials,[51] to require federal judges to engage in arcane efforts to guess what state law might be, to flout the basic idea of federalism, to foster the idea that state courts are second-rate, and to remove any incentive for the influential segment of the bar representing nonresident corporations to work for the improvement of state courts.

But before there can be a rational allocation of roles between federal and state courts, there must be stable and adequate funding of state courts to ensure that state courts are manned by a quality judiciary. And there must be more movement to abolish the election of judges, particularly their partisan election, and so to ensure that state courts are manned by an independent judiciary.

This objective, state court systems of excellence and independence, is of equal interest to all those participating within our dual federal-state justice system and to citizens at large on whom the health of our most serious activities depends.

4

In Chambers

I. The Workplace

We have borrowed from English barristers and judges the word "chambers" to signify a judge's suite of offices. The word still has a musty connotation. Almost half a century ago, Reginald Hine, in *Confessions of an Uncommon Attorney*,[1] after mourning the changes in the legal profession wrought "in this pestering age," wistfully reflected, "Gone, too, is that ruminating, spider-like existence that a lawyer used to lead in his be-cobwebbed chambers." He recalled his own professional beginnings as an articled clerk in 1901, when "documents of title [were] elegantly scrivened on sheepskin, not vulgarly typed as now on parchment paper."

Today's judge may not lead a "spider-like existence," the chambers may not be "be-cobwebbed," and documents may no longer be scrivened on sheepskin, nor even vulgarly typed on parchment paper or any other paper, but rumination is still the crucial activity. Contemporary law offices, particularly the multistoried offices of a large firm, radiate a highly charged, electric sense of activity—young associates striding the corridors, overnight crews working the computers, banks of sophisticated electronic equipment, busy conference rooms. The chambers of a trial judge, when the judge is not in court, are likely to see a constant flow of lawyers taking their turn in pre-trial conferences. But the chambers of an appellate judge house only the permanent occupants—the judge, the secretary, the law clerks. The only noises are those of quiet conversation and the muted clack of computer keys.

In a sense this quiet is misleading. It obscures the fact that what is going on is reading, thinking, writing in an effort to resolve in a principled way some question that has locked the parties in combat, tapped the energies and judgment of a trial judge, jury, or administrative agency, and is thought close enough to warrant an appeal. In short, though the work is quiet and solitary, it is rigorous. It prospers best in an environment conducive to sustained reflectiveness. So the time-honored English designation "chambers" signals a hope to preserve something of the serenity, dignity, and grace associated with more leisurely and reflective times. And even though the rise in caseloads and the infusion of electronic aids have forced a faster pace, a nurturing stillness yet survives.

My own chambers are a suite of three rooms abutting the chambers of the chief judge of the district (Maine) in which I live and do most of my work. I like to tell friends that in nearly half a century my career has taken me only six inches. For that is the width of the wall between my present chambers and the room I occupied as law clerk to *my* district judge some forty-seven years ago. I can remember that in first reporting for duty, I met the venerable predecessor of my judge, who looked with disdain upon such an encumbrance as a law clerk and wrote all his opinions at a stand-up desk with a quill pen.

What a far remove from the computers at every desk (including my own), the copying machine, the facsimile (fax) equipment for transmission of documents, and access to computerized legal research connecting chambers with almost any book in any library! And although this is the age of the computer, the torrent of books shows no signs of abating. In my time on the bench, now well beyond a quarter of a century, I have seen the reports of United States Supreme Court decisions expand from Volume 384 to nearly Volume 500—a 30 percent growth in my life as a judge. Even more awesome are the facts that the volumes of the Federal Reporter, Second Series ("Fed Second"), which contain the opinions of federal courts of appeal, first reported my own opinions in Volume 355 and now, at this writing, are approaching Volume 1000—an increase of over six hundred volumes occupying, I might add, forty-six shelves and some 123 linear feet. My mind boggles when I try to estimate the number of volumes of reports issuing from the state courts of last resort and intermediate appellate courts during the same time span.

In my own sanctum sanctorum, in addition to the shelves of Fed Second, there are scores of monographs and law review articles, some treatises, copies of procedural rules, and, on the walls, a few paintings and some photographs of cherished colleagues. Beyond my door is the middle room of three, the domain of my secretary. Here is her workstation—desk, computer, printer, telephone, all of the Supreme Court reports, a large copying machine, and file cabinets for current cases. And on the wall, two large panels of photographs of my clerk family, fifty-eight of them, with spouses and children.

Finally, the clerks' workroom. Over the entrance is a sign, the age and origins of which are lost to memory: "It's hard to soar with eagles when you fly with a bunch of turkeys." Each clerk has a computer adjacent to what I suppose is a desk. "Suppose" because the surface is usually covered with books of case reports, treatises, briefs, opinion drafts, and raw notes. A fax machine reposes in a corner, ready to spew forth drafts of colleagues' opinions. Around the room are shelved another collection of Fed Second, many volumes of federal district court opinions (Federal Supplement or "Fed Supp"), some fifty volumes of the United States Code Annotated, several key treatises, and a digest of federal cases . . . and near the door is a miniature basketball net toward which a frustrated clerk may occasionally lob a soft ball.

II. The Chambers Family

A. Secretary-Administrator

For nearly thirty years I had the good fortune to have an excellent secretary, who served me in all three branches of the federal government. For two thirds of this time she was my judicial secretary. And for most of this time her duties were mainly secretarial. That is, she was, in the traditional sense, my amanuensis—an ancient word derived from the Latin *servus a manu*, which might be literally translated as "slave to handwriting." Indeed, though she was equipped first with a manual typewriter, then an electric, and finally a word processor, her time was more than occupied with taking dictation and copying my handwriting or clerks' typescript. Copying and recopying. I shudder as I think of all the drafts that had to be completely retyped because of a few stylistic changes.

There always have been other functions. My secretary had the responsibility of generally supervising the running of the office, working with the clerks to see that basic procedures were followed, helping me with my committee work and court administrative duties, ordering supplies and equipment, and keeping records. But the most important part of her work was the secretarial.

As I reflect on the spectrum of duties of my present secretary, I am struck by the reversal of priorities. Today the secretarial element, while remaining important, is not dominant. Because of the computer, both I and my clerks can turn out clean copy of our drafts. All corrections are easily made. The last step is simply to send the disk containing the final draft to our court clerk for publication. No more typesetting. No more hot lead.

But four other functions have become more demanding and complex. Office administration involves liaison with other chambers and offices in the judicial branch, developing procedures and systems, governing activity in chambers and ensuring conformity with circuit policy, and keeping on top of supplies and office maintenance. Personnel responsibilities require intimate knowledge of all the rules, requirements, and procedures governing grade and quality step increases, sick leave, travel, and government benefits. The keeping of records and reporting of statistics relating to cases, equal opportunity compliance, and book and equipment inventories are increasingly demanding. And finally, the responsibility of being our in-house expert on computers is critical; my secretary trains all of us, monitors our equipment, does troubleshooting herself or calls in outside help, and makes recommendations for new software and other equipment.

After becoming fully aware of the extent to which the ancient position of secretary has changed, even in the past half-dozen years, I have recommended that the position be renamed "judicial assistant administrator." Perhaps in time it will be rechristened to conform with reality.

B. Law Clerks

1. Origin and Basic Concept. This brings me to the subject of law clerks. Their importance to the work and life of a judge and the court on which he sits cannot be stressed too much, particularly since the contemporary role of the law clerk is still too little understood. The institution of the law clerk was invented by Horace Gray when, as chief justice of the Massachusetts Supreme Judicial Court, he began in 1875 the practice of annually employing a Harvard Law School graduate to assist him. When Gray, an obviously well-organized, methodical jurist, became an Associate Justice of the Supreme Court in 1882, he continued the custom, relying on his brilliant half brother, Professor John Chipman Gray, to select the clerk of the year.[2] Justice Oliver Wendell Holmes, Jr., succeeding Gray, continued the practice. The future Justice Felix Frankfurter, while a professor at Harvard Law School, undertook to pick out bright young third-year students and send them on to Washington to serve as clerks to various justices. Karl Llewellyn, of the Columbia Law

School, wrote, "I should be inclined to rate it as Frankfurter's greatest contribution to our law that his vision, energy, and persuasiveness turned this two-judge idiosyncrasy into what shows high possibility of becoming a pervasive American legal institution."[3] Pervasive indeed this institution has become, there now being over two thousand law clerks serving federal judges and over six hundred other clerks serving bankruptcy judges and magistrates.[4] A similar number must be serving state courts of last resort, intermediate appellate courts, and trial courts.

A century ago, it may well have been that many law clerks were kept busy and useful simply checking citations, correcting galley proofs, preparing research memoranda on specific questions of law, and running errands. But although there may be some judges today who claim such a limited role on the part of their clerks, I suspect that the crabbed, wholly mechanical role has seldom found eager aspirants among the best and brightest of young law graduates. Indeed, Justice Gray, the creator and first sponsor, probably used his clerks in a more spacious and challenging manner. Samuel Williston, celebrated professor and scholar, late in life wrote about his service as a law clerk to Justice Gray in 1888. He wrote that in addition to being asked to look over briefs and records of argued cases,

> I would also frequently be asked to write an opinion on the cases that had been assigned to the Judge. I do not wish, however, to give the impression that my work served for more than a stimulus for the judge's own mind. He was a careful man and examined cases for himself, and wrote his own opinions; my work served only as a suggestion.[5]

My own suspicion is that if young Williston served up an admirable piece of work, the Justice would not consider it degrading to borrow liberally from it. Indeed, Professors Oakley and Thompson have likened Williston's role to that of clerks a century later—"[n]either a Rasputin nor a ghostwriter"[6]—and have called Justice Gray's use of law clerks "the taproot of a tradition."[7]

The *Judicial Writing Manual* published by the Federal Judicial Center reports the following spectrum of contemporary law clerk usage: (1) limiting clerks to research, bench memos, editing, cite-checking, and commenting on the judge's drafts; (2) assigning clerks to write first drafts in routine cases only; (3) assigning clerks the task of rewriting the judge's first draft before final polishing; and (4) assigning clerks to write first drafts in even the most complex cases.[8]

I suspect that the judges who genuinely limit their clerks to (1) and (2) are, as one sage put it, "in shallow water and sinking fast." Generally, the concepts of law clerk as citation checker and writer of memoranda and insubstantial opinion drafts have outlived any time when they could fairly be said to reflect reality in most chambers. There may yet remain the rare judge who, because of prodigious facility or chronic inability to delegate, can claim authorship in minute detail of every substantial opinion. But most of us could not hope to cope with the exponential increase in volume and complexity of both state and federal appellate caseloads without much more substantial help from our clerks.

Apart from any other consideration, the demands on a judge's time make it critically important to use law clerk assistance with maximum effectiveness. A typical appeals judge, after three to five days in court hearing arguments, will return to chambers for three or four weeks with from six to ten opinions to draft. Perhaps one or two will be insubstantial and easily disposed of, although such cases are usually eliminated by the screening process. From two to four will be of middling complexity, either because some legal issues will require considerable research or because a lengthy record has to be read. But there will remain two or three heavy cases, of which one may require up to a month's time in research and writing. Over the course of a year an appellate judge will produce fifty or more published opinions and perhaps an equal number of unpublished opinions, an output at least three times that of a judge in the 1960s. The *Judicial Opinion Writing Manual* of the American Bar Association reports that "many appellate judges who were writing fewer than 40 opinions per year in the early 1970s are writing well over 100 opinions per year in the 1990s."[9]

Today, as we shall see in greater detail in Chapter 11, the collaboration between clerk and judge is much more than proffering only a suggestion, doing research, preparing memoranda, and cite-checking. Although the number of variations in collaboration probably equals the number of appellate judges, there are three major modes.

The first is the authoritarian mode. In this mode, work of very substantial importance is entrusted to a law clerk, but under a tight leash and with rather precise instructions. For example, the clerk is assigned to draft an opinion, but only after an outline has been approved by the judge. Or, the judge has in mind a theory and the intuition that there are cases to support it; the clerk is to put flesh on the bare bones. This kind of collaboration is closest to that which formerly existed between a skilled medical specialist and his technical assistants and resident interns as he made his rounds of patients.

The distinguished doctor-essayist Lewis Thomas has given us a snapshot of his ward "clerkship" in internal medicine, years ago, under the supervision of a masterful diagnostician, Dr. Hermann Blumgart:

> Ward rounds with Dr. Blumgart were an intellectual pleasure, also good for the soul. . . . He had the special gift of perceiving, almost instantaneously, while still approaching the bedside of a new patient, whether the problem was a serious one or not. . . . To watch a master of physical diagnosis in the execution of a complete physical examination is something of an aesthetic experience, rather like observing a great ballet dancer or a concert cellist. Blumgart did all this swiftly, then asked a few more questions, then drew us away to the corridor outside the ward for his discussion, and then his diagnosis, sometimes a death sentence.[10]

With such a master in charge, assistants and interns fulfilled their duties by carrying out assigned chores punctiliously. I venture to say that there are very few appellate judges today who come to a difficult case with quite the same confidence.

More suited to our general condition is a second mode. It

is more permissive and might be called the discretionary mode. While the obviously basic decisions are made by the judge, there is room for minor decision-making by the clerk. This is a creative collaboration which calls up in my mind the interaction between a master and his apprentices in a Renaissance artist's studio. Irving Stone described the master's studio, or *bottega*, of the Florentine painter Domenico Ghirlandaio as it was at the time the young Michelangelo was apprenticed to learn the art of painting:

> Ghirlandaio created the over-design, the composition within each panel and the harmonious relation of one panel to the many others. He did most of the important portraits, but the hundred others were distributed throughout the studio. . . . Where there was an excellent angle of visibility from the church [in which the frescoed panel would be installed], Ghirlandaio did the entire panel himself. Otherwise major portions were painted by [senior apprentices]. On the lateral lunettes, which were hard to see, he let [the junior apprentices] practice.[11]

There can develop from this kind of master-apprentice relationship a third mode, which I call the collegial. In this mode the collaboration takes on the collegial character of several colleagues devoting their entire efforts to the pursuit of a shared common objective. The bedrock responsibility of the judge is so understood that it needs no explicit expression. The ample discretion lodged in the clerk is a product of the trust earned by experience. In our chambers, we have reached this level of trust in no small part because of the continued service for ten years of my career law clerk. Through her mediation, in addition to whatever I can impart, my clerks are generally sensitized early on to my values and approaches and are able to help in the design of many issues. Although my clerks willingly wear the cloak of anonymity, they take just as much pride as I do in the work product of "our chambers."

A fly on the wall, listening to our discussions as we come to decision on even the largest of issues, would, with rare exceptions, detect no hierarchy of authority. Of course, as George Orwell put it in *Animal Farm*, "All animals are equal but some animals are more equal than others." And in chambers, because of my appointment by the President, confirmation by the Senate, and my oath of office, I am more equal than my associates. But the collegial mode suits us, even though it may not be feasible for every chambers.

Whatever the mode of collaboration between judge and clerks, all realize the vitalizing contribution of the clerkship institution. Clerks bring to chambers their recent exposure to excellent professors from all parts of the country. They are experienced in ways denied an older generation, they possess high intelligence and energy, and they are questioning, articulate, and idealistic. They provide the judge with a continuing seminar that cannot fail to keep the mind open and mental juices flowing. The pleasure of their company is one of a judge's most precious fringe benefits.

2. Recruiting Clerks. The business of choosing clerks is a vital function of the judge and her chamber associates. Although it may occupy only a truncated period of time, the effort invested—by student applicants, their professors, the judge, her secretary, and law clerks—is enormous and intense. I cannot begin to reflect the efforts of the student who in the midst of the middle year of law school must somehow assemble a résumé, acquire a transcript of grades, polish, complete, or create a writing sample, prevail on busy professors to write a personal letter of appraisal, and compose a covering letter that will be suitably deferential but not overtly ingratiating and will suggest a special interest in serving the reader while being appropriate for the mailing list of ten, twenty, or fifty judges.

As if this task were not difficult enough, it must be carried out in the presently chaotic context surrounding clerk selection. Because of a deep-rooted fear on the part of judges in one area that judges in another will skim the cream from each new class of law graduates, the choice of law clerks is being moved back earlier and earlier—to the point where only one third of a student's law school experience can be taken into account. Attempts are periodically made to defer decisions until a certain date, at which time the equivalent of a California Gold Rush takes place, when judges phone offers, applicants accept, reject, or want time to think, and judges and students end with a deep distaste for the process.

Although I have had unwavering success in recruiting law clerks who have served with high competence and have become close friends, I can boast no set formula. My clerks have come from law schools all over the country. Their undergraduate majors have varied from mathematics to philosophy. Their non-law occupations have included operating a restaurant, being a carpenter, being a newspaper reporter, and working with the handicapped, the poor, and the illiterate. Since a clerk's work for me requires high productivity in research, writing, and editing, I generally look for someone who has had substantial responsibility in putting out a school law journal.

I am also looking for a clerk who, in addition to all other qualities, can write with some facility prose that is clean, unadorned, vigorous, and free from jargon. Small order? No, but I have been blessed by clerks who have learned to write well. The first clue to an applicant's writing ability is the letter of application. At one extreme is the utterly drab, wooden, boilerplate letter. At the other is almost stream-of-consciousness rambling about one's aspirations in life, often presented in purple prose. Somewhere in between is the applicant I seek.

More substantively helpful is the applicant's writing sample. Are the sentences excessively long, or short and too choppy? Sometimes there are so many case citations and footnotes that I have a hard time following the flow of the applicant's reasoning. Sometimes an argument will be brigaded with plentiful scholarly apparatus, but on analysis will seem lame. This, of course, is not a matter of writing style, but of something more important: basic legal analytical ability. Writing samples do not have to be lengthy law review pieces, polished and ready for print. They can be pieces written under time pressures; indeed, such a sample may be the most useful, if the time taken is revealed. After browsing over a sample, sometimes reading a section with more care, my question to myself is: would I feel reasonably comfortable if I had written the sample? Ordinarily the final source is letters from professors and employers. Not all recommenders deal with writing ability, but I look for comments from professors whom I respect that give me some idea of writing ability.

While a clerk applicant's letter, résumé, writing sample, and recommendations tell me a great deal, personal interviews are of key importance. In this kind of competition, where almost every "finalist" is superb in every category, I inevitably look for a "something else." Sometimes I detect this attribute from the range of interests of the applicant, sometimes from the occasionally highly perceptive and personal letters of professors, and often from evidence that the student looks on a career in law as one which will enable him to contribute something to his fellow humans. But sometimes the personal interview communicates the spark or brightness of spirit that engages me, that makes me sit forward in my chair and relish the prospect of a year's company. I fear I am not intrigued by the applicant who comes with a buttoned-up look, with a slight aroma of arrogance and of unconcern with society in general. I know that I have let slip extraordinary clerk applicants just because I couldn't sense the something extra that, happily, I have managed to find so often.

Before I interview an applicant, he or she first spends a half hour or so talking with my present clerks about the way in which our chambers operates. Later we have lunch—the applicant, myself, my clerks, and my secretary. This is not a law-oriented occasion, but it has its importance. Once in a while we will find an excellent "paper" applicant whose demeanor seems to us to be contrived or who may, with ill-concealed difficulty, condescend to talk to my secretary. We let the applicant seek fame and fortune elsewhere.

3. The Basic Requirement: Confidentiality. The foundation of all relationships between a judge and his law clerks is assured confidentiality—extending throughout life. In an era when the public's right to know is asserted as to every governmental entity and function, it may seem archaic to value confidentiality for judicial chambers. But there must remain a veil over what is discussed among judges and between a judge and his law clerks. There is no reason to penetrate this veil to discover how a judge has voted or why, because the published opinion sets forth the facts, assumptions, authorities, reasoning, and conclusions by which alone the opinion is to be tested.

Disclosure of the informal communications, crossfire, negotiations, and concessions preceding the final opinion would only lead to the distortion of what is essentially a highly creative, tentative, testing, and experimental process—developing a collegial decision. The apprehension by a judge that one of his remarks, be it deliberate or random, said in contemplation or in exacerbation, could someday gain public currency would be a leaden blanket smothering discourse.

This counsel to clerks concerns not only what is talked about by judge and clerks. It applies also elsewhere. A clerk must not reveal which judge of a panel or court has the responsibility of writing the opinion. A law clerk should be particularly careful in conversing with attorneys who appear before the court. And there is even a caution about communicating with fellow clerks in the chambers of other judges; a clerk should always check with her or his judge as to whether clerk-to-clerk communication is desirable and at what level of revealing positions and reasoning.

4. Life with "the Clever." Our language abounds in suggestive collective nouns: a pod of whales, a gaggle of geese, a pride of lions. Long ago one of my law clerks found the proper collective for my law clerk family: a clever of clerks. The term, as we use it, is fun-poking rather than self-congratulatory. In a sense the lighter side of judge-clerk relationships has no place in a book that attempts to be serious about the appellate process. But not really. For the companionship between bright young clerks and judges is one of the ineffably precious perquisites of judging and helps keep alive the sacred fires of enthusiasm and creativity. In any event, I cannot leave a chapter concerning chambers without some mention of the ecstasy and occasional agony of living a great deal of my life with my clerks.

Over the years, we have found more and more of life's passages to celebrate. We (meaning my clerks and my wife and I) cherish get-togethers at our house, a clerk's lodging, or a restaurant to do decent homage to a birthday, to passing a bar examination, to getting a job, to departing or returning, to celebrating our secretary's length of service, to Christmas, Chanukah, sometimes the winter solstice, and weddings (at some of which I have been privileged to participate).

In addition to these conventional occasions, we have been known to climb small mountains and canoe on placid rivers in the autumn, tempt fate in ski outings in the winter, and visit Maine islands and feast on lobster at our ancient summer cottage. Every few years there is a homecoming clerk reunion and, whenever our travel plans allow, a gathering of former clerks in Washington, New York, and even San Francisco. Occasionally, my clerks have displayed frustrated thespian talents. Once we reenacted *Twelfth Night* between dinner courses. A memorable performance was "The Wizard of Laws," in which the tin man and his celebrated friends followed the yellow brick road to the land of Laws and finally exposed the Wizard . . . not a feckless Frank Morgan, but the redoubtable months-old daughter of a clerk.

Sadly, such performances degenerated into irreverent roasts of the clerks' hapless judge, one even being frozen for all time on videotape. And during the past decade a tradition of fiendishly clever gullery has, I am afraid, become a *fait accompli*—I being predictably gullible. The cozenage began with an impressive application for a clerkship from one Stanley Egret. So awed was I by the covering sheet of favorable appraisals by my clerks (who thought this might be a unique opportunity for affirmative action) and a quick glimpse at the detailed résumé and glowing letters from Stanford Law School professors that I took the file home for careful scrutiny. Only then did I read Stanley's obscure reference to his involvement "in a minor incident that led to my conviction of aggravated rape and to my commitment to San Quentin prison for a term of ten years." A letter from San Quentin's warden was reassuring: "[W]e have discovered that bolting a large chain to a heavy desk makes a full-time attendant unnecessary."

This kind of nonsense has unfortunately led to what I call "clerkscam." On or about every April 1, some facially credible communication lands in my in-basket: a supposed letter from a law professor whose book I reviewed, humbly seeking guidance on how he could meet my criticisms; a formal memorandum from the director of the Administrative Office of U.S. Courts outlining cost-cutting measures, including eliminating secretarial and law clerk support by fully computerizing chambers . . . and requiring judges to "use their own resources to purchase the appropriate equipment"; a more recent—and poignant—memorandum announcing the requirement that senior judges must demonstrate a typing capacity of fifty words a minute to retain their chambers' computers; and, most recently and impertinently, a forged letter (on W. W. Norton stationery) from my editor, Don Fusting, telling me that an associate had a client who felt that this book was "the perfect vehicle for . . . either a primetime television drama or a full-length feature film about the workings of a judicial chambers."

I regret to say that so far I have not managed to retaliate with any significant success, but someday . . .

Before we see an appellate chambers at work, we must pause for a good look at where appeals begin, and where many of them are won or lost long before briefs reach an appellate chambers.

5

Where Appeals Begin

Paradoxically, we begin our detailed review of the appellate process at a stage and time long before an appeal has been taken. The locus of this chapter is the trial court or administrative agency where, from the very moment a complaint is filed or a prosecution begun, virtually every step taken or not taken may have profound influence on whatever appeal ultimately is pursued. Here is where many a seemingly meritorious appeal is unmade, where many a stable door is locked after the steed is stolen.

Indeed, the phenomenon of nonpreservation of claims of error has been the occasion for a rite of passage for many a law clerk. Fresh from law school, with a record of high achievement, a new clerk gleefully seizes on a new and challenging issue: here is a chance to play a role in the forging of new law. But before she spends too much time in research, I ask that the record appendix be consulted, to make sure that there was a proper objection, request, or motion and that the trial judge's ruling is fairly viewed in context. When all this has been done, we can all too often invoke Tallulah Bankhead's mordant comment after lunching with the celebrated clique of pundits at the Algonquin: "There is less here than meets the eye." Making new law has to wait.

If new law clerks need to be sensitized to the importance of error preservation, how much more compelling is the need for practitioners to develop an awareness of this *terra incognita*.

I. Where the Die Is Cast

A. The American Tradition

We have noted, in Chapter 2, that appellate courts in civil law jurisdictions will review issues of fact with little deference to trial court findings and will even receive new evidence. The same is true, to a lesser extent, in the Court of Appeal in England. But in the United States, ironically for this newest of traditions, the ancient writ-of-error way of thinking still holds sway—the concept that the target of an appeal is the alleged error(s) of the trial judge, not whether a fresh view of facts and legal issues would command a different result. Consequently, our appellate courts step into the shoes of the trial judge and view the facts and issues as they were presented to him.

But there is more than history and tradition supporting our adherence to the record made below. There is an instinct of fairness due both the trial judge or agency and a litigant's adversary, a sense that one's opponent should have a chance to defend, explain, or rebut some challenged ruling and that the trial judge should have a clear first chance to address the issue. Indeed, if appellate courts were to consider some unpreserved issues but not others, depending on gradations of sympathy, the result would be an extremely uneven playing field.

There is also the canny recognition that if late-blooming issues were allowed to be raised for the first time on appeal, this would be an incentive for game-playing by counsel, for acquiescing through silence when risky rulings are made, and, when they can no longer be corrected at the trial level, unveiling them as new weapons on appeal. Finally, there is an element of institutional self-preservation in closing the door to what could be a flood of open-ended appellate opportunities.

Isn't this attitude overly technical? I should quickly acknowledge the existence of an escape hatch for egregious error. All appellate courts will consider an issue not preserved below if otherwise a "gross miscarriage of justice" would ensue, or if the issue concerned the court's jurisdiction, or, in a criminal case, if a very basic or "plain" error was committed. And some courts are somewhat more permissive than others. But I venture to predict that with ever-increasing caseloads, there will be ever more rigorous insistence on the general requirement of preservation of issues.

B. The Trial Court Minefield

It is not my purpose to present a definitive or encyclopedic panorama of all of the steps in the course of a litigation where issue preservation traps and mines may be encountered. My aim is the more modest one of developing awareness in the student and practitioner in an impressionistic manner. Accordingly, I offer Chart 3 as a graphic catalogue of threats and opportunities during the pre-trial period, during trial itself, and during the post-trial period preceding appellate consideration.

1. Pleadings. The hazard of waiving issues begins with the pleadings. Perhaps the commonest predicament is that of the plaintiff whose complaint, say, of conspiracy to violate his civil rights is long on vituperative conclusions but bereft of specific facts concerning dates, participants, and events. This complaint is a prime candidate for dismissal. Plaintiffs have also seen their cases narrowly confined and ultimately lost because of the omission in the complaint of causes of action that the facts reasonably suggest. One example: A plaintiff who alleged only an intentional infliction of emotional injury lost the chance to claim damages for the easier-to-prove tort of negligent infliction of such injury. Another

CHART 3
On the Way to Appeal

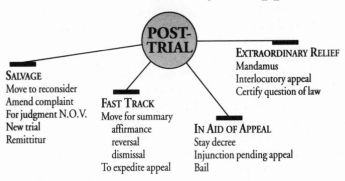

POST-TRIAL

SALVAGE
Move to reconsider
Amend complaint
For judgment N.O.V.
New trial
Remittitur

FAST TRACK
Move for summary
   affirmance
   reversal
   dismissal
To expedite appeal

IN AID OF APPEAL
Stay decree
Injunction pending appeal
Bail

EXTRAORDINARY RELIEF
Mandamus
Interlocutory appeal
Certify question of law

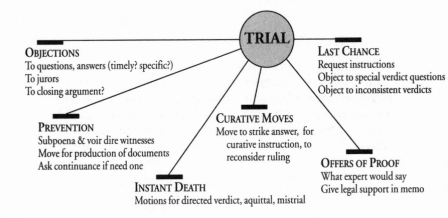

TRIAL

OBJECTIONS
To questions, answers (timely? specific?)
To jurors
To closing argument?

PREVENTION
Subpoena & voir dire witnesses
Move for production of documents
Ask continuance if need one

INSTANT DEATH
Motions for directed verdict, aquittal, mistrial

CURATIVE MOVES
Move to strike answer, for
   curative instruction, to
   reconsider ruling

LAST CHANCE
Request instructions
Object to special verdict questions
Object to inconsistent verdicts

OFFERS OF PROOF
What expert would say
Give legal support in memo

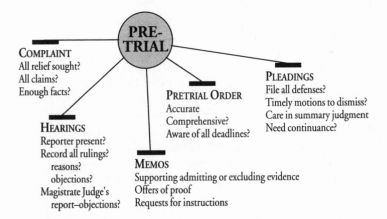

PRE-TRIAL

COMPLAINT
All relief sought?
All claims?
Enough facts?

HEARINGS
Reporter present?
Record all rulings?
   reasons?
   objections?
Magistrate Judge's
   report–objections?

MEMOS
Supporting admitting or excluding evidence
Offers of proof
Requests for instructions

PRETRIAL ORDER
Accurate
Comprehensive?
Aware of all deadlines?

PLEADINGS
File all defenses?
Timely motions to dismiss?
Care in summary judgment
Need continuance?

example: The failure to allege a cause of action in contract in addition to one in tort resulted in the case being dismissed because the shorter limitations period for torts had run. Sometimes a possible recovery of damages is frustrated by failure to name as a party the only solvent person or institution, or the only chance for some remedy goes out the window because the complaint failed to add a request for injunctive relief to that for damages.

Pleadings (and motions) are a snare not only for plaintiffs. Defendants have lost the chance to raise certain defenses to personal jurisdiction, venue (the proper place for trial), service of process, the suppression of evidence, or severance of charges or parties by not taking timely action as mandated by rules of procedure. Failure to raise affirmative defenses can hobble a defendant just as much as failure to raise claims can hobble a plaintiff.

2. Pre-trial Proceedings. There has been increasing resort, in pre-trial proceedings, to the precipitate remedy of summary judgment when pleadings, affidavits, depositions, and exhibits demonstrate that there is no "genuine" issue of "material fact." Great care is called for, both on the part of a litigant who seeks summary judgment and of one who opposes it. Quite often a party against whom such a judgment has issued will cry foul on appeal because of inadequate time to discover what the facts really are. But all too often the claim fails because counsel has failed to take advantage of a rule allowing a continuance if specific reasons are given to explain the need for more time.

A party can lose the ball game by a failure either to object to or to correct an ill-advised admission. For example, a party is bound by the recommendations a federal magistrate judge makes to a district judge if he does not make a timely objection. A party also is bound by a judge's pre-trial order if he allows an erroneous statement of his position to remain uncorrected.

A graphic illustration of the price paid for failing to correct or update earlier concessions is provided by the following excerpt from an actual case. The issue was whether a buyer of goods could recover for certain defects. The seller attempted to raise a defense under the Uniform Commercial Code that the buyer had not given timely notice after discovering the defects. The following colloquy took place on appeal:

> JUDGE: Where in your pretrial statement did you raise that point [timely notice]?
> COUNSEL: We did not specifically raise it, Your Honor.
> JUDGE: Not only did you not specifically but the answer says just the opposite—that you admit due notification.
> COUNSEL: But two and one half years after we filed that answer, we discovered that they knew about the defects in June and not in September as we had originally—
> JUDGE: After you filed the pretrial memorandum?
> COUNSEL: No, Your Honor, before that.
> JUDGE: That was the time, wasn't it?
> COUNSEL: Yes, Your Honor, we did discover—
> JUDGE: All right, go on to your next point. As far as I'm concerned, you're dead on this one.

3. Trial. The seasoned advocate will come to trial with one eye cocked on the possibility of appeal. She will come armed with memoranda covering anticipated problems and opportunities, an ability distilled from experience to make quick decisions, a knowledge of the rules of court, and unflagging alertness. The following situations require these weapons in varying degrees.

The weapon of preparation, happily, is as much a source of strength for the beginner as for the veteran, for the plodder as for the genius. This lies behind all discovery and supports arguments for or against the admission of evidence, the making of offers of proof, and the submission of requests for instructing the jury. But, though necessary, preparation may not be sufficient armament.

Appropriate action in offering or objecting to contested evidence, for example, is likely to be the product of a number of prior court experiences. Unsuccessful experiences may well be the best teachers. The ingredients of effective action decisions at trial are (1) sensing wisely whether to object or not, (2) making a timely objection, request, or response, (3) making one's point in a few words, with elaboration to follow if there is opportunity, (4) covering all the relevant grounds, (5) seeing to it that record is made of the objection, the argument, and the ruling, and (6) repeating one's objection when attempts are made to raise the same issue again.

Sometimes the "evidence" objected to is some nontestimonial happening, such as a judge's disapproving facial gestures. In one case that came before our court, counsel had approached the bench to request the trial judge to cease making disparaging faces during his cross-examination. While we found in the record no danger that the jury could have been improperly influenced, we added the following advice in our opinion:

> Although we rule against counsel, we think that he took the proper action to protect his client. Counsel should not, once he has determined that some protest at body or facial "English" is necessary, hesitate to approach the court at side bar as counsel did here. And judges, just as did the judge here, should not take umbrage at criticism, excepting of course obviously frivolous and uncalled-for protests.[1]

Curative action is available if a lawyer has been too slow in objecting. If the stable door has only just been opened, there is a chance to get the horse—or most of it—back inside. Motions to strike objectionable answers, requests for curative instructions to repair damage, and requests for reconsideration of rulings may not be as effective as preventing damage in the first place, but they often have weight on appeal in persuading the appellate court to deal with an issue.

Nearing the end of a trial, counsel can face several critical points for action. If a defendant has moved for a directed verdict at the end of plaintiff's case because of insufficient evidence, that motion must be renewed at the end of all evidence to preserve the issue of sufficiency of evidence. If one's adversary is making an improper closing argument, counsel must balance tact and politeness against necessity and, on occasion, interrupt and register an objection. If prudence dictates silence, counsel must seek a curative instruction as soon as possible, or, in an extreme situation, a mistrial.

Then come the judge's instructions to the jury. Many an appellate advocate has been laid low by a record showing that an objection was made before the trial judge delivered jury instructions, but that counsel remained silent thereafter. Many court rules, including Federal Rule of Civil Procedure 51, require a party to object to the failure to give an instruction before the jury retires. And in many jurisdictions a party's precise objection to a charge must be renewed even if it is perfectly clear that the trial judge is unbudgeable and even though she has assured counsel, "Your objection will be preserved."[2]

Finally, vigilance must not abate even after the jury has retired to deliberate. If the case is complicated, and if special verdicts have been requested, a jury may return verdicts that are internally inconsistent. The time to cure such a defect is at that moment, when correction is still possible, not after the jury has been discharged.

C. Two Cases: The Naive Neophyte and the Feckless Firm

In order to demonstrate the all-too-common phenomenon of waiver of issues on appeal, I present two models. The first is a hypothetical appeal brought by an obvious beginner. Although the appeal is hypothetical, the errors committed are typical of many such cases. The second case is more mournful, for it is based on a real appeal brought by a large and reputable law firm which shall be nameless. The moral of these tales is that attorneys manage to lose a formidable number of appeals before they come within sight of an appellate court.

* * *

The Naive Neophyte

Once upon a time Attorney Anon. Dogood, in striving to be of use to society, was assigned to represent a prisoner who had been committed to solitary confinement in an unheated cell for several weeks, because of an alleged breach of prison shaving regulations. The execrable conditions, the triviality of the alleged offense, and the length of the confinement suggested to Dogood the prosecution of a civil rights complaint charging violation of the prisoner's constitutional Eighth Amendment right not to be subjected to cruel and unusual punishment. Suit was duly brought against prison guards, the warden, and the commissioner of corrections. The prayer for relief sought damages in the amount of $500,000.

Dogood, brimming with energy and enthusiasm, not only interviewed his client meticulously but obtained an examination by a psychiatrist, who agreed to testify to the effects of extensive isolated confinement on the prisoner. He also had the good luck, on the eve of trial, to identify a former prison official who was willing to testify to heated debate within the prison as to the propriety of imposing extended solitary confinement on recalcitrant or troublemaking inmates. Here were the makings of a significant case.

This is what happened. The prisoner testified movingly that he had refrained from shaving because of a skin rash and that the solitary confinement had brought him extreme discomfort. From here, however, the road was downhill. When Attorney Dogood called the psychiatrist, the defense objected to his qualifications on the flimsy ground that the doctor had retired within the past month. Unaccountably, the judge ruled that the witness was not qualified. It did not occur to Dogood to make an offer of proof as to what the doctor's testimony would be, i.e., submit to the judge a summary of what the doctor would say.

Matters worsened when the former prison official was called to the stand. Dogood had forgotten that one of the terms of the pre-trial order was to give the other side notice of all witnesses expected to be called, and had not attempted to justify his failure to comply, even at the eleventh hour. The witness was excluded. The defense called a fellow inmate who, at one point in his testimony, referred to a paper in his hands which reported that the plaintiff had been involved in a number of earlier prison disturbances. Dogood fiercely objected to allowing the witness to read this information into the record—on the sole ground that it was irrelevant, it apparently not occurring to him to object on the ground that a fellow inmate was not a particularly reliable source to authenticate a prison record.

Finally the trial ground to an end. Dogood vigorously objected to the judge's failure to instruct the jury that the fellow inmate's testimony should be carefully scrutinized, in light of his admission on cross-examination that he had been promised some consideration for his cooperation in upcoming parole proceedings. He also objected to the judge's instruction that damages could be awarded only if plaintiff had suffered a pecuniary loss or a lasting deterioration in his health. But he neither offered alternative instructions nor did he renew his objections after the instructions had been given.

The jury deliberated for a considerable period of time—several hours. At one point the jury sent a note to the judge asking whether, if it did not assess damages, it could register its displeasure at the practice of solitary confinement as evidenced in this case. The judge, after consultation with counsel, told the jury that it had been asked for only its judgment on damages. It of course did not occur to Dogood to move to amend the complaint to ask for expungement of any reference to solitary confinement in his personnel file or injunctive relief.

Dogood went home, deeply disillusioned by the injustices permitted by the law. His client went back to his cell, his contempt of the legal profession renewed.

In sum, Attorney Dogood had managed to commit at least eight errors during trial which not only foredoomed his case before the jury, but foreclosed any chance of a successful appeal: too narrow a prayer for relief in the complaint; no attempt to conform or excuse nonconformance with the pretrial order; no attempt to obtain a continuance to allow the defense to prepare to deal with the "surprise" witness; no offer of proof of vital testimony expected from the psychiatrist; objecting to the prison record only on the ground of relevance, without questioning its authenticity; failure to offer alternative instructions; failure to renew the two objections to the instructions after they had been given; and failure to attempt to amend the complaint to include a prayer for broader relief. Not all of these efforts might have succeeded. But the probability is that Dogood would have won some kind of a jury verdict, and the certainty is that he would have obtained a new trial on appeal if he had preserved his issues.

* * *

The Feckless Firm

This appeal arose from an antitrust case which plaintiff had brought against a large number of his sales competitors and local, regional, state, and national trade associations. Plaintiff alleged that defendants had not only boycotted his operation but conspired to monopolize his sector of business, in violation of the Sherman Antitrust Act. After a long trial, the jury had found for all defendants. What follows is a brief summary of a substantial portion of plaintiff's arguments on appeal and of their common Achilles heel, a failure to preserve the issue.

Argument One: The jury finding that defendants exercised no substantial effect on interstate commerce was against the weight of the evidence. *But*—to test the weight of evidence supporting this jury verdict for defendant, there must be a motion for new trial, which was not made in this case.

Argument Two: Special questions put to the jury used the wrong legal standard for determining impact on interstate commerce. *But*—plaintiff only generally addressed the issue, proposed no language, said he would not belabor the point, and said nothing at the end of the court's charge.

Argument Three: The jury's answers to the special questions were inconsistent. *But*—plaintiff made only a conclusory statement about inconsistent answers, suggesting a "possible" mistrial without pressing such, did not request that the issue be resubmitted to the jury, and, when asked by the judge for suggestions before he recalled the jury, replied that he had none.

Argument Four: The jury erred in finding that defendants had no specific intent to monopolize. *But*—plaintiff did not object to the special question on this issue submitted to the jury.

Argument Five: The jury was given the wrong definition of causation. *But*—the ground of objection was not stated with sufficient specificity.

Argument Six: The judge's instructions contained merely abstract statements without legal content or application of law to the facts. *But*—the language of the objection defied parsing, merely referring to various types of antitrust claims without indicating where and why the judge erred.

I have always wondered whether either the client or the lawyer's partners ever knew just how amateurish a performance had taken place.

D. Advice to the Advocate

With the hope that the reader may never be in the position of counsel in either of the two cases just described, I offer the following.

The lawyer who is engaged in the trial of a case, with a decent appreciation of the fact that both action and inaction in the courtroom are also the seedbed of any appeal, has several delicate missions. She first must assess the sensitivity of the trial judge and the jury to objections, requests, motions for reconsideration, and suggestions. Does the judge feel that any intimation that there could be an appeal is an insult? Some trial judges feel that when the door of the courtroom closes, the only world is that of the trial and they are the supreme sovereigns of that world. Others may not resent the idea of an appeal but may have little interest in the case, or may exhibit some bias on a particular issue, or may resent any implied criticism of their handling of the case. Still others may be so chary of any chance of reversal that they are overly free in allowing objections and granting requests. Finally, there is the desired norm, the judge who listens, who reflects, who reads submitted memos, who is not afraid to change her mind.

The advocate's course will accommodate each of these types. He may be more restrained and selective, and perhaps even more deferential. But he must not, on a central issue, be cowed. If the judge is peremptory and rules before counsel can speak, counsel must respectfully ask to be heard. Even if refused, counsel has made a record. Patience and persistence are the guiding principles, for sometimes, after the novelty and heat of a colloquy has passed, a judge may be able to reconsider a ruling with serenity.

At the same time that the advocate is trying to respond effectively to the judge, he must keep a delicate balance. There are two extreme types of trial lawyer: one is the rough-and-tumble jury lawyer who is out to win a verdict and looks no further; the other deeply distrusts both judge and jury and seeks only to build a record for the inevitable appeal. The sophisticated advocate will pursue a happy mean. This means maintaining a sense of proportion, resisting the making of objections if the question can easily be rephrased or if the evidence does not draw blood.

In addition to reacting sensitively to the trial judge and jury, without ignoring or overstressing issues for appeal, the advocate must constantly keep in mind how the cold record will look to a reviewing court. One must remember that the first concern of most appellate judges is whether the advocate gave the trial judge a reasonable opportunity to understand an objection and to correct any error. The advocate should imagine himself some ten months or a year in the future answering such questions as these by a panel of appellate judges:

—Did you call this to the trial judge's attention?

—What specifically did you say?

—Did the judge's reply indicate a continuing misunderstanding of your objection? Did you try to point it out?

—After the judge made the ruling, did you move for reconsideration, giving your reasons?

In sum, the appeal-conscious lawyer will turn on a two-tier thought process immediately after the critical interview with his client that signals the commencement of litigation. He will, of course, be concerned with preparing for the trial— obtaining all relevant facts, developing a theory of the case, and marshaling all legal authorities. But at the same time he will be thinking of a whole range of issues that could be relevant to an appeal, whether his client eventually becomes an appellant or appellee.

I must add this caveat. I have written the above as if the same lawyer handles both trial and appeal. But a great deal of the major litigation is in the hands of very large firms, which employ different groups of lawyers to specialize in trial and appellate work. In such a situation, appellate lawyers may wisely engage in missionary work with their trial colleagues to the end that all important issues be preserved.

II. The Decision to Appeal

A. Questions to Ask

When Senior Circuit Judge John C. Godbold was chief judge of the Eleventh Circuit Court of Appeals, he wrote the following trenchant comment:

Whether an appeal should be taken is an unexplored frontier of litigation. Texts abound on how to prepare and try a case and how to handle an appeal. No text that I have seen devotes more than passing interest to whether a party dissatisfied with the result of trial should appeal. There is similarly a stark contrast between counsel's approach to the question of whether to go to trial and his approach to whether to appeal. The able lawyer will appraise with microscopic care his chances of winning at trial. He will exhaust the full spectrum of available options to avoid a trial that in his judgment he cannot win. But having been through trial of a case—good or bad—and having lost, the same able counsel will appeal without a precise appraisal of his case.[3]

Amen. A decade and a half after this comment was made, overt discussion of the decision whether or not to appeal and of the lawyer-client relationship on this issue remains largely virgin territory. Before going to trial, seasoned lawyers leave no stone unturned to make their clients weigh carefully the pros and cons. But I have the impression that after a case has been lost there is all too little discussion between lawyer and client. Too often the marching order seems to be "Damn the torpedoes; full speed ahead." The investment by trial counsel in the case may be too great for objectivity at this stage. The hazard, not always recognized, is that this is precisely when the standards shift dramatically. As we shall see, the importance of the standard of review that will apply to the appeal cannot be overstated.

An appeal-at-any-cost syndrome is at odds with the statistics. Usually around 80 percent (plus or minus several points) of civil appeals and 90 percent of criminal appeals are unsuccessful, with most decisions being unanimous. This being so, the hard facts are that lawyers have spent a great deal of fruitless (although compensated) time, clients have fruitlessly spent a great amount of money, and panels of judges and their law clerks have fruitlessly invested a great deal of scarce time on causes that ultimately were found to have been decided below without significant error. Today, the pressures on all appellate courts, state and federal, demand a consciousness-raising effort on the part of the litigating bar.

Of course, a client may reasonably conclude that the costs of appeal in time and money are justified by the chances of success: the judge, the jury, or both may have committed serious error; or even if no error was committed under the law to date, there may be a sound basis for believing that the appellate court would be willing to abandon obsolete precedent. And, quite apart from the likelihood of securing a reversal on appeal, there may be a realistic chance to narrow the scope of the trial court's holding or to narrow the remedy. Or it simply may be of great importance to the future conduct of one's client's business that a question of law be finally settled.

There are other reasons commonly relied on to justify appeal that need deeper scrutiny. In criminal cases, a lawyer may understandably want to delay the inevitable incarceration of her client as long as possible, but there comes a point where such a decision is irresponsible. Then there is a pragmatic reason. Under Supreme Court teaching, a court-appointed lawyer for an indigent defendant must, if her client insists on prosecuting an appeal, and if she wishes to withdraw from the case, advance all grounds that could "arguably" support an appeal—an exercise which may require almost as much investment of time as writing a full brief and arguing the appeal. One cannot blame the hapless lawyer for pushing ahead with the full appeal. Finally, there is timidity. A lawyer who sees no merit in an appeal and withdraws risks the unpleasantness of being the focus of a future habeas corpus suit brought by her former client, based on ineffective assistance of counsel. Only counsel possessing a healthy amount of self-confidence and a solid reputation for competence are likely to attempt to urge their convicted clients that an appeal would be frivolous.

Questionable and possibly sanctionable reasons for prosecuting a civil appeal include exploiting the advantages of the running of time, whether the time is used to permit a client to continue polluting the environment, to retain the use of the funds in question for as long as possible, to extend for a year or two the nonrecognition of a bargaining unit for employees, or to force a victorious but impecunious plaintiff to accept a minimal settlement.

Whether a client is contemplating a civil or a criminal appeal, counsel must ask hard questions. Were the errors such as to affect the result, or can they be perceived as harmless? Do the chances of success justify the costs of appeal, which include not only one's own fees and expenses, but possibly an award of costs and attorney's fees to the other side, as well as the interest which will have accumulated on the judgment? Even if a retrial is obtained, what are the chances of prevailing in the subsequent trial? Is there another way, beyond further court proceedings, to bring the dispute to an end?

In a close case, where the wisdom of pursuing an appeal is in doubt, an objective judgment should be sought. Robert Stern has urged the assistance of "the greater objectivity which a lawyer who did not try the case can bring to an appeal." He elaborated:

> The lawyer who lost is often too easily persuaded that all rulings adverse to him were completely erroneous, or even outrageous. Appellate judges will not start off with this bias, and neither will a new lawyer whose appraisal of the case, at the beginning at least, is more likely to coincide with that of the judges who are also seeing the case afresh. He will therefore be better able to advise as to the chances of winning the appeal and also as to which arguments, if any, are likely to be persuasive [quotation omitted]. Such advice may be invaluable in determining whether an appeal should be taken. Consulting a different lawyer (who may, of course, be a member of the same firm) at this stage of the case will often be extremely important, even if he is not given complete or primary responsibility for the appeal.[4]

B. The New Era of Sanctions

There is a new urgency surrounding a decision to appeal. The rules of the game have changed with the increasing proclivity of appellate courts to invoke sanctions. This stems from the awesome increases in caseloads, causing both federal and state courts to resort to measures designed to protect them from unworthy or technically deficient causes. This has not arisen from a selfish interest in the courts' convenience but rather from a realization that time given to frivolous cases is time that might have been given to other and more worthy appeals. And while in a more placid era there might have been time enough for both categories, today's constraints of traffic and time compel a choice.

1. The Range of Sanctions. So today both state and federal appellate courts are imposing, with increasing frequency, punitive measures on parties and even their counsel for both actions and failure or delinquency in taking action. There are two broad sources of sanctions: the violation of technical rules regarding the time and content of documents to be filed on appeal, and the more general proscription against the filing of frivolous appeals and unjustified delay in prosecuting any appeal.

In the federal courts, Rule 31(c) of the Federal Rules of Appellate Procedure provides for the possible dismissal of appeals for failure of an appellant to file a brief timely; in the case of a delinquent appellee, the sanction is loss of opportunity to make an oral argument. In the state courts, all but one or two states have similar or even more stringent sanctions. Failure to observe the rules regarding the filing of documents can result in (in order of severity) a reprimand, a letter to bar ethics authorities, a return of the brief for revision, the imposition of costs for excess or irrelevant matter, damages for delay, the dismissal of an appellant's case, the loss of oral argument for an appellee and the acceptance of facts as set forth in an appellant's brief, an adjudication of contempt of court, a fine, and a revocation of one's license to practice in the appellate court.

Beyond specific rules there is the broad policy of discouraging meritless appeals. In the federal courts, Rule 38 of the Federal Rules of Appellate Procedure provides: "If a court of appeals shall determine that an appeal is frivolous, it may award just damages and single or double costs to the appellee." "Damages" is interpreted as allowing the imposition of reasonable attorneys' fees. As of the time of the writing of this chapter, there were twenty-four pages of fine print in double columns noting federal appellate decisions under this rule assessing costs and fees against parties *and* against counsel. Moreover, a statute, 28 U.S.C. §1927, provides that any attorney "who so multiplies the proceedings in any case unreasonably" must personally satisfy "the excess costs, expenses, and attorneys' fees reasonably incurred." As of this writing, there are twenty-one pages of fine-print annotations of cases implementing this provision. Obviously, the time has passed when lawyers can afford to take a laissez-faire position on whether or not to appeal.

Not all, but an overwhelming majority of state courts have specific authority to sanction the bringing of frivolous appeals or the engaging in delaying tactics. The range of sanctions, from the slight to the serious, includes the imposition of single costs, double costs, treble costs, damages (including reasonable attorneys' fees), *actual* attorneys' fees, citation for contempt of court, a recovery of from 10 to 25 percent of a money judgment appealed (if the appellant did not prosecute the appeal and brought the appeal chiefly to delay), affirmance of the judgment, and appropriate discipline.

What should particularly pique a lawyer's interest is that this new era of sanctions affects not only parties but counsel. Here is an attorney-sanctions case from my own circuit. In a personal injury case involving a complaint in ten counts, the jury held for defendants on all claims. Appellant appealed, "alleging a host of evidentiary and procedural errors as well as a general bias against him on the part of the district court."[5] Appellant not only failed to argue in his brief many issues listed as points for appeal, but presented "little or no discussion of any of them."[6] Nevertheless, the court did discuss several issues, finding no merit in any, and concluding:

> We believe this is an appropriate case in which to assess against appellant's counsel personally appellee's costs and reasonable attorneys' fees on appeal. The absence of meaningful argument in the brief filed on behalf of appellant rendered this appeal frivolous and needlessly burdened appellees.[7]

2. Advice to Counsel. The first caution emerging from a consideration of this newly and rapidly developing field of sanctions for rule violation or frivolous appeal is that appellate counsel must master a new subdiscipline, what an attorney friend of mine calls "client control." At bottom this means a more activist role in arriving at the decision to appeal. A lawyer must increasingly balance the issues he or she thinks merit another chance and how a busy court, perhaps prompted by one's adversary, may view them. At this juncture, a "second opinion" is useful.

In any event, a lawyer, in any case where forecasting the court's ultimate ruling on frivolousness is difficult, should document his or her advice on the decision to appeal. A former law clerk of mine has told me of an appeal for a major client which resulted not only in losing the appeal but in a vigorous chastisement from the appellate court. When the client made known its displeasure to the law firm, the firm produced a copy of its letter advising the client in strong terms that the appeal was unlikely to succeed, even though there were issues legitimately to be discussed, and that sanctions were possible. The firm kept its client.

Sometimes, perhaps with increasing frequency, a lawyer may have to bite the bullet and withdraw from the case rather than prosecute an appeal. Balancing one's duty to a client against the loss of credibility and the possibility of incurring sanctions from the appellate court may well be an excruciating decision. Sometimes, of course, the lawyer, convinced that a rule of law has long outlived its day, will have every confidence that the client's cause ought to prevail; but a court might ultimately find that the lawyer was unjustifiably tilting against windmills. This contretemps is—alas—always possible.

If the choice facing the retained lawyer is difficult, that facing the appointed lawyer is almost impossible. That is, when a court-appointed lawyer comes to the conclusion that the client's appeal has no merit, he or she must, under current Supreme Court requirements, present to the appellate court a document presenting every issue which could reasonably be argued for the client, before being relieved from continuing with the appeal. It is simpler for most to proceed with ordinary briefing and argument.

A final note for counsel. In this new era of sanctions, a lawyer must ponder whether duty to the client requires that he or she include in the brief a request for sanctions against the other party. This flies in the face of "professional courtesy," yet courts often refrain from any action on a sanctions issue, absent any request by counsel. If an appeal has been truly meritless and undertaken only to delay the day of reckoning, one's obligations both to client and court are to request sanctions.

3. Questions for the Court. If attorneys face a *terra incognita* in the new era of sanctions, so do courts. Although most of the controversy between bench and bar has concerned sanctions at the trial level, there remains considerable potential for misunderstanding and tension at the appellate level. The application of sanctions for rule violations is perhaps the easier area. Rules, after all, are definite, and compliance is usually not too much to expect from the bar.

The more difficult questions arise when an appellate court concludes that an appeal is frivolous or has been unduly delayed. A court must not, after weeks of deliberation have shown the way to an agreed result, be quick to draw upon its painstakingly won hindsight and pronounce a judgment of frivolousness. When it does make the judgment, it should spell out the factors which have led to its conclusion so that a common law relating to sanctions can be built up. And if the situation calling for such sanctions as dismissal is ambiguous, or if it is uncertain from the record whether the fault lies with the party or with its counsel, notice and opportunity to respond should be afforded, as some state rules specifically provide.

III. On the Road to Appeal

A. Interlocutory Appeals: A Selective Opportunity

The record is not entirely complete when the trial is over. The window between final judgment and the time, months later, when one addresses the appellate court affords opportunity for aiding one's cause. In the first place, there are obvious curative motions such as a motion for reconsideration, a motion asking for a statement of reasons (if there were none with the order), a motion for judgment notwithstanding the verdict, or a motion for new trial. But when all chances of changing the result at the trial level have been exhausted, there remains a menu of opportunities to invoke the early attention of the appellate court. These are opportunities to engage the attention of the appellate court on some issue relating to the case before considering the formal, full-fledged appeal. They are called interlocutory appeals.

A responsible and seasoned appellate advocate will not lightly or automatically mount an interlocutory appeal. She does not wish to expend her credit with the court on a premature effort. But there will be occasions when a motion to stay the judgment, to enjoin enforcement of the order pending appeal, to grant bail to a criminal defendant, to grant summary affirmance or reversal, or to expedite the appeal may be worth making. These motions and accompanying memoranda must be unusually clear and succinct. Their first audience will be seasoned and skeptical staff attorneys, interested only in facts of record and hard legal points, not rhetoric. Their second audience will be rather harried motions or emergency judges working under stringent time pressures.

If, however, the occasion justifies and the briefing is effective, a number of positive results are within range: if the trial judge is way off base, a quick victory and prompt reversal or remand; if a stay, injunction, or bail is granted, a possible presage of ultimate victory; even if, after deliberation, the motion is denied, education of one and possibly more judges and the stimulation of interest in the appeal; at a minimum, expedited scheduling of the appeal.

B. Assembling the Record

What one might suppose to be a very low-level, grubby piece of work—assembling, organizing, and presenting the record appendix in an appeal—actually contains both hazard and opportunity for the advocate. The hazard is that if an appellant fails to include some testimony, colloquy, ruling, or exhibit that is necessary for the decision of an issue, the court may very well not probe the original record.

The opportunity lies in assisting the appellate court in doing its job in an expeditious manner. By this I mean including no more transcript of testimony or other evidence than is necessary; presenting an appendix with a clear table of contents and orderly pagination, with all printed matter reproduced in easily readable form; incorporating in an addendum to one's brief the most critical passages of testimony, the judge's charge, a key exhibit, and the trial court's decision; and being alert to opportunities to supplement the record if the need arises. The best advice I can give on such matters is to ask personnel in the office of the clerk of the court not only for local rules and information booklets but for information about the court's preferences and antipathies.

C. Waiver Traps

Finally, as noted above, there are risks of waiving issues in the appellate court, although not as many as in the trial court. Issues stated as points for appeal but not briefed are waived. Beyond this, issues argued in only a cursory manner, tucked away in some footnote, may be deemed waived. Sometimes by not discussing an issue until a reply brief is filed, an appellant will find himself out of court on that issue. Even a changed basis for arguing an issue will be held to constitute an abandonment of the issue.

This account of the perils encountered on the long ascent to the appellate court is reminiscent of *Pilgrim's Progress*. If the advocate can survive the Slough of Despond, skirt the Valley of Humiliation, overcome Doubting Castle, and succeed in preserving all issues, he or she has most certainly earned the right to address them on their merits in the Celestial City of Appeals.

6

Briefs: Reflections of an Advocates' Consumer

I know of no other field of human endeavor where a limited number of pages of written and structured argument can be so decisive as in appellate decision-making. The heavy artillery of appellate practice *is* the brief. And it is as difficult for the lawyer of general accomplishments to master the collection of skills and judgments that together make up the art of writing an effective brief as it is for a successful novelist to master the art of writing a moving short story. In my own library I possess scores of articles and a dozen books expatiating on the do's and don't's of brief writing; there are hundreds more.

It is not my purpose to join this worthy throng. My aim is to try to inculcate a basic attitude of reverence for the art form that will help the practitioner realize his or her fullest potential. There is no one prescribed formula, even though there are certain ground-level principles. The goal is how to make a document of ten to fifty or more pages as readable, complete, fair, and persuasive as possible.

The first thing I would say to a writer of briefs is that a brief must serve at least three audiences. At the threshold, the brief must seek to persuade a seasoned if not cynical cadre of appellate court staff attorneys that the case does indeed deserve oral argument and should not be summarily affirmed or dismissed with a brief opinion. Even though a screening panel of judges must join in any decision to take a case off the oral argument list, the initial impressions of the staff attorney are significant. The second audience consists of all the judges who will sit on the case and their law clerks; the brief is their first introduction. For the audiences in both stage one and stage two, clarity in stating issues and simplicity in fleshing them out are vital. The third audience is the most important: the judge who has been assigned to write the opinion and his law clerks. Even though surface clarity and simplicity must somehow be managed, there must be enough picky detailed argument and citation to facts and law to furnish the fodder for a favorable appellate opinion.

While all these audiences are important, I propose to try to describe how I use briefs, what I look for, what helps me, what irritates me, what infuriates me, and how in general I prepare in my chambers for the oral argument in the courtroom—and for the ensuing process of decision. If writing about my own tastes as a consumer of thousands of briefs seems a bit parochial, I should add that I suspect my reactions are far from unique.

I. The Reading of Briefs

A. The Reading Context

A very significant segment of an appellate judge's work life is devoted to the reading of briefs. With the thought that it will help the writer of briefs if he can visualize what happens when his product is read, I invite him into my chambers.

1. The Brief-Reading Scenario. A term or sitting of the appellate court is held every month or six weeks. Some two weeks before the court convenes, some twenty to thirty sets of briefs and accompanying volumes of appendices arrive in chambers. The briefs will range from fifteen to one hundred pages or more; the total will amount to from two thousand to three thousand pages, with another three thousand to five thousand pages of appendices (which include pleadings, motions, transcripts of hearings and trials, exhibits, and rulings of the trial court). The briefs alone would form a stack from one to two feet high.

The eager writer of briefs would do well to keep in mind that he is in competition with two dozen or so peers, each claiming precious minutes of reading time from three or more judges and an equal or larger number of law clerks. Moreover, this reading matter does not lend itself to pellucid, aesthetically pleasing, or fast-moving prose. It embraces tales of either (depending upon whether the writer is for the appellant or the appellee) hard-won triumphs of right over wrong or lamentable miscarriages of justice. The subjects range from a simple street arrest to the most technically complex environmental, antitrust, or product liability issues.

My own routine in reading briefs has evolved from an after-hours evening activity, conducted after my work on current opinions was put aside, to a mainstream activity taking place during my time in chambers. I find that the added alertness which daytime reading affords outweighs any "saving" of daytime for other chores. At best, rather ample blocks of time should be reserved for reading so that, in substantial cases, appendices may be looked into or cited cases may be read. I will attempt to read all of the briefs on all cases, but not all with equal thoroughness. My objective is to become familiar enough with the briefs to profit from a discussion with my law clerks, each of whom will have read her share of the briefs with greater attention to detail. I long ago abandoned requiring my clerks to write bench memoranda containing summaries of facts, issues, arguments, and comments. For me it has been more productive to require less writing from clerks at this juncture and to substitute extended discussion of cases, during which I make such notes as I think necessary.

2. A Tale of Shifting Biases. At this point my cyclical agony begins. If the first brief I pick up is reasonably good, I begin my meandering perambulation toward decision. I call the process, at least for me, graduated decision-making. Instead of either arriving at a firm conviction early in the process or maintaining perfect balance until the end, my mind continually tacks like a sailboat going upwind. Or, to change the metaphor, decision for me is much like tracing the source of a river, following each minor tributary back to its origin in a swamp, only to return to the main channel, which narrows as one goes upstream to the one final true source.

One reads a good brief from the appellant; the position seems reasonable. But a good brief from appellee, bolstered by a trial judge's opinion, seems incontrovertible. Then discussion with law clerks in chambers casts doubt on my tentative position. Any such doubt may then be demolished by oral argument, only to give rise to a new bias, which in turn may be shaken by the post-argument conference among the judges. As research and writing reveal new problems, the tentative disposition of the panel of judges may appear to be wrong. The opinion is written and circulated, producing reactions from the other judges, which again may change the thrust, the rationale, or even the result. Only when the process has ended can one say that the decision has been made, after as many as seven turns in the road.

In my view, the guarantee of a judge's impartiality lies not in suspending judgment throughout the process but in recognizing that each successive judgment is tentative, fragile, and likely to be modified or set aside as a consequence of deepened insight. The non-lawyer may expect a judge to be a model of decisiveness. This characteristic better fits a trial judge. The truth is more likely that the appellate judge in a difficult case is consigned to the unpleasant state of prolonged indecisiveness.

B. The Preliminaries

1. First Impressions. When I pick up a brief, the first thing I look for is the name of the attorney or the firm. This is generally a neutral exercise. I may not know or have heard of the writer of the brief or the firm. Or, if I do have some memory, it may be unilluminating. But I must confess that if I associate the name with earlier briefs and arguments that were misleading, useless, or otherwise unreliable, I start with a special wariness. By the same token, if the name recalls to me earlier candid, competent, and highly professional performances, I relax and prepare to enjoy the experience.

My next inquiry is to find out who was the judge in the trial court. This, too, is quite an irrelevant quest for the most part. Yet I cannot deny that my prior experience has something to do with my attitude at the outset of the consideration of an appeal. Most of the time, a particular trial judge would stand in my mind for an unremembered set of rulings, most of them sound, a few of them found reversible. But I might remember a judge as the author of rulings rather consistently reversed by the appellate court. I cannot help approaching an appeal from such a judge with a slight skepticism. Finally there are trial judges who stand out in my mind as consistently open, sensitive, careful, and splendid. Here, too, I am afraid I tend to begin with a bias, predisposed to think that reversal is not likely.

Without spending more than a passing moment on these preliminaries, which may well prove of no significance, I next want to see what kind of a case this is. There are three signposts: the table of contents, the statement of issues, and the summary of the argument. It never ceases to amaze me that notwithstanding these three aids, I can sometimes, too often for comfort, glance at all three without a glimmer of what the case is all about.

2. The Decision Below. My first spadeful of real digging into the case itself comes with a reading of the ruling or opinion of the lower court or agency. I like to read what the previous supposedly impartial adjudicator has said about the case before I plunge into the partisan accounts of appellant and appellee, when, all too often, I receive the impression that we are dealing with two very different cases. If counsel is at all sensitive, she will include this ruling or opinion or order as an addendum to the brief.

Sometimes I find no help from this source; the judge may have merely made a marginal note, "motion granted" or "denied" or "dismissed." Sometimes the judge will have rendered a very short, conclusory ruling that gives the appellate court very little understanding of the reasons for the ruling. But sometimes there is a thorough opinion in which the key facts are set forth, showing how they are supported by the evidence, together with clear reasoning linking relevant authorities to the facts and leading to conclusions of law. In such cases there is nothing quite so gratifying to an appellate court as to "affirm on the opinion below." But even if the lower court opinion does not readily dispose of the case, its account of the facts, procedural history, issues raised, arguments, and the court's own reasoning provide an invaluable, generally balanced context and starting point for the appellate court.

3. Threshold Inquiries

a. *Jurisdiction.* The first question for any appellate judge is: is this case properly before us? Such a question is compelled by the very nature of law, which both empowers and limits courts. An appellate court is empowered to hear an appeal only if it has been given authority to deal with the particular kind of controversy, if the parties are properly before it, and if all necessary steps have been timely taken in earlier proceedings to allow the appeal to go forward. In other words, there must be subject-matter jurisdiction, personal jurisdiction, and appellate jurisdiction.

It is surprising how often an inquiry into jurisdiction will uncover a fatal flaw which the parties have either overlooked or perhaps have hoped would be overlooked by the court. So my clerks have standing orders to ask certain questions. Are all parties properly before the court? If it is a federal court of appeals, is there a real diversity of citizenship? To ask a hypertechnical but necessary question, have all parties been named or identified in the appeal papers? Is the order or judgment below final or the kind of interlocutory order that is appealable? Is the decision of the trial court or agency one which is reviewable at all? Have all time deadlines been met? Have all requirements to exhaust administrative and judicial remedies been met? Have events since the decision below made the whole case moot?

If a likely jurisdictional flaw has been discovered early enough, a judge should make the effort to consult with colleagues with the objective of alerting parties to the need to discuss and brief the issue. If the press of time does not permit advance notice, an appellate court would probably welcome supplemental memoranda even after oral argument.

b. *Procedure.* Procedural rules are almost as sacrosanct as jurisdictional principles, although they are more subject to the discretion of the appellate court. As the discussion in the previous chapter has underscored, what an appellate court will consider is almost always limited to what has been adequately preserved in the record of proceedings in the agency or trial court. So, even before I begin a careful reading of an appellant's brief, I will look at appellee's table of contents to see whether there are any issues alleged not to have been preserved. If nothing has been said, my clerks have instructions to check the record to see if objections, requests, offers of proof, and identification of issues on appeal have been made. If my reading of the lower court's opinion contains no mention of an argument made in an appellant's brief, I scout the possibility of an eleventh-hour attempt to revive an issue that has been allowed to perish. But not only must the issue be preserved below; it must also be raised on appeal. If it is not clearly raised in an appellant's main brief, it is in deep trouble. Mention of the issue in a footnote or in a reply brief may not do the job.

c. *Standard of Review.* My third threshold inquiry is to identify the precise standard or standards of review—the rules that tell appellate courts to what extent they can substitute their views as to both facts and law for those of the trial court or agency. There is a wide range within which we must choose the appropriate guide. In some cases, as when we review a decision which has by law been committed to the discretion of the agency, our "window" is limited to decisions which can only be termed capricious; at the opposite pole are cases where the question is one solely of law and where we have carte blanche to substitute our own views.

What this means for reviewing judges is that in most cases we know that we must be prepared to acquiesce in decisions that we would not make ourselves, but are not sufficiently unsupported or unreasonable to allow us to reverse. So it is important that counsel help us in their briefs by identifying the appropriate standard of review. Sometimes there will be issues requiring different standards, as when a judge's conclusion presents a mixed question of fact and law. A clear, succinct, and authority-supported statement of standard of review gets me off to a good start.

C. The Merits

1. Reading for Facts. With the preliminaries over, I turn to the case itself. Sometimes the facts are all stipulated, or not in dispute. Sometimes they are simply and briefly set forth. But sometimes, as in a complex commercial contract case involving highly technical devices or methods and trade secrets protection, one must spend hours to comprehend the facts and the arguments.

Beyond the briefs, it is usually worthwhile to read those parts of the record which are at the root of the case: the actual words of the complaint, the whole instruction given the jury by the judge, key exhibits, the actual words used by counsel in making an objection, the key testimony of a witness, and the entire network of statutes and regulations being challenged or interpreted. The prudent advocate will include such matters in an addendum to the brief. Obviously, the more one reads, the more one understands. But time must be austerely rationed. The art involved in the first reading of the facts, beyond acquiring a general understanding, is to identify points and areas which suggest the need for extra work by law clerks or questions to be asked counsel at argument, or both.

Indispensable to this end is something developed over time by a judge—what I call a judicial nose. Such an organ is exquisitely sensitive, if not allergic, to both strong and faint odors that the briefs exude. The judicial nose, if it is to serve its possessor properly, must distinguish between the scents that are merely unpleasant and those that signify the presence of some endemic disease or weakness. The former are regrettable, reflect no credit on the drafters of the brief, and test the fortitude of the reading judge, but may not indicate malignancy. This kind of benign, if unhelpful, condition is typified by dullness, lengthy sentences, passive verbs, unclear referents, gigantic paragraphs, jargon, misspelling, obsequious tone, pretentious anger, and snide innuendo concerning the integrity of one's adversary.

More serious, and occasionally fatal, are such emanations as the following:

—An important fact is misstated. Brief: There was no evidence of the reliability of the government's informant. Fact: Officer's affidavit stated that informant had provided accurate information on six earlier occasions.

—An important fact is omitted. Brief: A request for an instruction to the jury was erroneously refused. Fact: The request was indeed made, *but* it was not renewed *after* the charge was given.

—Testimony is selectively reproduced. Brief: Appellant was in the kitchen when the officers arrived. Fact: Appellant did so testify *but* the officers testified that she was in the cellar where the cocaine was being cut . . . and credibility judgments are generally not appealable.

—Facts are set forth blithely, without any references to pages in the record.

—Facts are set forth in exhaustive detail. After plowing through a score of pages of narrative, involving a half-dozen persons, dozens of conversations, and events at different places, with no apparent focus, a judge is tempted to wonder whether the object of the brief writer was not to divert the reader from discovering that the brief was going nowhere. Example: After nineteen pages of facts, there follow five pages of lame argument, citing only one case authority.

—A complex network of statutes and regulations is set forth with no effort to reduce the complexity. The brief writer has not attempted to mislead but has become so mired in the minutiae that he expects the reader to read with the sophistication and background of the specialist.

—Facts are unnecessarily repeated. Example: A brief first presents the facts in the statement of the case; they are substantially repeated in describing what happened at the sentencing proceeding; they reappear in an introduction to the argument; and they surface once again in the argument on the merits.

2. Reading for Legal Reasoning. The ways in which issues are treated, arguments are advanced, and authorities are dealt with often send signals of weakness to me. For starters, here are some leading candidates:

—An issue is overlooked. In a complex case with many issues, a quick reading may leave the reader with the impression of the brief's overwhelming strength. A careful rereading (and comparison with the opposing brief) may bring to light the missing issue, which may well not have been treated because there was no persuasive way to deal with it or, more innocently, because the writer thought it unimportant. But it may well be decisive.

—An issue is misstated. When this happens, it suggests the tawdry device of setting up and knocking down a straw man. For example, an appellant attacks a trial judge's refusal to depart downward from sentencing guidelines. The government devotes its argument to underscoring the wide amount of discretion lodged in the judge. But appellant's point is that the trial judge based his refusal on what he perceived as a lack of authority to depart downward, not on any exercise of discretion.

—There is a blizzard of issues. When a judge reads a brief in which a dozen or more issues are presented, there is a likely risk that all will share in a perceived diminution of importance. The brief writer has flunked the tests of selectivity and prioritization.

—There is a plethora of arguments on one issue. Occasionally an issue in a closely contested case will finally appear at the appellate stage so one-sided that a half dozen reasons in support or opposition can be marshaled. In such a case, as one of my colleagues likes to say, "All roads lead to Rome." More often, however, I find that when several good arguments are followed by increasingly fanciful or far-fetched arguments, I become skeptical of the whole array.

—There is a sloppy or slippery use of case authorities. The judicial nose sniffs when a brief uses old authority within the state or federal circuit, rather than recent case law; when a brief fails to deal with cases cited by the other side; when cases are cited in a long string and without description; when quotations from opinions, on examination, are found to be lifted out of context; and, most of all, when cited cases have been overruled, withdrawn, or sharply limited by subsequent rulings.

3. Reading for Policy. An appeal may present only the narrowest of questions. What do the decided cases demand? What does the statute mean? Was the trial ruling erroneous? Did the evidence support the verdict? In such cases there is no room for an appellate court to be concerned with policy implications. But if the question presented is a novel one, if legal authority is divided, if the statute is ambiguous, or— sometimes—if legal doctrine, though clear, is outrageous, the reviewing court ought to be concerned with policy in the broadest sense. This does not mean that the court should try to act like a legislature, but it should always keep in sight the polestar question: if we decide this case in this way, what is the underlying principle, and are we prepared to universalize it and apply it generally? We may have no trouble at all in saying that the seasoned intuition of the police ought to be enough justification for a warrantless search of a rumored Mafia headquarters. But what about allowing Internal Revenue agents to ransack a business office on mere suspicion of tax violations? Yet is there a principled difference between the two cases?

The veteran appellate advocate and scholar Robert L. Stern has addressed what he calls "The Importance of 'Why,'" saying: "Judges want to know whether a decision one way or the other will be fair and just, not only to the parties but to the public or the public interest, and what the general consequences of the ruling will be."[1] He also quotes the venerable yet currently relevant comment of Justice Rutledge, when he was a federal circuit judge:

> Perhaps my own major criticism of briefs, apart from that relating to analysis, would be the lack of discussion on principle. Some cases are ruled so clearly by authority, directly in point and controlling, that discussion of principle is superfluous. But these are not many. It has been surprising to find how many appealed cases present issues not directly or exactly ruled by precedent.

4. Ancillary Decisions. Apart from the result to be reached in the appeal under consideration, there are several other types of decision a court must make which are all too often not suggested by the briefs. A primary question is often whether a case should be decided on the narrowest possible ground so that the decision will have little precedential value, or whether the court should paint with a broader brush. Then there is a subtle objective: to choose the best approach to the agreed-on result. For example, a judgment based on a ruling excluding evidence could be affirmed because the court had no jurisdiction. But if the jurisdictional issue is difficult and vexing and the ruling on the merits was obviously correct, a court may be forgiven for affirming on the merits, saving the jurisdictional issue for another day.

Another objective, probably in the back of one's mind at this early stage, is whether it may be useful to have the opinion contain some dicta, that is, statements that are not necessary for decision but may indicate an attitude on the part of the court that could give some helpful guidance to judges and lawyers in the future. Sometimes this sense that guidance is needed will persuade an appellate court to base its ruling not on preexisting law but on the exercise of its inherent supervisory power.

Some other questions to consider are whether there is a need for an expedited decision, whether the decision can rest on the opinion of the trial judge, whether a full-scale opinion or a shorter memorandum is called for, and whether the opinion merits publication. There is also the question of remedy. In both conventional litigation and in class-action litigation seeking institutional reform, the most difficult question may not be liability; it may be what to do about it. Finally, if the appeal has fallen too far short of having merit, there remains the unpleasant question whether a party or counsel, or both, should be sanctioned.

Astute counsel will consider this range of ancillary decisions that may be of interest to the court and will make any comment that might be helpful.

D. My List of Likes

The literature on the writing of briefs is replete with the writers' favorite lists of commandments. All are probably useful. But in addition to the received wisdom in this area, I have devised my own short list of things that particularly please me and give me the feeling that someone out there is helping me.

—I like to read a brief that reflects a carefully constructed outline. I can feel the effects, even if the outline is camouflaged by the text; one point leads to the next with the minimum number of words. Just as I salute the discipline of outlining for a judge in Chapter 9, so I commend it to a writer of briefs. The attorney who outlines well is invoking the sense of order to which the judge gravitates in crafting an opinion.

—I like to find annexed to the brief as an addendum critical material such as the decision of the trial judge, statutes, a key part of instructions to the jury, or an important colloquy between judge and counsel.

—I like an informative table of contents, valuing it more than a statement of the issues. I like it when it is selective and prioritized, i.e., when it does not include too many issues.

—I like a brief that shows the signs of an organizing and discriminating mind: no swamping with unnecessary facts, or facts which one's adversary has fairly represented; and a brief so written that I can quickly scan it in preparation for oral argument but can find further riches if I have been assigned the opinion to write.

—I like to see the most important issues faced up front. Of course, I expect to see what the writer considers her adversary's most vulnerable point; what I rejoice to see is a writer candidly recognizing what appears to the reading judge as her own most vulnerable issue and dealing with it.

—As I have noted, I like to see the policy implications of a decision fully explored.

—I like to read, at the end of the brief, precisely what counsel wants us to do, giving us a menu of possible dispositions.

—I like, very much, a reply brief that does not attempt to traverse terrain already covered.

—I like, to the point of being unduly swayed, a brief that contains not one pejorative adjective or innuendo concerning one's opponent or the trial judge.

If all my likes have been satisfied, I know that I have read a brief, the first draft of which has been painstakingly edited and rewritten—perhaps more than once.

II. Pre-argument Discussions with Law Clerks

After reading the briefs for our next session of court, I then summon my clerks to discuss what we have read. They will have read in greater detail critical parts of the record, and perhaps even done some research. I call our discussions "seminars" in which I generally am not the teacher but the student. Most often they will begin with a brown-bag lunch around my desk and continue for two to three hours, during which time we will discuss three or four cases. The clerk who has been given primary responsibility for a case will lead off the discussion with a brief summary statement of what it is all about. From then on the seminar is a free-for-all.

A. Objectives

The primary purpose of these conferences is the simple one of helping me assimilate the relevant information I will need to understand the argument, to ask intelligent questions, and to contribute to the conference among the judges. In an uncomplicated case, our discussion will be brief, perhaps only a few minutes. It will confirm my preliminary understanding and will enable me to view the key problem with more precision—in short, to get more of a handle on the case.

In more complex cases, the seminar is more than merely confirmatory. If a brief totals a hundred pages or more, with a formidable maze of facts involving a dozen issues of law, a law clerk can spend a day or more unraveling, distilling, selecting, and outlining so that he or she can in a half hour convey to me the essential facts, issues, and arguments. Though I cannot hope to know enough about the case to form any binding opinion, a good seminar will enable me in perhaps an hour and a half to become a reasonably intelligent listener.

B. Seminars Preceding "A Day in Court"

To convey something of the nature of these pre-argument seminars, let us reconstruct what might have been the preparation for the oral arguments described in Chapter 1. The first case was argued before the entire court, *en banc*. This was the second time around for this case, for there had already been an opinion issued by a panel of three judges and since withdrawn pending full court reconsideration. So the territory was familiar. Not only were the facts, issues, and arguments familiar, but by this time the concerns of the individual judges. In rereading the original opinion, I could see statements which were needlessly broad or otherwise likely to trigger some judge's sensitive nerve. As one member of the court still disposed to uphold the panel's rationale and approach, I saw my job as that of trying to narrow the opinion and avoid all unnecessary controversy; whether this effort would succeed in gaining a majority I could not, of course, predict. But my discussion with my clerks centered on identifying areas where the prior opinion could be modified so as to minimize tension between the dictates of the Rehabilitation Act and university autonomy, without sacrificing its basic principle and outcome.

The second case was the appeal from a drug conviction, where any claimed error by the judge in instructing the jury had been waived by failure to object or request a specific instruction. The government's brief had made the case a simple one. Our discussion was summary and centered on whether costs or counsel fees should be assessed against the appellant or his counsel. Since counsel had been court-appointed and could have withdrawn from the case only with difficulty, I quickly abandoned any thought of suggesting sanctions.

The toxic waste insurance policy case created a lively discussion. My clerks were in disagreement over whether the violent rainstorm was a "sudden and accidental" discharge within the meaning of the policy. This was the big issue in the case, although there were several others that would have to be faced if the trial court was upheld on this main issue. A considerable amount of case law and the voluminous record of the trial would have to be read with care. Moreover, this was a case where our decision would have serious practical implications for both assureds and insurers far beyond this case. I would hear argument with no idea of the correct result. In such a case I would not expect to have a handle on the proper approach or result.

The fourth appeal was that which was brought by a black police officer on his own behalf, protesting the dismissal, without a jury trial, of his complaint of discriminatory discharge. The large question addressed in the briefs was whether a civil rights statute barring racial discrimination in the making and enforcing of contracts applied to this case. The Supreme Court had recently held that the statute applied to discrimination in *hiring*. Did this ruling also cover discriminatory *discharge*? Other courts had reached opposite results. We would have to take a position. Our seminar left me in a state of uncertainty. A day or so later, however, my law clerk, who had done more reading of the record, came back with the suggestion that the trial judge might not have paid sufficient attention to other allegations in the complaint which might fall under a broader civil rights statute protecting a person's equal protection right to be free from discrimination carried out under color of state law. The complaint seemed to suggest that the officials responsible for plaintiff's discharge might have final policymaking authority; if so, their actions would bind the city. But neither party had briefed this issue. We would have to explore this at argument.

The labor-management case, where the employer was resisting an order to resume collective bargaining with a union, seemed to be a close one. The company's general record in its dealings with organized labor was good; the evidence of employee loyalty to the union was ambiguous; much time had gone by. On the other hand, the Labor Board is entitled to substantial deference. This would be a delicate exercise in trying to see where a line should be drawn. Both the record and case law must be studied. But wholly apart from the facts and the law, there was a question relating to remedy. Given the general record of the company, the less than compelling evidence of employee loyalty, and the passage of substantial time, was the Labor Board's order too severe?

The final case to be heard was the appeal from a denial of habeas corpus relief. This occupied almost no time in our discussions, because there had been no attempt to present the issues to the state court and very little effort to preserve objections at trial in any event.

C. Follow-up Tasks

This review of what might have been the preparatory seminars in one day's diet of cases illustrates some of the directions taken by such discussions. Though time is short between our pre-argument seminar and the opening of court, discussion often opens up new areas for quick research. If a case is heavily relied on by a party, it may be advisable for the clerk to check the subsequent history of that case to see if it has been affirmed, followed by others, criticized, or simply ignored. If certain testimony appears critically important, the law clerk may well read it in context and report back. If the briefs contain selective quotations from legislative history and if there is time before this case is reached, the clerk should try to locate and read the whole committee report. If the issue on appeal has been commented on in a respected treatise or law review article, the clerk could sample the comment and report on his impressions.

Other follow-up tasks include the following. I might ask a clerk to frame a hypothetical question for me, to bring out, for example, how far counsel would push the principle he urges. I might ask a clerk to give me a status report on circuits which are for or against the argument being made. I frequently ask for a chronology of significant events. An organization chart may be useful in a dispute involving corporations, subsidiaries, contractors, subcontractors, and insurers. I will need Xerox copies of key court opinions.

Even with the reading that I will have done, the reading my clerks have done, and the give-and-take of our seminars, I know that I will still feel inadequate as I hear difficult and complex cases being argued. I will admire colleagues who may have mastered a case with which I am still struggling and may say to myself, after a particularly brilliant intervention by a colleague, "I wish I had said that." But I remind myself that I should not despair, that it is too early to feel mastery, and that at least I have started the process that will eventually deliver me to the point of conviction about a decision.

7

Oral Argument: Conversing with the Court

This chapter does not attempt to say everything there is to be said about pleading to an appellate court. We shall begin with a handful of observations of a general nature which seem to me to stand above the rest of the forest, like virgin growth: the current conditions that transform a crystallized art form, "oral argument," into an infinitely varied conversation with the court and endow it with unique challenges; what uses can be expected of argument by judges and lawyers; and a distillation of "first principles" into a basic twosome.

These things having been said, we then move to the particular: the ingredients of effective preparation; a battery of likely questions that should be anticipated; and the only wisdom I can give on the critical problem of retaining a semblance of control over one's precious few minutes in the face of a sometimes overheated, overactive court. We shall close with a contemporary vignette of an argument by a late master of the art.

I. A Changing Art Form

A. The Golden Age

Throughout most of history, we have thought of the presentation the advocate makes to a high tribunal as the epitome of polished and elegant rhetoric. The ultimate example of the classic mode, subsequent to Demosthenes and Cicero, was to be found at the lectern of the United States Supreme Court in the nineteenth century, particularly when the advocate was Daniel Webster.

His argument in *Trustees of Dartmouth College* v. *Woodward*[1] was perhaps the apogee of the formal style. The entire arguments of both sides took three days. Webster's opening presentation occupied four hours. In challenging a state statute which in effect would convert a historically private institution into a public one, Webster began with the common law, English tradition, ancient Roman law, Magna Charta, and natural law, and then sallied forth into interpreting the Contract Clause of the Constitution, with overtones of substantive due process. In his peroration, he uttered the deliberately understated sentences that have entered our common memory: "It is, Sir, as I have said, a small college. And yet there are those who love it."

Webster continued, in language that few would have the effrontery to utter in a contemporary courtroom:

> Sir, I know not how others may feel, but, for myself, when I see my Alma Mater surrounded like Caesar in the senate-house, by those who are reiterating stab upon stab, I would not, for this right hand, have her turn to me and say, Et tu quoque mi filii! And thou too, my son.![2]

Justice Story recalled the scene: "The whole audience had been wrought up to the highest excitement; many were dissolved in tears; many betrayed the most agitating mental struggles; many were sinking under exhausting efforts to conceal their own emotions."[3]

Such was the Golden Age when the rich ore of rhetoric could be mined, crafted, and presented in unhurried grandiloquence.

B. The Age of Tungsten

If we can choose a metal to denominate the current praxis of oral argument, I would opt for tungsten, said to have the highest melting point of any metal. For the pressures of modern argument apply maximum heat in minimum time to the appellate advocate. A typical appellate court will hear from eighteen to twenty-five or more oral arguments in three or four days at the rate of five or six a day, with "impression conferences" (or, to use the French equivalent, as my court does, "sembles") among the judges at the end of the day when tentative decisions are made.

This means, as a practical matter, that most cases can be allotted no more than half an hour. The result of these arrangements is that the advocate knows three things about the exercise he or she is about to participate in. First, her side of the argument will be given no more than fifteen minutes. Second, three or more judges and at least as many law clerks will have read and discussed the briefs in the case and at least some of the judges will come to argument with probing questions on their minds. Third, this is a pregnant moment in the life of this case, for it may be the only time that the judges are physically together to talk about it, and in most cases the final decision will be made within a few hours of the time counsel conclude their presentations. The advocate who does not melt under these pressures of foreshortened time and activist judicial questioning and succeeds in presenting a client's case in the strongest light permitted by the facts and the law is truly made of tungsten.

Those who teach and write about oral argument tend to try to describe a paradigm argument to serve as a model. It might go something like this. The appellant briskly touches on the underpinnings of jurisdiction and the procedural posture of the case, then succinctly limns the essential facts, going on from there to address the key issue, with a casual

reference to other issues left to the brief, and ends by pointing out the rank injustice resulting from a usually praise-
worthy trial judge. Then the appellee has his innings. He
concedes the accuracy of the factual and procedural background as presented by his adversary, but notes that if the
grounds relied on by the trial judge are not deemed sufficient,
the appellate court could and should take note of a ground
not relied on below, namely, that appellant has no standing
to raise the point and in any event waived it. He then deftly
marshals the evidence, demonstrating its sufficiency, and
directs the judges' attention to the trial judge's instructions
as a whole. He ends with a ringing reminder that the lower
court is entitled to a large dollop of deference.

Such arguments do occur. But they arise from fairly routine,
dull, or trivial cases. The judges in effect abandon the field to
the lawyers. The advocate must be prepared to fill a fifteen-
minute void in a constructive and interesting manner, or, better still, to sit down after ascertaining that no more need be
said. A most welcomed conclusion in such a case is "Unless
the court has questions, I shall rest on my brief."

But in most cases one, some, or all the judges will have
developed a lively interest in and will have read and thought
about the case. What will unfold is likely to be an unstructured and unpredictable conversation with and among the
judges, which, depending upon the skill and preparation of
the advocate, will be more or less productive, rational, and
helpful.

Counsel will hardly have finished stating his name when
a judge asks a question about some earlier stage in the litigation, which proves to be quite irrelevant. Counsel offers an
answer and returns to the facts, only to be queried about a
particular colloquy with the trial judge on a point of evidence. Finally the first real issue is reached, but it becomes
apparent that one judge has misperceived it. By the time
counsel has straightened out the judge, another has opened
up an entirely unforeseen area. Time runs out as counsel
bravely tries to think on his feet. The court, in the goodness
of its heart, gives the advocate an extra minute.

What has taken place was an unstaged, fortuitous discussion of a small segment of the case. The discussion was far from comprehensive, organized, balanced, or conclusive. The advocate may well have felt that nothing was accomplished. But the exchange between court and counsel was spirited; interest was aroused; one and possibly more judges were educated; and it may well have been that the issues not reached posed no problem for the court. The final assessment might properly be characterized as creative disorder.

C. The Arguments in "A Day in Court"

The six oral arguments briefly described in Chapter 1 may be viewed against this spectrum of textbook orderliness at one end and creative chaos at the other. The second case, a rather routine drug prosecution, fits the paradigm. Defendant's counsel did everything possible with a case that lost below. But the prosecutor came with arguments several ranks deep. Each attorney probably said everything he or she wanted to say. The *en banc* case of the dyslexic medical student, however, was nearer the chaos end of the spectrum. With seven judges primed to question and even debate among themselves issues as disparate as academic freedom and the dry, technical point whether there was a material issue of fact in dispute, counsel on both sides undoubtedly left the courtroom in states of high frustration.

The arguments in the pollution case saw counsel grappling with the problems of trying to present a complex factual situation and an intricate statutory scheme with some clarity and still leave a little time for arguing several issues on which the trial judge had ruled. The appeal argued *pro se* by the appellant policeman himself was one-sided, in the sense that the court allowed the lay appellant to use his time as he wished but pressed the prosecutor far more vigorously— and on different grounds—than he had anticipated. He saw what he had thought would be an easy victory suddenly become a possible reversal.

The labor case was similar in this respect, for usually the principle of deference to the findings of such an agency as the National Labor Relations Board proves insuperable for an appellant. In this case, however, the judges had obviously been impressed by the argument of the employer's attorney. The final case, the habeas corpus case so miserably tried, briefed, and argued, was one where, in retrospect, the appellee need not have argued at all. The only merit in having put this case on the oral argument calendar was to give the poor state prisoner the assurance that his plea was being heard by judges, not disposed of by hidden clerks or staff.

Our day at court, then, revealed to some extent the variety in chaos and order encountered in appellate arguments. It underscored the fact that there is no all-purpose model. But even though there is no single prescription for excellent advocacy, there are a few principles to pursue, more than a few potholes to avoid, and a rigorous discipline to cultivate. Before I say more, I ask the questions which lie at the back of the reader's mind. Is the game worth the candle? If judges are expected to decide a case correctly, despite any differences in the ability of the lawyers, what is the value of a good performance? Does excellent oral argument perform sufficient service to judges and attorneys to justify the required investment of time and effort?

II. The Uses of Argument

A. To the Judges

The variety and importance of the uses of oral argument-conversation to appellate benches are widely recognized. I identify five major functions served.

1. The oral argument gives judges a convenient and efficient way to increase their understanding—and eliminate any misunderstanding—of facts, procedural history, issues, and law. Based on their pre-argument reading and discussions with clerks, they can probe suspected weak spots.

2. Moving beyond clarifying their understanding, judges who think they may have discovered a hidden issue or a novel way of disposing of the case may test their ideas.

3. By their questions and comments to counsel, judges

telegraph their concerns and preferences to the other judges. Oral argument is really the first stage of the conferencing among the judges. How often I have begun argument with a clear idea of the strength or weakness of the decision being appealed, only to realize from a colleague's questioning that there was much, much more to the case than met my eye.

4. All of the above uses combine to enhance the confidence of judges that their final decision will be sound. In those cases which are decided without oral argument, without the chance for an exchange with knowledgeable counsel, there is always the possibility, even though a remote one, that some important happening in the court below, such as a stipulation, has been fatally overlooked.

5. Finally, important public goals are served. Accountability is advanced when real live judges can be seen by the public, exhibiting their energy or lassitude, their brilliance or stupidity, their civility or rudeness. Whatever impression is conveyed, the observer knows that judges themselves, not faceless staffs, are grappling with the case. Public understanding is also enhanced. As I wrote in *A Lexicon of Oral Advocacy*,

> An important part of the decision process is open to the press, the public, and to the parties themselves. To the extent that both the advocates and the judges have invested effort in preparation to make oral presentation and colloquy as useful as possible will respect for the process be engendered.[4]

B. To the Advocates

Unlike the judges, whose shared goal is to reach the right decision, the lawyers have diametrically opposite goals. While both appellant and appellee share some of the uses of argument, the difference in hoped-for result dictates an important divergence in attitudes. The first five of the following uses are shared, the sixth is solely the appellee's, and the seventh belongs to appellant.

1. One of the durable gems from the lore of appellate advocacy is that the function of briefs is to show the court

how to decide in one's favor, while the function of oral argument is to make the court *want* to decide in one's favor. Of course, a brief should touch on all reasons why the court should accept the writer's position, but the opportunity to engage in a sharply focused oral exchange with an informed and attentive group of judges offers the advocate a final and precious chance to persuade. And in the event that the brief was written in haste or by an inexperienced associate, the advocate has an invaluable second chance.

2. Just as the judges seek a better understanding of the case, one of the critical missions of the advocate is to sense and clear up possible misunderstandings of fact, procedure, and jurisdiction.

3. The substantive job that the advocate has to do can be summed up as making one's best points as forcefully as possible and dealing with one's weakest point by reducing it to nondispositive status.

4. While the judges are in effect opening their post-argument conference, the advocates are having their own opportunity to participate in that conference by guiding and advancing the discussion.

5. Advocates enjoy an external relations opportunity similar to the judges' interest in public exposure and accountability. They, too, are on display before judges and other lawyers, as well as the general public. The level of their performance will subtly affect their most important asset, reputation.

6. The seasoned appellee looks on oral argument not as opportunity to make new gains but as an encounter fraught with risks of losing what he has won. His chief objective is to avoid losing ground. Some of the ways open to him, as I noted in *A Lexicon of Oral Advocacy*, are that he "may concede noncrucial points, distinguish troublesome cases, acknowledge that his argument need not be carried to its logical extent and agree that relief may be limited to avoid the prospect of opening a floodgate."[5] To the extent that he feels unscathed after hearing the appellant, the course of wisdom is to say as little as possible.

7. The appellant, on the other hand, must view oral argu-

ment as a chance to add to the force of her brief, enough to tip the scales. How realistic is it to hope that what the advocate says in a brief period frequently interrupted by judges' questions can change minds? Such evidence as exists is largely the impressions of individual judges about their own experiences but is nonetheless persuasive that in a healthy minority of cases, oral argument can bring about a significant change of mind. When we consider that to effect such a change in the mind of only one judge may change the decision of the court, the following testimonies become even more impressive.

First we hear from the United States Supreme Court. Chief Justice Rehnquist: "[Oral argument] does make a difference: I think that in a significant minority of the cases in which I have heard oral argument, I have left the bench feeling different about the case than I did when I came on the bench. The change is seldom a full one-hundred-and-eighty-degree swing. . . ."[6] This estimate is corroborated by Justice Blackmun: "It is not rare that a justice says in conference that oral argument turned me around."[7] And Justice Brennan: "I have had too many occasions when my judgment of a decision has turned on what happened in oral argument, not to be terribly concerned for myself were I to be denied oral argument."[8]

Veteran appellate judges from lower courts, including state supreme court justices and intermediate appellate court justices, hold the same views. Perhaps the most ambitious quantitative analysis was made by federal circuit judges Myron Bright and Richard Arnold of the Eighth Circuit. For ten months in 1982 and 1983 they kept records of their impressions of the effect of arguments, noting whether oral argument had changed their tentative opinions. Judge Bright reported his opinion changed in 37 percent of all cases heard, and Judge Arnold reported a change in 17 percent.[9]

While there are appellate judges who take a dimmer view of the potential of oral arguments, I would say that it makes the game definitely worth the candle if a seasoned advocate can sense a serious error in a ruling at trial, a misreading of the law, an overbroad ruling, a finding unsupported by the facts, or a remedy in excess of a justified need.

III. The Demands
of Contemporary Advocacy

A. "First Principles"

The literature on oral argument is rich in recommended principles to guide conduct. One of the most widely quoted is the decalogue of perhaps the preeminent appellate advocate of the mid-twentieth century, John W. Davis.[10] But as the nature of oral argument has changed from a set speech to unpredictable, focused conversations, the array of really universal principles worthy of the name has dwindled. One group of admonitions contains such pearls of wisdom as: speak up, but not too rapidly; keep eye contact; avoid cuteness and indulging in personalities; know the record; don't read at great length. As to such guides as these, a New York practitioner, Milton S. Gould, in a salty riposte to Davis's decalogue, gibed, "I have no comment on these rules. I am also on record as opposing child labor and the Hindu custom of suttee."[11] Similarly, in *A Lexicon of Oral Advocacy*[12] I have sketched an alphabet of advocate types from actor, Cheshire Cat, and dancer to hare, scribbler, and tortoise. In so doing, I was more concerned with caricaturing the human condition than with announcing profundities.

Another group of propositions belongs under the rubric "It depends." For example, three of Davis's rules are: state the nature of the case and, briefly, its prior history; state the facts; state the applicable rules of law. I have trouble remembering any case argued before me in which all three kinds of statements were made. Indeed, in most cases all three are dispensed with as judges and lawyers home in on the crucial issues. At most, this trilogy is reserved for a case where the court has not been interested enough to ask any questions.

So also with another Davis rule: "Rejoice when the Court asks questions." Generally it *is* advisable to answer a judge's question on the spot and to pursue one's answer until the judge is satisfied. But sometimes it is not. And in many cases a judge's question may be anything but a cause for rejoicing. I try to discuss this helpfully in a later section of this chapter, "The Problem of Control."

This carping critique reduces the list of first principles to two rules: change places (in one's mind) with the court, and "go for the jugular vein." In fact, they are really one principle and have never been stated better than by Quintilian, the world's first official professor of law, who, writing in the first century, advised young lawyers thusly:

> After having . . . thoroughly examined a cause, and brought before his eyes everything that may promote or hinder its success, let him . . . put himself in the place of the judge, and imagine the cause to be pleaded before him; and whatever arguments would move him most if he really had to give judgment on the matter, let him suppose that those arguments will have most effect upon any judge before whom it may be brought. Thus the result will seldom disappoint him; or, if it does, it will be the fault of the judge.[13]

One way of defining "jugular" is, therefore, whatever arguments would move the court the most. This requires a bit of rethinking about "jugular." In the first place, I quibble with the choice of a vein, even such an important and vulnerable one as a jugular. In the appellate (as opposed to a jury trial) context, I would have chosen a carotid artery, which leads to the brain rather than to the heart. But beyond this, use of the expression is probably derived from the world of feral beasts, where victory goes to the animal that first sinks its incisors into the foe's neck. The figure of speech, if taken too literally, does a disservice to what ought to be, and is, at its best, civil discourse. The metaphor still has force in appellate argumentation, but it is incomplete.

Solely to aim for the adversary's most vulnerable point misses the fact that, generally, in the most significant cases on appeal, the sides are approaching balance. Each side has strengths and weaknesses. Hence, even though it is not pleasant to concentrate on the weakest part of one's own case, it is likely that *that* is what worries the court. And when the advocate has identified that part, acknowledged the appearance or actuality of weakness, and then, with as much forcefulness as the issue permits, has shown the appearance to be misleading or the weakness to be counterbalanced by other strengths, he will have "gone for the jugular" in the most effective way. He will have done just about all he could have done in oral argument. Implicit in this instinct for the jugular is credibility, the earned respect of the court for the advocate's candor in presenting the whole of his case, defects and all.

B. Preparation for Argument

All that I have endorsed as "first principles" undergirds and directs the advocate's preparation for oral argument. The attorney possessing a normal range of thinking, writing, and speaking talents can take comfort in knowing that preparation is the great leveler in appellate advocacy, minimizing if not eliminating any advantage initially handed out to the brilliant analyst and the compelling speaker.

For the advocate who is determined to exploit oral argument to the fullest, the ratio of preparation time to argument time is immensely disproportionate. It would range from four or eight to one (i.e., one or two hours to fifteen minutes) in the simplest of cases to, say, sixty-four to one in a case of some difficulty. This translates into sixteen hours of preparation for a fifteen-minute exposure. I think it is a fairly conservative estimate when one takes into account the things that have to be done. And in the most complex and delicate cases, top advocates may spend considerably more time in preparation.

The first step in preparation for an oral argument is to consider the nature of the court. Judge Murray Gurfein of the federal Second Circuit once wrote:

> Some appellate courts are "hot"; some are "cold." Some advocates like them hot and some like them cold. On a cold court the judges generally have not read the briefs and the relevant parts of the appendix before argument. The worst bench—and this must be the rare exception—is one on which at least one but not all the judges have studied the appeal before argument.

A court should not blow hot and cold because that is unfair to the advocate who is sidetracked by giving answers that the other judges already know. The good advocate will be ready for all the vagaries of individual judicial idiosyncrasies.[14]

Easier said than done. Nevertheless, unless one is sure of the level of preparation of the court, one must prepare for all three contingencies. If the panel or court proves to be "cold," the advocate should be prepared to fill the void by making an organized preparation, covering the essential procedural history of the case, stating the necessary facts, defining the issue or issues to be orally addressed, and discussing those issues. On the assumption that the court is well prepared, the advocate would do well to consider the range of questions reproduced below. And to prepare for the asymmetrical "hot-and-cold" court, the advocate must summon up courage to use some of the devices of control listed at the end of this chapter.

A second step in preparation is to master the record and the brief. If the advocate tried the case in the lower court or agency, the task is one of refreshing memory, by no means an insignificant one. But if the advocate comes new to the case on appeal, the importance of living with the record, making notes and cross references, and integrating these with the arguments and authorities in the brief is vital and the task formidable.

The third step is unstructured; it does not lend itself to formula or specific advice. It is to hold one's own retreat or period of isolated pondering, of thinking about the case, winnowing out what is less important from what is its essence, of discerning an underlying theme if possible, but, if not, of developing a clear sense of priorities. From this time of introspection will emerge the sense of the jugular (and the carotid) that distinguishes excellent advocacy.

The fourth step is rehearsal. It is, I think, a common experience, after a period of intense intellectual submersion in thinking through and writing out a presentation, for one to feel so on top of every argument that nothing further is needed. This is a serious mistake, for what passes for good writing very often does not make persuasive oral discourse. And while one may have full confidence in one's grasp of a problem, a ready and convincing answer may not come trippingly on the tongue. My own experience suggests a first set of rehearsals in solitude, to become used to talking aloud. It is surprising how clumsy one sounds in a first effort. After such warming up, including the possibly humiliating experience of looking in a mirror, the advocate should, if possible, speak to and be questioned by one or more colleagues who are reasonably knowledgeable about the case. One should not hesitate to make reruns in areas of weakness. But there is a risk in overdoing such exercises to the point where one feels stale and has lost an indispensable zeal.

C. A Catalogue of Critical Questions

As one goes through all these steps, the underlying goal is to anticipate what might be of concern to one or more judges and how best that concern can be allayed. If an advocate is fortunate, she will be given several uninterrupted minutes to say the few most important things. Then a judge will say, as Judge Richard Arnold of the Eighth Circuit does in close cases: "This is the problem with your case, as I see it. What can you say that will help me solve this problem in favor of your client?"[15] At this point, if the advocate has done her homework and anticipated questions just like this, she has a splendid opportunity to solidify or change minds. The specific question asked by the judge could be any one from the following catalogue.

1. Threshold Questions
—*How* did you get here, procedurally? Do you have a final judgment as to all parties and all issues?

—*When* did you appeal? Are you timely? Are you appealing too prematurely or too late?

—*Why* are you here? What is your jurisdictional ground? Is there a diversity of citizenship? Is there appellate jurisdiction? Are all parties named in the notice of appeal? Why isn't this case moot in light of developments since trial? Is the judgment below recorded on a separate document? Does your client have standing to raise this claim?

—*Where* in your complaint (or your answer) have you raised the issue you argue here?

—*What* is our standard of review? Clearly erroneous? Abuse of discretion? Substantial evidence? *De novo?* Error of law?

2. Waiver questions
—Before trial, did you make all necessary motions for discovery, hearings, rulings?

—Did you make a specific objection below? Did you move to strike an answer? When? What ground? Where is it in the record? Did you ask for a curative instruction?

—If you were surprised at trial by a document or testimony of a witness, did you ask for a continuance?

—Did you bring the authority you cite to us to the trial court's attention? Did you raise this issue below? How? Where in the record? And what did the court say?

—If you are complaining about the sufficiency of the evidence, did you request a directed verdict? Did you renew the request at the end of defendant's case?

—Did you make a specific request for instructions? Did you renew your request after the judge's charge?

—After the judge ruled, did you ask for reconsideration?

3. Obvious Questions
—How do you distinguish case X from case Y?

—Why didn't you cite our recent decision in *Y* v. *Z?*

—Where in the record are the facts relevant to this issue?

—What is the policy behind your argument?

4. Land Mine Questions
—If I understand your argument, you are relying *entirely* on *Y* v. *Z?* (Do not step quickly into this trap. Keep available an escape hatch.)

—Do you have any cases on point? (Seldom are there cases "on all fours," else you would not be here. There may be cases strongly analogous. Even if there aren't, this is no disgrace.)

—What is your best case? your strongest argument? your weakest case? (Beware of putting all your eggs in one basket.

You can politely say that one of your most compelling arguments is such-and-such, or that a case is weak only in that its facts are quite different, but its reasoning is fully applicable.)

—How would you deal with this hypothetical? If we hold for you, then won't we have to hold for the defendant in this hypo? Where do we draw the line? (Don't answer too quickly. On the other hand, don't be too reluctant. This is an opportunity for you to remind the court that although logic may extend to the absurd, it is the business of courts to draw sensible lines.)

—You are arguing for an exception to the general rule. How do we do this on a principled basis? Help us conclude this sentence: "Despite the general rule barring claims because of the statute of limitations, appellant is entitled to pursue this lawsuit because . . ." (This is not a question that can be answered by spur-of-the-moment inspiration. Woe to the advocate who has not wrestled with this one in advance.)

—Do you concede that . . . ? (Think twice. One can give the case away with an ill-advised concession. On the other hand, a concession that is justified by the facts and that will not harm your case may well be reasonable and enhance your rapport with the court.)

5. Ancillary Questions as to Remedy

These are questions of secondary importance. But it is embarrassing if counsel have not thought of answers that could help the court in the disposition of the case.

—If we disagree with the lower court, should we reverse or remand for further proceedings? Should we require (or permit) an evidentiary hearing? before the same or a different judge? with or without specific directions?

—What remedy should we order?

—Should we (if we are a federal court) certify this issue to the state court?

—Should we hold up our decision until the Supreme Court has acted on *Y* v. *Z*?

—Should the court impose sanctions on you? on your adversary? Why?

And finally, the rock-bottom advice from U.S. Circuit

Judge Thomas E. Fairchild, former chief judge of the Seventh Circuit: "If there is a material point you can't really answer, you should not have taken the appeal."[16]

D. The Problem of Control

Careful preparation gives the advocate confidence. Confidence should in turn foster candor. These two qualities are pearls of great price. But there is a third factor that depends on a combination of preparation, observation, experience, and just plain luck—retaining some residual control of one's limited argument time. In my view this has become the biggest problem facing even the best-prepared advocates as argument time has shrunk and judges have become more inquisitorial.

The standard advice is: be flexible, resilient, eager to deal immediately with a judge's question, whether or not it relates to the part of the case you are discussing. But there is such a thing as being too flexible. Not every question is a good one. Some are based on misinformation, some on misunderstanding of the law; some are premature, some totally irrelevant. I cannot begin to count the arguments where, after starting out impressively, counsel falters visibly as he or she pursues a will-o'-the-wisp down a judicially created blind alley. I wish I could produce a formula guaranteed to enable counsel, while being properly cooperative and deferential, to retain reasonable control over their few minutes of oral opportunity. Lacking such a formula, I offer the following modest suggestions.

First, be acutely aware of the court's level of comprehension. If you have sat through several earlier arguments, you'll have some idea of the court's preparation and interests. If not, or even if you have, it is prudent to ask the court if it has in mind a sufficient understanding of the basic facts and procedural posture. Then *listen* and guide yourself accordingly. Continue to listen as judges question both you and your adversary. Often you'll detect an erroneous assumption that you should correct. In any event, you will have avoided spending some time in talking about unnecessary matters.

Second, give special attention to the first dozen sentences you would like to say. Some courts, admirably, operate under a self-imposed rule of restraint, giving the first five minutes to counsel. Even without such a rule, an advocate can usually count on some uninterrupted time while judges are shuffling papers, consulting their notes, and finding the proper briefs. If you make each sentence count during this small window of opportunity, the chances are that you can generate a certain momentum. One goal would be to underscore your most important message. Another would be to identify the three or four issues you hope to cover. This may prompt a judge, when twelve minutes have been spent on issue number one, to inquire about the others.

Third, if a question is asked which relates to an issue you had planned to discuss later, you might say, as I heard one advocate say effectively, "You're skipping ahead, but I'll discuss it now if you like." Chances are that the judge will be content to wait. Another approach would be to give a short summary answer, saying that you will treat the question in more detail later.

Fourth, after, say, ten minutes, remind the court of the issues you still hope to touch upon. One way of making this reminder gracefully is to say, "I'm afraid we have not yet gotten to the core issue." Or, when considerable time has been spent on an issue and you sense a flagging interest even though the asking judge has not yet proclaimed his satisfaction, try saying, "I'd like to get to my second point." Even more graceful was this polite request to the court: "I'm almost out of time. Let me skip to . . ."

Fifth, if you have been peppered with questions and prevented from covering a vital issue, don't be afraid to ask for an extra minute or two. Most courts will graciously oblige.

As you wrestle with the problem of keeping some control over your time while being reasonably flexible and deferential, you should keep in the back of your mind the thought that even though you may leave one judge still thirsting for debate, you are likely to have two or more quiet supporters applauding your efforts.

IV. A Case in Point: A Strong Last Act

It is as difficult to capture the flavor of a masterful oral argument as it is to preserve the beauty of a butterfly in flight. Pinning the corpse to a display board does not quite do the job. But we can try.

We opened this chapter with a taste of Daniel Webster, the best of the Golden Age. We now close it with a taste of one of the ablest advocates in the Age of Tungsten, the late Edward Bennett Williams.

Williams, founder of the Washington, D.C., firm of Williams and Connolly, veteran litigator of many sensational trials, flamboyant part owner of the Washington Redskins and owner of the Baltimore Orioles, and legendary man-about-town,[17] was a single-minded professional when he undertook an appellate cause. He would seclude himself for days to absorb the record of a case and to think out his arguments and responses to questions.

I have witnessed the results of his preparation as he argued a case in our court. He was retained, after a trial, to pursue the appeal of a criminal defendant found guilty of evading income taxes. The prosecution had proceeded on a net-worth theory, a complex and indirect way of proving the receipt of unreported income by comparing the worth of a taxpayer at the beginning and end of a period, ascertaining the increase, then identifying and deducting all known expenditures, leaving a balance for which there is no legitimate explanation. The task of the advocate seeking reversal of a conviction in such a case demands exact knowledge of volumes of detailed, dry-as-dust data—a particularly awesome chore for someone who was not involved in the trial. But Williams had so prepared himself that he was absolute master of the huge record and could respond to any question with a quick reference to the volume and page containing the precise answer. Although he lost the case, he had done as much for his client as was professionally possible.

His professionalism did not mean that he spoke like a textbook or a judicial opinion. He had a flair for accurate, pungent, and memorable utterance. This was nowhere more evident than in his last major appearance on the appellate stage.

The case was a libel action brought in 1980 by William P. Tavoulareas, then president of Mobil Oil, against the *Washington Post* over an article stating that he had "set up" his son Peter as head of Atlas, a company chartering oil tankers, which did substantial business with Mobil. Williams represented the *Post*, a cherished client, and had struck out twice. Now, the entire court had decided to rehear the appeal *en banc*.

In September 1985, less than a month before argument, another cancer tumor showed up in Williams's liver. In obvious pain and discomfort, Williams worked over the case in his study, trying out arguments with two colleagues. At one point in their conversations, the three participants focused on one issue, whether the *Post* had harbored a malicious intent. To that end there had been some evidence that *Post* reporters had been urged to seek "sensationalist stories." One associate thought that such evidence was technically inadmissible. The other felt that they would not succeed in absolutely excluding all such evidence but that it was not very probative. As Williams's biographer reports it:

> Williams listened to this rather abstract debate for a while, and then he put the proposition a different way. "You mean," he said, "that the evidence has a ticket of admission, but only to the cheapest seats in the house?" Baine and Kendall smiled. In a single sentence, Williams had cut through a knotty problem that had tied Kendall up when he had unsuccessfully argued the case before a three-judge appellate panel in 1984. Williams, as always rehearsing his spontaneous quips, committed this one to memory, for use at the right moment.[18]

The oral argument took place in a packed courtroom. Williams did not look at all well. The night before, he had popped one of his stitches.[19] The time came to argue. Something of the flavor of Williams's performance is revealed in a contemporary legal newspaper report.[20] It was described by reporter David Lauter in these words:

He seemed at first cautious on his feet, beginning his argument while leaning on the lectern. But his voice and body appeared to gain strength as he argued, and he soon stepped back from the microphone and barged ahead, taking advantage early in the argument of being hard-of-hearing so he could talk through questions from the bench for which he did not want to pause.

After preliminary skirmishing over whether the plaintiff was a private or public figure, Williams was asked by then Judge Scalia whether there was not some testimony that *Post* reporters felt some pressure to find "sensationalist stories." Williams conceded the existence of some evidence and said, "It has a ticket of admission, but to the very cheapest seats in the house." There was a ripple of laughter and some judges smiled.[21] But, he continued with the utmost gravity, to say that there was any evidence of pressure to write false stories would be (the newspaper account reports him to say in a "thundering" manner) "a distortion and an abortion of this record."

Williams's final thrust was that on all the evidence the *Post*'s account was "a totally fair, truthful story." But, instead of contenting himself with this generality, he concluded by pointing to Peter's salary of $14,000 a year before his father's intervention, and saying:

> I say to you, that anyone who would believe that a $14,000 clerk went to a 75 percent owner of Atlas on the theory of meritocracy has to believe in the tooth fairy, and that's all the story said.

Not Webster. No Latin. Not nineteenth-century. Just Williams, colloquial, and twentieth-century. But the same art form, ever evolving.

The court of appeals ruled for him, seven to one, upholding the trial judge's action, concluding that "the fact that Tavoulareas 'set up' Peter in Atlas . . . is clear beyond reasonable dispute."[22] Judge Kenneth Starr wrote the opinion. He later said, "The tooth fairy line really got to me."[23]

8

The Judges' Conference

I. Three Models

Although the conferences held by judges after oral argument are as much beyond the ken of advocates as are the deliberations of a jury, it is important to have an idea of the nature and variety of these conferences—partly to appreciate how narrowly focused many are, and partly to be able to anticipate issues that might well determine the nature, scope, and consequences of the ruling, if not the very essence of it.

A. State Courts of Last Resort

In state courts of last resort, which generally have from seven to nine judges, who hear every oral argument, there is usually some structure and protocol governing the conference. But courts differ widely in their procedures. A few follow the practice of the United States Supreme Court, in which discussion proceeds in order of seniority, with the Chief Justice leading off. A greater number order the discussion in reverse seniority, beginning with the junior member. Others lead off with the judge who has already been assigned, by rotation or lot, to write the opinion (the "reporting judge"). And a minority of states allow random discussion.[1]

B. The Supreme Court

Quite different from conferences in state courts of last resort, which are usually driven by a desire for consensus or at least near-unanimity, and far removed from conferences in the federal courts of appeal, are those in the Supreme Court of the United States. Here, as in other areas, the differences reflect the uniqueness of that Court. Chief Justice Rehnquist describes his own experience:

> When I first went on the Court, I was both surprised and disappointed at how little interplay there was between the various justices during the process of conferring on a case. Each would state his views, and a junior justice could express agreement or disagreement with views expressed by a justice senior to him earlier in the discussion, but the converse did not apply; a junior justice's views were seldom commented upon, because votes had been already cast up the line.[2]

The prospects for any change are dim. The Chief Justice notes:

> [M]y sixteen years on the Court have convinced me that the true purpose of the conference discussion of argued cases is not to persuade one's colleagues through impassioned advocacy to alter their views, but instead by hearing each justice express his own views to determine therefrom the view of the majority of the Court.[3]

One perceptive insight, helping me to understand this kind of conference, was given me years ago by one of my law clerks who had gone on to clerk for a Supreme Court Justice. In commenting on the somewhat cursory discussions of cases that he had participated in with his Justice, he observed, "I guess this is because, by and large, the Supreme Court decides issues, not cases, and [my Justice] has known where he stands on most issues for years."

To some extent this comment—that issues may over-shadow cases—may also apply to state supreme courts, which have the task of setting judicial policy within their jurisdiction.

C. Federal Courts of Appeal

In the federal courts of appeal, however, the specific case is almost always the focus of a conference, rather than a transcendent issue. The focus of this chapter will therefore be confined to the federal courts of appeal, where judges sit in panels of three (unless the whole court is hearing a case *en banc*). There can therefore be far more informality than in the larger courts. Their conferences are generally held at the end of each argument day.

There are two general models. Some courts—a minority, I think—follow the practice of a number of state courts and preassign cases to judges for preparation of memoranda. This means that Judge X has looked into a given case far more deeply than her colleagues, has circulated a detailed memo-randum to her colleagues, is likely to take the lead in ques-tioning counsel and in the post-argument conference. This has the merit of producing an analysis of a case in some depth with minimum investment of judges' time.

More to my liking, perhaps because of my own court's approach, is the practice of calling on all judges to treat all cases as possible opinion-writing assignments and to defer assigning cases until after argument and conference. Each judge feels equally proprietary about cases; the oral argu-ment conversations reflect the judges' uninhibited points of view. And in conference any judge might begin the discus-sion, or the presiding judge might call on a colleague to give his views. It is by no means "orderly" or systematic. Each judge says what is uppermost in his mind. There are no memos in evidence, unless a judge has a case to cite or some testimony to quote. The conference on a particular case ranges from less than a minute to a half hour or more. Each judge takes a few notes; occasionally the presiding judge will prepare a summary of the discussions. Only after the conference will the presiding judge or, in some courts, the chief judge assign the cases.

II. A Critical and Unique Stage

Whether the judges' conference is a more structured one or a seemingly casual conversation among three judges, it is the most significant step in what I have characterized as a process of graduated decision-making. All the participants have read, discussed, listened, and asked questions about the case. They have absorbed insights from their clerks, the lawyers, and their own colleagues. They have already seen their own initial impressions change, perhaps several times. And they know that although their ideas might now be fairly well seasoned, they could change their minds again. The judges come to conference fresh from the most intense and concentrated exposure of oral argument. Most important, this is generally the only time when all judges will be discussing the case together. Even though their tentative disposition of the case in conference may change, it is safe to say that at least 90 percent of the decisions made at conference will stand.

The judges' conference, as a method of group decision-making, is unique. The outsider would find it remarkable that, notwithstanding the bundle of questions of fact and law that must accompany most cases deemed worthy of an appeal, case conferences are very often abbreviated, telescoped conversations hitting only a few issues. All judges are by now so immersed in the case that most questions have been answered. They know the points that bother them. Their talk is plain and to the point, cutting through the lengthy legalese of many of the briefs. There is generally no "hype" or salesmanship in their comments, no guile, simply a statement of how each judge reacts to the point being discussed, and perhaps some reference to a fact or case authority deemed crucial, and reasoning about policy implications. The tenor of comments is usually not combative or final. A judge who finds her initial views disputed by colleagues may say, "I didn't think this through very deeply. I will probably go along with both of you." Or a possible dissenter will end his comments by saying, "I'll listen. If you find some cases or show me in the record something to support your position, I'll be open."

During all these exchanges, no one knows who will be writing the opinion. Each judge carefully notes the concerns of colleagues; if he or she is to write the opinion, it is important to address those concerns and heed the nuances expressed in the conference. As we shall discover, much of the conversation may bear little relation to what was said at oral argument. Indeed, some issues may not be touched upon at all. Sometimes, because of failure to consider or deal adequately with a "sleeping" issue, the writer of the opinion may run into a roadblock and find that a quite different opinion must be written. For example, judges may have agreed that admitting evidence of prior crimes committed by a criminal defendant was proper. The writing judge may have discovered precedent that precluded such a decision, and therefore wrote a draft opinion holding that although the evidence was erroneously admitted, such error was, in the light of all the evidence, harmless. Or the draft opinion may go all the way and recommend reversal. Because of this always present possibility, the decisions at conference are not engraved in stone.

In an era when conferences are the commonest of devices, the judges' conference breaks all the rules. It has no fixed agenda for any case, staff, minutes, rules, or press release. It consists of informal conversation on the issues the judges find important. It is nonadversarial. It is nonbinding. No one stands to gain or lose prestige, position, or power by what he or she says or does not say. No one is trying to take advantage of another. Each has trust in the motives of the others.

III. A Spectrum of Case Conference Types

To convey something of the focus and flavor of appellate case conferencing, I have drawn upon my own rudimentary

conference notes of the past several years, with full awareness of the necessity to preserve the confidentiality that is
their foundation. No specific case discussion is reported.
But I think the following impressionistic survey of types or
models of case conferences is fairly representative of what
goes on in the federal courts. I suspect, also, that except for
somewhat greater protocol the same spectrum prevails in
state courts of last resort. I list case conference models beginning with the simplest and working toward the more complex, full-scale conferences.

A. On the Merits

Perceptive counsel can anticipate the nature of some of
these conferences, but the very nature of the process we
are dealing with—an evolving case analysis in which, as in
peeling an onion, new layers of facts, issues, interpretation,
and legal theory are revealed—more often defies prediction.

1. "Rope of Sand" Cases. These are cases in which the
judges in conference quickly agree, without detailed discussion, to affirm. Frivolous cases—like the sixth case heard on
our day in court, discussed in Chapter 1 (the hapless state
prisoner who sought a writ of habeas corpus without first
presenting all his issues to the state courts)—are, of course,
primary candidates for this treatment. But there are many
nonfrivolous cases which merit the same disposition. Whatever persuasiveness may have initially appeared in appellant's claims has, after much reading of briefs and listening
to argument, been dissipated—like a rope of sand before a
rising tide. Many criminal appeals challenging the sufficiency of evidence to support the jury's verdict are of this
kind. For example, a criminal appellant may urge earnestly
that the evidence established at most defendant's "mere
presence" at or near the scene of the crime. After the prosecution points to several bits of evidence indicating defendant's additional involvement in planning or otherwise
aiding in the commission of the crime, there is literally
nothing more to be said. The second case heard in our day

in court, a nonfrivolous but routine narcotics case, was of this nature.

2. "Cafeteria" Cases. These are cases presenting the judges with a choice of grounds on which to rest their decision—such as jurisdiction, procedural waiver, standing, the merits, and harmless error. Sometimes the choice is left to the writer of the opinion. But quite often judges feel strongly that the choice is important and needs discussion. If a difficult jurisdictional problem is posed, the court may wish to avoid deciding it and simply go to the merits, as long as the result is to be the same as if a finding of no jurisdiction were to be made. Similarly, although a strong case of procedural default has been made out (e.g., if a *pro se* prisoner has filed his appeal a day late), the court may nevertheless want to indicate, out of a desire to avoid the appearance of placing form above substance, that even if a point had not been waived, its view of the merits indicated that no injustice had been done. Or the judges may feel that the validity of a search warrant is such a close question that they would rather uphold the search on the ground that "exigent circumstances" existed, justifying the search, rather than write a pathfinding opinion interpreting the Fourth Amendment.

3. "Technical Weighing" Cases. Slightly more discussion than is given to the two types of cases just identified takes place when facts are to be weighed against a legal standard. Typical cases are those where a key issue is whether an error, though not preserved at trial, is so egregious as to be noticeable under the doctrine of "plain error"; where, in a criminal case, error was clearly committed and the issue was clearly preserved, but its impact was so minimal as to be "harmless error"; where the challenge is to the sufficiency of evidence, i.e., whether there was sufficient evidence to support the verdict or judgment; and where the question is whether the facts recited in an application for a search warrant add up to legal "probable cause."

In such cases there is initially likely to be room for differences as judges try to assemble all relevant facts and see if they measure up to the legal standard. Generally the discussion is not carried to the point where a final vote is taken; judges are likely to be content to await a more complete review of the trial record by the judge who ultimately is assigned to draft an opinion. When the draft opinion is later circulated, unanimity is highly likely. I have used the classification "technical weighing" for this kind of case in order to set it apart from the kind of case discussed in section 7, below, where the task of weighing or balancing is likely to be complicated by conflicts of values. Here, the question is solely whether the facts meet a neutral, value-free standard.

4. "Abuse of Discretion" Cases. Offering a wider range for discussion are cases where the issue is whether the trial judge, the hearing examiner, or the administrative agency abused the discretion granted by the law. The fifth case of our day in court, the appeal from a National Labor Relations Board ruling, was this kind of case. Abuse of discretion is a fuzzier question than whether the facts meet a legal standard. Each judge is not asking whether the action in the agency or lower court was correct or not. The judge begins with the assumption that the action below was not that which he would have taken; the question then is whether it was so wrong, arbitrary, or irrational that an abuse of discretion was committed. The question arises in myriad forms: Was the judge within her discretion in believing a certain witness? in admitting relevant but highly prejudicial evidence? in allowing or refusing to allow an amendment to the complaint? in refusing to reconsider a ruling? and in imposing sanctions on a party or a counsel?

Appellate judges generally are reluctant to find abuse of discretion. This is particularly true in the realm of the kind of judgment calls which I have just mentioned. What gives rise to more strain in sensing the boundary between abuse and nonabuse is the rare conduct of the trial judge who is so carried away by the illusion of absolute and unchecked power that he is curt and peremptory in his rulings and even insulting and threatening in his comments to counsel. When such conduct occurs, appellate judges squirm, bite their lips, and affirm conduct they deem going to the verge of the captious, autocratic, or quixotic. But if the trial judge has earlier been the subject of similar criticism, an appellate court may choose to bite, not its lips, but the proverbial bullet, admonish the judge, and perhaps even reverse and remand the case for retrial before a different judge. Sometimes the discussion over a judge's abuse is brought to a head by the question: if we don't reverse for this conduct, when would we ever reverse?

5. The Dispositive Fact. Once in a while a complicated case may eventually be found to turn on one fact—whether a paper was signed, whether a conversation took place, whether a notice was given. The briefs may range widely and miss such a fact. For example, an appellant's brief may cite ample evidence of breach of express and implied warranty, and even fraudulent representation, but skip over any mention of evidence of reliance on any such representations. Or the focus may be on a defendant's negligent, reckless, or even intentional conduct, without any indication of how such conduct could be found to have caused injury to the plaintiff. But oral argument, aided perhaps by the assiduous record-reading of a judge, may highlight the gap in the facts. In such cases, the conference is brief, although there is always the caveat: let the writing judge check the record thoroughly to be sure we are right.

6. The Dispositive Legal Issue. Sometimes a case focuses to the point where all judges recognize the dominance of a stark legal issue. Did the trial judge err in defining "reasonable doubt"? in defining "malice" as being implicit in "any very cruel act," whether spontaneous or deliberate? in defining "specific intent" in a criminal case as requiring an intent not merely to do a certain illegal act but to do it, knowing that a law was being violated? When legal doctrine is involved, judges are loath to decide quickly. They realize that much research needs to be done on the case law. So here, too, the decision is really to await the analysis of the writing judge.

7. The Value-Added Weighing Decision. The values of judges creep into the discussion of many cases. We discuss the varieties of these values—and their relative worth—in Chapter 13. Here, we pause to note how they may surface in a conference.

Values probably all stem from personal experience in some generalized sense. But some values may be traceable to the rather specific experience of a judge. For example, in a case where a police officer, on the strength of a warrant for civil arrest, signed by a court clerk, arrests and causes the imprisonment of a person, the question is whether a reasonable police officer should have known that a judge's authorization was needed and thus should have made sure such authority had been given. In such a situation, one judge may intuit, on the basis of his experience, that "everyone knows that any officer should get hold of a lawyer before he puts anyone in jail." Another judge might feel just as strongly that "if a warrant looks valid on its face, you can't expect a foot soldier to know the niceties of the law." Similarly, when, as often happens, trial judges sit on appellate panels, they bring quite a different perspective, as do appellate judges who have once served as trial judges. Sometimes this results in a plea for deferring to the trial judge; but sometimes it results in a searching review, the former trial judge feeling strongly that any sensible trial judge would never have acted as the judge below did.

Judges being human, the "value-added" component of judicial balancing sometimes exceeds professional bounds. Once in a while a judge will give vent to spleen, making such statements as "We shouldn't add to the burdens of the police or the trial judge. If we don't shut the door on this type of lawsuit, we'll be buried." Or such ad hominem remarks as "The judge below is a very good one; I'd hate to reverse. Besides, this defendant is obviously a very bad character—a record as long as your arm." Once such a statement is made, it appears to be what it is, a remark that has no place in the decision process. It reflects a value judgment—about burdening the police or the courts, the competence of a judge, or the worthlessness of a defendant—but nothing about the law, the facts, or the process of reaching a just decision in accordance with the law. In its very utterance, the remark generally seals its own doom. It is not unusual that a judge who has "sounded off" in unjudicial irritation will join or even write an opinion running contrary to her initial comments.

8. Judicial Creativity. Some of the most interesting conferences turn not on what the briefs and arguments have discussed but on some additional input from one of the judges. It might take the form of a novel theory that could dispose of the case in a more satisfactory manner than either side has suggested. For example, in a tax case where a company official has been held liable for his company's contributions to the social security credits of employees, despite heroic attempts by the official to stave off disaster and protect the employees, a judge might want to try to see if a respectable basis could be found for exonerating the official. Though the law might appear to foreclose such a result, it is likely that the other judges will at least give their colleague head room to try out her idea.

Here is another example. At the end of one day's arguments, our panel gathered to discuss the day's cases. After disposing of all but one, we confronted the remaining case. It was far from earth-shaking. It involved the internal affairs of some labor unions. But we spent perhaps an hour or more in discussion, gradually working toward approaches that were absent from the briefs and arguments of counsel. They had not been in our minds until after the give-and-take of our discussion had made us see the basic problem and an approach which might best reflect precedent, yet permit an equitable result. One of our panel was a visiting judge. It had been he who had come up with a brilliant resolution in the labor union case after some forty minutes of shared pondering. He expressed appreciation for this kind of leisurely probing, contrasting it with some conferences he had known where judges would simply announce seriatim their vote with perhaps a sentence of explanation.

My admiration of moments of creativity is tempered by a

word of caution. Such moments often reflect a judge's indepen-dent research of the law, or perhaps a detailed scrutiny of critical testimony or exhibits, placing the case in a new light. Or even a remedy that the parties did not consider. While such new insight is always welcome, a court is wise to pause at this juncture. It may be that somewhere in the lengthy history of the litigation the newly discovered "insight" was considered and either rejected or found irrelevant by the parties and the trial judge. Or the point may simply not have been raised on appeal and thus not be available as a basis for decision. So prudence often dictates that the new idea be broached to the parties and supplemental memoranda solicited.

9. "Blockbuster" Cases. At the "heavy" end of the spectrum of case conferences is the case which obviously will require a great deal of work by the opinion writer. A case may be a blockbuster for any one of several reasons. The most visible example is a case like that of our dyslexic medical student, which has already been deemed important enough for *en banc* consideration. A conference on such a case usually generates vigorous and lengthy discussion, for the issues have long been clear and views of all the judges have had a chance to become focused and refined. Some judges come to such a conference with their opposing views deeply entrenched. The excitement lies in seeing which way the "swing" judges, those who have been on the fence, lean. Usually the conference ends with two opinions assigned, one to represent the views of the putative majority and the other to represent the minority. I say "puta-tive" because a draft minority opinion has been known eventu-ally to command a majority.

Another blockbuster is the case which, because of the multiplicity of issues and huge record, will require an enor-mous investment of time. A typical example is the appeal from a successful prosecution of several defendants in a lengthy drug conspiracy trial. Of the dozen issues raised, none may prove troublesome in the final analysis, but read-ing the transcript, analyzing and researching all the issues, and organizing and writing a manageable opinion make the task a formidable one. At conference, however, there will seldom be extended discussion. A few issues which look close may be highlighted; the judges will note that the disposition is a probable affirmance; and the writer is charged to "read the record."

Then there is the occasional case involving complex issues of both law and fact. The third and fourth cases described in Chapter 1—the case testing whether the discharge of toxic waste was both "sudden" and "accidental" and thus covered by an insurance policy, and the case brought by a black policeman who claimed that his discharge was wrongful— were of this variety. Once in a while, if a judge has had the time and inclination to do some early digging into the record, he will provide his colleagues with insights which may guide decision. Or oral argument may succeed in distilling from a welter of contentions and facts a succinct, luminous, and compelling capsule that goes far to tip the balance. Generally, however, the conference is not lengthy, the judges knowing that they will not have any reliable "feel" until an in-depth, systematic, and comprehensive analysis has been accomplished. So they put down in their notes a big "?" and leave the initial job to the judge who will shortly be assigned to write the opinion.

B. Beyond the Merits

So far, we have reviewed conferences where the focus is on the decision as to the merits—which party wins, whether the vote will be for affirmance or reversal. But a great deal of conference time is devoted to dealing with other issues.

1. Fine-Tuning the Decision. Quite often an appellate court will spend more time in conference fine-tuning the decision than in deciding what the result should be. By fine-tuning I mean deciding the scope of the decision, its precision, or its basis. While a court generally will wish to decide a case on the narrowest basis, confining it to the kind of factual situation presented by the instant appeal, there are times when it will feel compelled to paint with a broader brush to clear up uncertainty and differences among trial courts. Appellate counsel most definitely have a role to play in trying to guide the court in one direction or the other. A similar question is whether, if a retrial is to be ordered, the court should try to decide all of the issues raised on appeal. Some issues should be put to rest, where the question seems likely to rise again and is sufficiently novel, but other questions may never see the light of day again, or should be left to the trial court for decision in a new context.

The basis of decision can produce a great deal of debate. For example, it is a sobering step to declare a statute unconstitutional; this means that future amendment or interpretation is unavailable. Courts are therefore expected to construe a statute to avoid a ruling of unconstitutionality, if this is possible. And sometimes, of course, interpreting or invalidating an implementing regulation will suffice.

Much conference time is spent on speculating about the impact of a decision on future cases. Courts are understandably chary of their ability to predict for the long run; they dislike making apocalyptic pronouncements that time can make obsolete. They therefore hesitate to draw bright lines, preferring to decide the instant case and leave for the future the "hard case." An example was a case where a defendant who had rented a room in a rather poor rooming house, which required him to share a bathroom with other tenants. Officers, who had been called to the house to investigate a threatened use of a sawed-off shotgun, broke into the bathroom and, reaching into an opening in the ceiling, saw and seized the weapon. The trial court held that defendant lacked "standing" to object to the search, since the bathroom was available to anyone on the premises. But, deeming this issue a very close call, we preferred to decide the case on the ground that the reported danger of someone using a shotgun was an "exigent circumstance" justifying the search. We left for another day any attempt to draw a precise boundary governing the extent of any privacy interest of tenants in a shared facility.

In some situations a court will seek to preserve some flexibility by refraining from a legal holding or ruling and contenting itself with an admonitory lecture aimed at prosecutors, other attorneys, or even trial judges. When best used, it puts on notice all the other professionals on whom the court depends that certain standards of conduct should be respected. In the face of continued flaunting of the standard, the appellate court can be expected to harden its stance, perhaps first by a rule of presumption, declaring certain conduct presumptively error unless adequately justified, and ultimately by a hard-and-fast *per se* rule. For example, a court might, when first presented with a claim that the trial judge erred in sending a message to a jury without communicating with all counsel, merely admonish the judge. A second such instance might produce a more strenuous exhortation. A third might lead to a reversal.

Sometimes newer judges are tempted to resort to "preachy" opinions, issuing admonitions about the future which they and their courts are unlikely to follow up with vigor. An example is the unhappiness of appellate courts with some of the closing arguments to the jury made by overzealous prosecutors. In an otherwise error-free case it is tempting to shake a judicial finger and say, "We shall not in the future permit such conduct." But the next case comes along, with overwhelming evidence of guilt and in the main a fair trial. An appellate court will be reluctant to reverse and will therefore look to see if objection was made to the offending argument, if the judge made an immediate curative instruction, and if in the context of the entire case the remarks were likely to have had any effect. One learns from long and frustrating experience that one reversal is worth a hundred lectures.

In such matters as these, affecting the manner in which cases are tried and the rules and standards governing judges and counsel, an appellate court may on occasion rest its decision, not on a constitution, statute, or regulation, or even upon case precedents, but upon its own supervisory authority over the agencies and courts within its jurisdiction. It is a power to be used sparingly, but does allow fine-tuning not confined to the precise issues raised by a particular case. When a panel of a federal court decides to take this route, it usually circulates its proposed rule to all members of the court for comment and agreement.

It is understandable that an attorney in an appellate court is so immersed in her case that her attention has been riveted on winning a victory. "Victory" is usually translated into the simple alternatives of affirmance or reversal. But the court itself must confront a number of collateral choices having to do with the basis of decision. Some of these choices will be seen as immensely important to the litigants and their counsel. Some chiefly concern the internal workings of the court. But all are worth some thought on the part of counsel, in order to be of help both to themselves and the court.

2. Unfinished Business. Before a conference ends, the court must reflect on whether decision is the next step. It may be that before a novel approach is taken, supplemental memoranda should be requested. Or perhaps at oral argument they already have been. Or it may be that, at oral argument, the court has suggested that the parties attempt to settle the case, or that a compromise resolution be explored. And sometimes, when a case involving the same issue is pending before the Supreme Court, the court will simply defer its decision until the Supreme Court acts.

3. Disposition Choices. The two options for a final decision are, of course, to affirm or reverse. An added subtlety is a decision whether or not to have the mandate (the document that evidences the fact that the decision is now effective) issue immediately or to allow some time for a petition for certiorari (i.e., a request that the case be accepted for review) to be presented to the Supreme Court of the United States.

Decisions that are somewhat less than final are those which remand the case to the trial court. There are many variants: a remand with instructions only to "institute proceedings in accordance with this opinion"; a remand with specific instructions (e.g., in a successful habeas corpus appeal, a remand to the federal district court with instructions to grant the prisoner's freedom unless the state initiates a new trial within ninety days); a remand for clarification of the court's reasoning, or for essential fact-finding; a remand with or without a requirement to open the record for additional evidence; and a remand to a different judge. Each one of these possibilities could be fraught with significance for a litigant; an advocate would do well to anticipate these choices and be prepared to give advice to the court.

Then there are critical choices as to timing. A basic question is whether a new rule or an extension of existing law should be applicable prospectively or retrospectively. But there are timing questions relating to the issuance of the instant decision. Sometimes the panel (if it is a federal court of appeals) knows that one of the issues is being considered by another panel in another case; some checking with that panel is indicated. The result is that the decision may be held in order to await the other panel's decision. Similarly, as we have noted in section 2 above, prudence may dictate awaiting the issuance of a pending Supreme Court decision involving one of the issues under consideration. Finally, delay may be caused by the decision of the panel to certify a controlling question of law to a state supreme court. Counsel must be prepared to respond to questions probing any of these possibilities.

4. Variants of Form. Sometimes the nature of the case is so clear that the judges in conference can also agree on the degree of formality that should accompany decision. In many cases, however, that decision must await the recommendation of the writing judge. In the continuum of increasing formality, decisions may be ranked as follows: a one-sentence or several-sentence order affirming under a rule or a cited authority; a sentence indicating adoption of the opinion of the trial court, sometimes with a few added comments; a *per curiam* opinion (i.e., unsigned, without indication of individual authorship) of a paragraph or two, usually unpublished; a full opinion, but so fact-bound and lacking in precedent that it is not to be published and is often unsigned; a full opinion, signed, and to be published.

Although counsel have little to say about the form a decision takes, they do have a later opportunity to have their say on publication. Parties may have a significant interest in this matter. For example, a company may not want an adverse decision to have broad prospective authority; it may hope, therefore, for a low-profile, unpublished opinion. On the other hand, a government agency may want the widest possible circulation and influence of a favorable opinion. If a party has reason to think that the opinion should be published, the chances are that a court would grant a supported request for publication.

5. Sanctions. As we have learned in Chapter 5, courts, both trial and appellate, are increasingly invoking their statutory authority to impose sanctions on parties—and even counsel—for cases brought or contentions or defenses advanced that are so lacking in merit as to be deemed frivolous and an imposition on the court, its time, and processes. Accordingly, counsel must have in mind the full range of sanctions available. The range begins with a reprimand, continues with the usually modest monetary assessment of double costs (to cover the printing of briefs and record), and escalates to a monetary fee to be assessed against the party, counsel, or both. In extreme cases, the court might refer the issue to a disciplinary board.

Appellant's counsel must be sensitive to any vulnerability, making sure of a sufficient justification if a sanctions issue arises. Conversely, appellee's counsel should anticipate the issue and decide for herself whether appellant's case merits the imposition of sanctions.

6. Remedy. Counsel, who have been so engaged in striving to win, must give thought to the many ways in which they could win . . . or lose. They want to win as broadly as possible, but if one is to lose, he or she wants to lose as narrowly as possible. The choices open to the court are sometimes quite wide; to help influence the choice is the opportunity of counsel. We have discussed in section 1 above what is perhaps the weakest form of winning while losing: a hortatory lecture by the court to the judge or prosecutor. Sometimes, however, if the litigant or the lawyer expects to appear repeatedly in the future before the court, the lecture provides a good base for increasingly strong argument in the future. Another option at the weaker end of the spectrum is a declaration of rights, more than a dictum or a lecture, less than an immediate grant of a right or compensation. If an official enjoys qualified or absolute immunity and is therefore immune to a suit for damages, injunctive relief is still available. If, on the other hand, a claimant has been reinstated in his job, injunctive relief may be foreclosed, but damages are still available. If the case for compensatory damages is weak, there may still be a viable claim for substantial punitive damages. Then there are the added subtleties of back pay, front pay, pre-judgment interest and post-judgment interest, not to mention attorney's fees.

Counsel are well advised to dissect the claims of their clients in order to have clearly in mind their relevance to available remedies. And in complex class-action claims against institutions such as prisons, school boards, and mental institutions, imaginative counsel can be of immense help to a court in proposing imaginative and constructive remedial steps and phases. Here there is more room for improvisation, common sense, and ingenuity than in more traditional areas of the law where case law and statutes more narrowly restrict options.

Merely to review the kinds of comments and decisions made in conference cannot begin to convey the quality and variety of interactions that make this step one of the most fascinating in the entire process of appellate decision-making. Because it brings together the impressions, biases, and studied views, relevant and irrelevant, of judges in a free-wheeling and nonbinding way, it is unpredictable and unfailingly provocative and helpful.

The judges themselves bring to a case different strengths and interests, with offsetting weaknesses and blind spots. The result is that in a day's conference, one judge will be brilliantly analytical in technical matters, and another judge will start with a preferred result and try to work backward toward a respectable supporting analysis. There may be one judge who views some of the cases through a broad philosophical framework; he will be balanced by one who keeps everyone's feet on the ground with her solid common sense. To make matters more intriguing, the judges may swap these roles, attitudes, and functions from case to case.

The image that comes to mind as we discuss case conferences is that of a large stewpot sitting on a low flame, just enough to make it simmer, not boil, while various ingredients are gently added. The judge who is assigned to write the opinion remembers the exchanges, takes them into account, and both consciously and subconsciously adapts his or her draft opinion to the views so expressed. And thus the conference serves its purpose as the principal centripetal force in the graduated process of maturation that is appellate decision-making.

IV. The Assignment of Opinions

The last item of business for the judges' conference is the assignment of cases to particular judges for the writing of a suitable opinion, whether it be hard or easy, long or short, signed or *per curiam*, published or unpublished. Folkways vary as to when and how such assignment takes place.

In some courts, such as the United States Supreme Court, conferences are not held until the end of a week's arguments. Assignments are made at that time. In my own court, and other federal courts of appeal in which I have sat, assignments immediately follow the conferencing of the day's cases.

In such courts, the assignment is made by the presiding judge, subject, perhaps, to final approval by the chief judge. Up to that point, no judge has known who would be chosen; consequently, each judge will have taken equal responsibility in preparing for argument and conference. In many state and some federal appellate courts, the cases are assigned, before argument, by rotation or by lot. Under these systems, one judge has a special responsibility for preparation. While this more intensive preparation by one judge may save some judicial time, there is a danger that other judges may defer too much to the assigned judge, to the disadvantage of a true multi-judge decision.[4]

The objective of an automatic assignment system is, of course, to be fair and to avoid the reality and appearance of manipulative assignments. But my own experience has revealed no evidence of any such motives in the assigning judge. Instead, such a judge must wrestle with several questions. How can the burden of the term's cases be most equitably shared? To what extent should a colleague who is behind in his or her work be given less of a load? How can interesting cases be fairly spread around? To what extent should the proven expertise of a colleague in a particular field be utilized without risking overexploitation and overspecialization? To what extent should colleagues be asked what cases they would particularly like to write or like to avoid? And, in cases of divided opinion, what judge is most likely to command a majority?

Other idiosyncratic aspects of the cases themselves may guide the assignment. If a decision is to make new circuit precedent, a local rather than a visiting judge may be chosen. Sometimes, however, an "outsider" is preferred, as, for example, when a trial judge or counsel is to receive criticism—on the theory that the criticism should not appear to be merely the result of parochial pique. Some cases in which the decisions would criticize judges or other officials or would strike down actions of official bodies require considerable sensitivity; the chief judge or a judge known for a velvet pen may well receive the assignment. I have been known to author an opinion which, in subsequent years, a panel has decided to overrule; if I agree with my colleagues that the case was wrongly decided from the beginning, or has been overtaken by events and later authorities, I willingly agree to write the overruling opinion. By so doing, I have removed any concern over my sensitivity. Finally, if an opinion is to make a significant policy change affecting court procedures or the conduct of trial judges, prosecutors, the bar generally, or government entities, the chief judge or the presiding judge may well undertake the task.

The assignments now having been made, the judges decamp to their respective chambers and begin the solitary incubation of a new round of opinions.

9

Opinions I: Organizing the Workload and Doing an Opinion

I. Introduction
to Opinions I, II, and III

We now enter the heartland of the appellate process, the court's opinion. Though the opinions drafted by a judge are by no means all of her total work product, they are her most visible and enduring contribution to the legal system. They reflect the judge's unique qualities, values, methods, tone, and approaches. Moreover, the construction of an opinion is the core of appellate judging. This is where the fun and challenge, the agony and frustration are.

The appellate opinion serves three functions: it decides a case, ending at least one dispute between the parties; it continues the story by making some law, from a little bit of interstitial law to a huge chunk; and it projects the story into the future by giving intimations of further directions. It occupies a far more central position in the United States' legal universe than in either civil law countries or the United Kingdom and its followers.

But as we have learned in Chapter 3, there are, in addition to the United States Supreme Court, 113 federal and state appellate courts, nearly 1,400 appellate judges, and 517,000 appeals processed each year. Most of the opinions written by most of the judges on all of the courts (except the United States Supreme Court) will not be considered magisterial, seminal, or of enduring importance. Yet some of them will, at least for a significant time, play an important part in the development of the law. Perhaps the critical challenge today for an appellate judge is to discern which opinions fall into these two categories and to organize his or her chambers to deal appropriately with each group.

The next three chapters will be concerned with this challenge. In this chapter we shall consider both the responsibilities of a judge in organizing the workload and what "doing" an opinion from beginning to end involves. I use the word "doing" rather than "writing" because the act of putting words to paper comes rather late in the process. In Chapter 10 we shall explore how this judge works with law clerks in a collective or chambers opinion writing effort. And in Chapter 11 we shall look at judicial collegiality and the relations among judges as they engage in the creation of consensus, and, when consensus is not achieved, in the crafting of dissenting and concurring opinions.

I add quickly that these chapters will not attempt to be a handbook on opinion writing. I recognize the existence of valuable manuals, articles, and even books on the subject.[1] I also recognize that there are as many ways of crafting excellent opinions as there are excellent appellate judges. My aim is a humble one: to describe in some detail how I go about my work. I do this with the hope that my fellow judges will gain something from this, even as I have gained from reading about them.

I also write for the practitioner, for I have the conviction that the more an appellate advocate knows about the work ways and thought ways of appellate judges, the more effective an advocate he or she will be. One year when I was teaching a law school course in appellate advocacy, I had my students take on the role of appellate judge and write opinions, after reading briefs and hearing oral arguments by

their peers. It was illuminating to me how far from reality
these opinions were, even though written by sophisticated
law students who had spent two years doing little else but
studying appellate opinions. Most wrote in what I call the
pronouncement mode, being overly brief and sketchy in getting to the bottom line, where they would baldly announce
a holding. They apparently thought it was good form to adopt
a tone of impatience, if not shrillness, and a patronizing
attitude. They hurdled difficult questions without much discussion, never indicated that a question was close, and usually opted for an extreme all-or-nothing affirmance or
reversal. They generally fell far short of the consensus mode,
based on the guiding motivation of the writing judge to accommodate the hesitant and attract the uncommitted.

It was my hope that putting oneself in the shoes of a judge
might help the future advocate to be clear about the standard
of review, to recognize the virtue in stating an adversary's
case fairly and even acknowledging the closeness of the issue, to build logically on precedent, to spell out policy implications, to seek as narrow a decision as comports with the
client's interest, and to think through a viable remedy.

There is another, little recognized, reason why insight into
the work of appellate judges can be useful to the practitioner.
As attorney-scholar John W. Cooley reports, after a study of
appellate decision-making,

> [N]egotiation plays a crucial role in how appellate panels reach
> decisions.
> . . . .
> Lawyers now have much to learn from judges about the negoti-
> ation process and problem solving, and appellate judges have
> much to learn from each other and from negotiation experts
> about their problem solving function.[2]

He concludes, "If we can teach law students how to be
good judges, they cannot help but be good lawyers."[3] It is
with this hope that I invite the reader into my chambers as
we undertake our opinion production work.

II. Organizing the Workload

After a term of court, my return to chambers signals a distinct change of style and pace in work, the onset of a period of solitary labors, enlivened by discussions with my clerks. My mind is buzzing with memories, impressions, and insights from the arguments of from forty to sixty lawyers and the questions and views of my colleagues, expressed both on the bench and in conference. Before memory fades, I try to analyze the extent of the workload added by the new opinions I have been assigned and to organize it so that we can come close to being "written up" when next I go to court for a new round of arguments. This goal is seldom fully realized, but continually monitoring my chambers production helps me avoid falling too far behind and failing in my ultimate and rock-bottom aim—to begin a new judicial year (in September) with all opinion-writing responsibilities from the year just ended fully discharged.

A. The Judge's Debriefing

My first mission, on settling back into chambers, is to bring my clerks "up to speed" on all the new cases by telling them the salient points discussed in the judges' conference. Of course, I am sensitive to my duty to protect confidences exchanged among the judges. But just as I exact from my clerks a solemn lifetime pledge to respect the confidences of our work in chambers, so do I feel that if they are to be of real help to me, they must share not only the tentative results agreed upon by the judges, but the give-and-take among the judges concerning approaches, points to avoid, points to emphasize. To the extent that I can sensitize my clerks to the nuances of my colleagues' predilections and aversions I can avoid later unnecessary controversy, negotiation, and rewriting.

For this post-argument debriefing I rely somewhat on my notes, but they are skeletal. Their chief utility lies in spurring my memory, still reasonably fresh. I should note that some judges I know follow the practice of reducing to writing a very detailed summary of the conference. In some courts it is the custom for the presiding judge to perform this task and circulate the summaries to his colleagues. Such a summary must be of considerable value, but, for me at least, does not pass a cost-benefit test. I would rather invest my time elsewhere.

I have said that my debriefing covers all the cases heard, not just those assigned to me for opinion-writing. I follow this practice because I expect my clerks to follow the cases in which they have studied the briefs before argument and to help me review the opinions drafted on those cases by my colleagues. And in all of the debriefing, all clerks are present. This stems from my view of clerks' work within a chambers as being just as collegial as judges' work on a court. That is, my clerks are not separately cabined and confined in either the location of their desks or their work on opinions, whether mine or my colleagues'. I expect collegial discussion among them whenever it might be profitable.

B. The Necessity for Rational Triage

As we discuss the cases assigned to me for the writing of an opinion, I have in mind the stark necessity of weighing their probable demands on our time so that I can do three things: determine priorities, make my intra-chamber assignments of work to clerks, and give both myself and my clerks a rough sense of the time that should be spent on each case. If we fail to keep in mind that a new bundle of briefs will be on our doorstep in perhaps two more weeks, with a new round of arguments no more than four weeks distant, we begin to dig a trench that soon will blot out the sky. Without a sense of the relative importance of cases, both I and my clerks will be tempted to lavish time and care on every case, whether routine or significant—because every case poses its challenge of substance or style and beckons to the perfectionist within. We would soon find ourselves falling behind and working on older and older cases. And the older the cases, the harder it is to recall what we have read, heard, and discussed. The opinion thus becomes more difficult and time-consuming than it should be, and the cycle becomes more vicious.

This time-conscious evaluation of cases does not mean triage in the sense used to describe the terrible dilemma faced by medics at a wartime front, who are forced to decide which of the badly wounded to try to save and which to abandon. Classifying cases does not mean that some cases will be decided incorrectly; what is open to sacrifice is not the result—which in all cases ought to be determined by the application of relevant legal authorities to facts properly determined—but the length, depth, and elegance of the reasoning. What I mean by "triage" is the sense conveyed by the *Oxford English Dictionary*. Of French origin in the fourteenth century, it means "the action of sorting according to quality." And the first example given is taken from the 1727–41 *Chambers Encyclopedia*: "Each fleece consists of wool of divers qualities, and degrees of fineness, which the dealers therein take care to separate."[4] So we have in mind sorting the workload to reflect the degrees of fineness of the expected opinion.

While the infinite diversity of cases defies any hard-and-fast categorization, I have tried to outline a threefold division of cases in terms of normally expectable time investment and to identify the types of opinion-writing called for under each part. The reader should be alerted to the fact that opinion-writing differs from decision-making. In Chapter 8 we considered a classification of cases, listed roughly in the order of the difficulty they posed to the judges when they had their decision-making conference after oral arguments. Some cases, like the "rope of sand" nonfrivolous but routine criminal case, are easy to decide but may require substantial work in drafting a suitable opinion. Other cases take little time in conference because the vote is to await what the writer produces. Another category is the case that is very difficult to decide, but, once a decision has been made— for example, whether or not a trial judge has abused his discretion—the writing is not difficult. Finally, there are many cases—the "blockbusters"—where the difficulty to decide is matched by the difficulty of writing the opinion.

The following listing, therefore, will end with the types of cases that fall into this joint category of difficulty.

C. A Topography of Cases

1. Light. Cases in which the disposition, order, or opinion can ordinarily be expected to take from one or two hours to no more than half a day.

a. *Affirm on the Opinion Below.* Where the trial judge has taken the trouble to draft a thoughtful opinion, the appellate court, after reviewing the briefs, record, and lower court opinion, may well conclude that there is no need to reinvent the wheel. By affirming on that opinion, with or without some additional comments by way of supplementing or indicating nonreliance on part of the opinion, the court not only saves itself considerable time but shows the trial court that it recognizes work well done.

b. *A Short Order of Several Lines.* The trial court may not have issued a sufficient, free-standing opinion, but the facts and the legal implications are so clear that a simple order should suffice, either a reference to a rule requiring summary affirmances where no substantial question is presented, or a few sentences saying that the court has read the record and briefs, heard arguments, and decided that there *was* sufficient evidence to support the verdict. Particularly when oral argument has taken place, with meaningful conversation between court and counsel, is such a short-form disposition justified.

c. *Memorandum Opinion or Per Curiam.* The court feels impelled to go beyond summary conclusions and to give, in short compass, its reasoning. The vehicle for such a disposition is a short memorandum opinion or unsigned *per curiam*.

2. Moderate. Cases in which an opinion should ordinarily be prepared in from two or three days to a week.

a. *A Simple, Fact-Intensive Unpublished Opinion.* This kind of opinion states no new principle, no unusual application of law to fact. Indeed, there is usually no need to repeat all the facts, since the opinion is only for the parties' benefit. But sometimes the integrity of the reasoning demands a presentation of the facts, in which case the opinion becomes a sizable task.

b. *A Straightforward Application of Law to Facts.* This is a run-of-the-mill case which may or may not merit publication, depending upon whether the way in which law and facts interact could shed light on future decisions. But it does entail considerable work.

c. *Line Drawing.* This is the kind of case that could be either "moderate" or "blockbuster." Sometimes the court is clear as to where it wishes to draw a line, say, as to what blood or other relationships fall outside the concept of "family" or when the power of law enforcement authorities to interrogate suspects arises or ceases.

d. *Statutory Construction.* Like item a, this could be either a moderate or a heavy case. The inquiry starts with a scrutiny of the words of a statute, then may go on to a consideration of the sense and purpose and to the legislative history. Sometimes the divination of legislative intent can involve a labyrinthine investigation. By the time I talk with my clerks, the dimensions of the task usually are apparent.

3. Heavy—the Blockbusters. Cases in which, for various reasons, the expected time investment is substantial. By "substantial" I mean from two to six weeks. The advent of such a case in a chambers requires careful planning and readjustment of work schedules so that the remaining work goes forward as the "biggie" slowly moves forward.

a. *The Multi-issue, Multi-defendant Case.* The paradigm of this kind of case is the criminal prosecution of a drug conspiracy, involving many defendants, wiretaps, one or more searches and seizures, incriminating conversations with codefendants, exclusion of some evidence and admission of some, rulings on expert witnesses, alleged prosecutor overreaching in argument, refusal to sever trials of various defendants, challenges to sufficiency of evidence as to some, and claimed errors in the instructions to the jury. The very magnitude of the trial record and the multiplicity of issues assure me that a very large piece of work is involved, requiring up to four weeks of a law clerk's time and from a day or so to several days of my time.

b. *An Overarching Legal Issue.* The facts may be relatively few, uncomplicated, and undisputed. But the task of legal analysis is a heavy one. It may take a number of forms: a crucial, threshold decision (is a municipal ordinance content-based? Is a suspect "in custody"?); a delicate balancing act (do institutional interests outweigh individual rights?); a deep policy analysis (should sectarian high schools be more immune to church-state establishment clause scrutiny than sectarian universities? Or, as in *Burbine* v. *Moran*, which we discussed in Chapter 3, should police be permitted to lie to the attorney of a suspect presently in custody and being interrogated?); study of a cluster of diametrically opposed cases to decide which group is to be followed; or a microscopic study of an enigmatic Supreme Court decision.

c. *An Overarching Factual Question.* This type of case requires the opinion writer to master a lengthy transcript and many exhibits. Examples are an antitrust case turning on market share, a case involving a decision by the Food and Drug Administration not to approve a new drug for use, and a challenge to the sufficiency of an environmental impact statement issued in connection with the proposed construction of a major air terminal.

d. *Court Policy.* A case may not turn on any case law, statute, regulation, or constitution, but on the court's supervisory power over courts within the appellate court's jurisdiction. Matters of practice and standards of behavior affecting judges and lawyers are frequent subjects. Because any decision dealing with such issues must be clear, fair, and practicable, great care in phrasing is required and usually all members of the court are invited to comment.

D. Assigning Work on Opinion Drafts

After my debriefing, I go over work assignments with my clerks. My decision is made on the basis of various factors indicating where the comparative advantage lies. The advantage lies with my doing the initial draft in such cases as the following. There is the "quickie" opinion, where the goal is to say just enough to explain to the parties why the court reached its result. Doing such an opinion quickly is easier for me—and for any judge—than for a law clerk because the judge has enough experience to know that not every contention need be addressed nor authority cited for every proposition in a simple case where the law is clear. A conscientious clerk, particularly a new one, might feel that she has to justify even the obvious.

Another category is the opinion which reverses a trial court for abuse of discretion. Here, a judge is best qualified to deal sensitively with a colleague. The challenge in the opinion is not law but delicacy. Similarly, if the issue has wide public interest, I may feel that my language should be in the opinion draft from the beginning to assure the utmost clarity and persuasiveness of which I am capable. One consideration in my mind as I think about assigning cases is, of course, the caseload pressures I have mentioned in Chapter 4. But quite apart from the quantity of cases, I must always take into account the amount of uninterrupted time likely to be at my disposal. Cases involving a huge trial record and a plethora of issues require the complete and sustained absorption of the writer for substantial blocks of time—time the active judge seldom can arrange.

As I write these words, I am a senior judge, with fewer responsibilities than an active judge. But the average day in the life of an active judge would be something like the following. From one to two hours as a member of a duty panel dealing with emergency motions or appeals, reviewing draft orders, screening cases to be decided without oral argument; another hour or two reviewing colleagues' drafts, writing or reviewing draft responses, receiving and making telephone calls to colleagues about cases; constant study of reports, correspondence, telephone calls, and attendance at meetings in connection with one's court, or a committee of the judicial council of one's state or circuit, or of the Judicial Conference of the United States; preparation for and participation in educational workshops and seminars; reading briefs for the next session of court; and, in between or after these activities, several hours consulting with clerks, reviewing their drafts, and doing research and writing on the draft opinions which the judge has undertaken to write in the first instance.

It is not out of line to estimate the demands of bureaucratic, administrative, governance, reporting, and educational duties to amount to more than one third of the time of an active judge. Another third is judicial time, but time devoted to motions panel work, colleagues' drafts, and reading briefs. This leaves perhaps one third of a judge's time for work on the opinions assigned to him or her.

So, one key factor in my decision to assign cases for drafting opinions is the amount of time involved. I know that I cannot, without exceptional circumstances, spend from two to four weeks on one case. A case, therefore, that contains a voluminous record, which must be read, or many legal issues, each of which requires detailed study, is assigned to a clerk to come up with a proposed draft.

Other considerations influencing me in my allocation decisions are the following. Who is farthest behind in opinion draft production to date? Who has special knowledge or interest in this field? Who has had more than his share of criminal cases and needs a change? Who has had more than her share of tedious, dull cases, and really needs a case challenging creativity?

I make my assignments, reflecting my ideas of the time that should be required. As I assign the cases, I reiterate my instruction that if my law clerk unearths some fact or authority or public policy that throws doubt on our tentative decision, she should think a bit, assemble the relevant transcript and copies of decisions, and claim some time from me, after doing some focused reading, for a problem-solving discussion.

After a representative term of court, including the day described in Chapter 1, I drew six cases. Two were argued on the day described. I was assigned two: the dyslexic medical student and the black policeman's case. From the rest of our sitting, I was assigned four more. I assigned to myself the medical student case because it had been heard *en banc*, after our panel's decision, and every judge had voiced an opinion, either from the bench or in our conference. I felt that I was closer to the feelings and thoughts of my colleagues than a clerk could be. I had the best chance of finding common ground. This was a "heavy" in importance but not in expenditure of time. I also took a case involving a challenge to the composition of the jury; but no adequate contemporary objection had been made. This was a very quick and short opinion.

The policeman's case I assigned to a clerk, for it would involve a thorough rereading of the record and considerable research of the law. Moreover, the clerk had already demonstrated a good grip on the case, by opening up a question that neither party had briefed. To another clerk I assigned a criminal prosecution with First Amendment overtones, with three defendants proffering different grounds for reversal. This obviously would call for "a job of work." There were two more cases, not easy, not hard. One was a typical criminal appeal challenging the sufficiency of evidence to support the verdict and the length of the sentence imposed. The other was a civil case, an employment discrimination case, where the facts did not support the allegations of the complaint. I did not assign these immediately, waiting to see whether and when I or my clerks would be available for a new case.

III. Doing an Opinion

A. Immersion in the Case

After my clerks and I have discussed the new cases and I have assigned the work, they go off to their desks and I settle in at mine. I may first toss off a quick memorandum opinion. But then, facing up to serious work, I hibernate. I go through a ritual. It seems to serve me well, whether the case is a big one or a small one.

My first step is to immerse myself in the case totally, drawing first upon everything the parties and the judge below have said. The case at this point is like a tidal pool, recently stirred by the tide. Everything is cloudy and in motion. My faith is that if I just wait long enough and observe closely enough, the water will clear. So I begin my rereading and note-taking. I start with my very brief and impressionistic argument notes, just to refresh my memory as to lively issues. Then I look at my very skeletal notes of our conference to see if either of my colleagues had voiced some idea that I should keep in mind. Then I pick up the briefs.

I have sifted through them lightly before argument. This time around, I read (figuratively) with a magnifying glass, noting every reference to the record, every major case cited. I begin to construct my index, recording arguments with page numbers. I also depart from the briefs to follow up leads—a promising record citation or case. Very early in this exercise I realize that there is an opinion of the trial court in the addendum to the brief, and I drop everything to read it again, this time making fairly detailed notes of the points made. As I read a few cases, I do two things: I mark lightly with pencil in the margin of the case reporter (usually the Federal Reporter, Second Series), so that I will not have to hunt for what is relevant; and I write a small précis of the relevant holding on a separate slip of paper. (This enables me later to arrange the slips in order of my use of them.) The last task I undertake in the reading of briefs is to cross-check.

By that I mean that I check each brief to see what response is made to each argument in the other; if there is no response to a particular argument, no opposing case citation, or what looks like a very weak argument, I sense vulnerability.

The briefs having been read, I realize that I shall not really "know" the case until I have gone through the record. But I know that I can spend several entrancing hours with a record and retain only general impressions unless I can retrace my tracks. So I emulate Theseus when he entered the Minotaur's maze and leave a thread behind me as I go forward. This thread, in the form of a crude index of major facts and the pages on which they are found, is my assurance that I can retrace my steps and, when I am in danger of being overwhelmed by detail, see with some perspective the relation of events. I have no doubt that today a judge with greater word-processing sophistication than I possess could make a computer program that does for judges what the thread did for Theseus.

Sometimes, if fancy suggests and time allows, I shall go beyond the briefs and record, and browse. I shall look into law review articles that have long lain on my desk or I shall open a treatise or two and "read around" the issues. Once in a while I find some ore worth mining. What this kind of experience teaches me is that when one sets forth to work on what could be a significant opinion, it is a pearl of great price not to be harassed by tight deadlines.

B. Pause for Bearings

After this solitary musing, rereading, and immersion in the appeal, it is time to come up for air, to look around and ask, "What do I really think?" This is a critical stage in the opinion-creation process. The Federal Judicial Center's *Judicial Writing Manual* takes note of the important distinction Professor Richard Wasserstrom drew between "the procedure by which a conclusion is reached . . . the 'process of discovery' and the procedure by which a conclusion is justified . . . the 'process of justification.' "[5] It concludes, "A judge should have completed the process of discovery and reached a conclusion—if only a tentative one—before beginning to write. Setting down the reasons in writing then constitutes the process of justification."[6]

I prepare for this by holding a solitary retreat, going over all my notes, and redlining important facts, cases, and thoughts (including my own). I note issues as to which I think I have a clear answer. I note others on which more work has to be done. But what I am really interested in is resolving some big issues. At this point I summon my troops, my clerks, and we have a wide-ranging discussion. In this kind of case, just exactly what *is* the standard of review? Even if there was a waiver of this objection, should we nevertheless reach the merits? If one issue proves dispositive, should we deal with any of the other? Should we decide on a narrow or a broader ground? Do we want to make a ringing precedent, or should we minimize the precedent by affirming on alternate grounds? Invariably I leave such a conference refreshed and inspired.

This is the point of decision. Not decision on everything, but decision on the most difficult issue or issues. Until I feel I have a handle on them, I will not even attempt an outline, much less any opinion drafting.

Once in a great while, I reach this moment of truth and realize that our tentative decision at conference is probably not going to "write." In such a case I write my colleagues of my predicament and ask for a license to proceed in another direction. Very rarely I resort to a more cowardly device: I send my colleagues two opinions, the one they voted for, and the one I think is better.

At this point I have confidence that I know the general approach I shall take on the major issues. I have done enough work to feel comfortable with my grasp of the law and the factual record. My discussions with my clerks have helped clear up the major questions I have had. True, there is much more research to be done and perhaps some changes in thinking lie ahead, but not on the result or the dispositive issues. I am ready to begin the construction of the opinion.

C. The Road to Justification

1. The Preliminaries. When I say that I am ready to begin construction, I do not mean that I am ready to write. I am in the position of a tourist who knows he wants to drive from Boston to San Francisco, visiting in Chicago and Denver en route, but has not yet mapped out the highways and turnpikes that will yield the best trip. My threshold task, therefore, is to make my own road map or outline.

For me, outlining is the *sine qua non* of creating any opinion containing more than two or three paragraphs. Particularly in this age of writing with word processor is outlining necessary to keep one's writing lean. One of the seductions of the computer is the ease of spewing out one word after another on a cosmetically pleasing screen. If one's thought processes have been sloppy, the temptation of the writer is to think, "Why use one word when two will do?"

Outlining is not a task that I perform all at once. I do my outlining not only in sequential stages, but in different layers of detail. I first concern myself with outlining the preliminaries—everything leading up to my analysis and discussion of the merits. I do not attempt an outline of the merits at this point. Also, in outlining both the preliminaries and the merits, I act again like the cross-country traveler: when I come to a big city like Chicago (or a complex section of an opinion), I need a more detailed road map on a larger scale. So I make sub-outlines.

It may seem odd, but I view the outlining and writing of the "preliminaries" as the hardest job in doing an opinion. The very first paragraph presents a unique challenge to the writer—to say a great deal in very short compass and, if possible, in an interesting way. At a minimum it should identify the parties, the nature of the litigation, what the appeal is about, and, generally, the decision of the appellate court. Writing this may require its own little outline. This opener probably goes through more rewriting than any other part of the opinion. And the final rewriting will often be done after the rest of the opinion has been completed.

The next challenge is to tell the minimally necessary story

of the case: what happened between the parties to create the lawsuit; what needs to be said about what happened in the lower court or agency; and what needs to be said about the decision being appealed. This can be tedious work, for it often gives the writer no sense of being creative. This is not where the judge has to put on his thinking cap. Yet even here there is room for a sense of pride in one's work. If the facts are set forth with scrupulous fidelity to the record, are presented in a way to interest the reader, and have been so threshed that no chaff remains; if the procedural history of the case has similarly been clearly and sparsely told; and if the reasoning of the lower court and the parties' contentions have been fairly summarized, the achievement is not insignificant.

At this juncture, it is appropriate to state the issue or issues with more precision than the opening paragraph permitted. The statement should flow easily from what has just been said about the decision below and the parties' contentions.

An important part of what I have called the preliminaries goes beyond setting the stage. It deals with legal issues that have been, or should be, raised, and that may guide the analysis of the merits but are not themselves dispositive. As we have seen in Chapter 6, jurisdiction is a foremost consideration for any appellate court. Other preliminary issues include such technical ones as mootness, the standing of a party to raise an issue, and waiver of issues by failure to object in the court below. These have obviously been resolved in a manner to allow the court to proceed to the merits, but must be dealt with. Still other preliminaries exercise great influence over how the court proceeds. They include the always important issue of the proper standard of review, choice of the applicable law (state or federal), and identifying which party has the burden of proof.

All this done, I am ready for the merits.

2. The Merits. By this time, much of the bone labor lies in the past. The meat of the opinion lies ahead. Even though I have read the briefs, the record, and some cases, I know more work has to be done before I can even make a good outline. So I follow any leads in the briefs or in cases to other authorities. The time comes when I feel that I "know the territory." This means that I have come to the point where I feel I am aware of all relevant authorities, and where pursuing further research would be a misuse of time.

By this time also my long work table–desk is completely overrun by law report volumes in long ranks two deep, like soldiers awaiting the order to advance. Sometimes scouting parties, gathered on subordinate issues, camp out on a distant table, on my library ladder, or even on the floor. I now rummage through all the slips containing my notes on the cases and sort them out. I can discard older cases from a state or federal circuit if I have a more recent one. I must be careful to recognize cases right on point from those where the issue was slightly different or where the court's pronouncement was mere dictum, not a holding.

After I have made my case selections and prioritized them, I turn to policy. I always look for the policy implications of any decision we might be making. In some cases we realize that the decision of the trial court, necessarily made without the luxury of time to reflect which is vouchsafed appellate courts, may have done "justice" as between the parties, but, if made generally applicable—the test of a principled decision—would be unworkable. In other cases, where we might also chafe at the decision below, further thought might convince us that a reversal would only pave the way to chaotic future decisions drawing on the same principle. I think any appellate opinion is strengthened and made more understandable if such policy implications are spelled out.

I am now ready to outline my treatment of the merits. Of course, the first decision will be to determine the order in which the issues, if there are more than one, should be discussed. I suspect that generally the most important issue should lead off. But not necessarily. It may be that disposing of less important issues will clear out the underbrush and lead logically to the final and dispositive issue. As priority of issues is considered, I also am thinking of grouping issues, some deserving very summary treatment, and some deserving no treatment at all.

I am now ready to begin writing. I realize that I still shall have to stop along the way to make a more detailed sub-outline if an issue warrants it. At this point, I usually sense a welling of enthusiasm as I begin to express the fruits of more creativity. I cannot help but make two comments by way of contrasting what I do today with what I recorded back in 1980 in *The Ways of a Judge*.[7] First, in those days I was not only an "active" judge but chief judge of my circuit. My days were full of administrative matters, emergency cases, and other duties; the major opportunity for sustained work on opinions was at night. Today as a "senior" judge, I have most of my daytime hours available for work on opinions. I confess this is a change for the better.

A second change lies in the writing instrument. In *The Ways of a Judge* I wrote the following phrases:

> The writing now begins . . . with my placing a long pad of paper on my desk. . . . The first paragraph . . . soon becomes a mess of cross-outs, inserts, and rearrangements. . . .
> . . . .
> After four or five hours of steady work . . . I find my pen flying over the pages.
> . . . .
> As I go over my copy before giving it to my secretary, I realize with some apprehension what a collage I expect her to interpret. Not only does my writing degenerate into minute hen tracks, but carets and arrows and inserts affixed with paper clips force me to give a guide's talk on the sequence of each "page," which may consist of a half-dozen pieces of paper.[8]

Today, at the left end of my desk sit a computer screen and keyboard. There is still, as the reader now knows, plenty of pen-and-pad work. But they are engaged only in the outlining process, a process which I think has been made more important by the computer. That is, when I wrote opinions with a pen and had a new idea or afterthought, I could always clip another piece of paper onto the text at the proper place, cross out captions, renumber or reletter. While text can easily be moved around with a computer, I prefer to keep the moving of blocks to a minimum. There is for me something formidable about a blank screen that makes me want my road map before I sully the virgin space.

Yet similarities remain. If enough good thinking about the merits and the structure of the opinion has been done, momentum increases and the clicking of the keys proceeds apace, just as the pen used to fly. Finally, the issues have been addressed, with cases presented and discussed or distinguished in an orderly way, and with policy implications made manifest. There remains a minor but important task: to make clear what the outcome is and what, if anything, is expected by the court below.

I have one final checkpoint before I turn my draft over to my clerks for editing. I listen to the tape recording of the oral argument. I may have listened to this earlier and made notes from it, but in any event I give the lawyers one final chance to speak to me on the off chance that I have overlooked some point worth noting.

D. Final Touches

1. Editing. After the first copy comes off the printer, I will quickly make obvious repairs, but not do a deep review. I have for the moment had enough and am ready for other work. It is to my law clerks that I look for a rigorous editing job, as to both substance and style. This is not always a pleasant experience for me. No matter what may be the conventional wisdom, there *is* a pride of authorship, and I have not yet learned to see a favorite phrase excised without wincing. Sometimes the criticism digs deeper. I may have been carried away and made my conclusion more sweeping than it needed to be. I may have been sloppy in citing a case as "exactly on point." Indeed, I may find that some of my choicest arguments do not hold water. Chastened though I may be, I know the opinion has been improved.

2. Circulating the Draft. The moment finally comes when we send the draft opinion to my two colleagues (unless the opinion is to speak for the entire court). Usually no comment is needed except to make a recommendation as to whether the opinion has enough novelty or interest or other significance as to merit publication, rather than merely dissemination to the parties. But sometimes I may want to call attention to a close issue, to a tricky problem, to a change in our earlier agreed-to position. There may also be matters such as the assessment of costs or counsel fees worth noting. At this point there is nothing left for me to do but hope that I have met the expectations of my colleagues and either reflected their views faithfully or persuaded them that the draft contains better ones.

I have pointed out some of the differences in opinion-writing that have developed since my earlier book was written. But the essence remains the same. I can do no better than end this chapter with the sentence that began my section "On Working Up an Opinion" in *The Ways of a Judge*:

> Sometimes, often enough to make me aware of the privilege of being an appellate judge, the process of working up an opinion from the raw materials of the cold record, the contesting briefs, the existing law, history, logic, custom, and such considerations of policy and social justice as the case permits, becomes an intense, all-engulfing, and fulfilling experience.[9]

10
Opinions II: Working with Law Clerks

I. Role of the Judge

In this chapter we shall examine in some detail the ways in which this judge works with his law clerks—on the opinions he has initially drafted, on those for which a clerk has done the initial draft, and on those sent out from other judges' chambers for comment. These are subjects of increasing importance, and as yet the literature on them is sparse indeed. Even though any discussion is bound to reflect the idiosyncrasies of individual judges, there is a need for the sharing of practices and experience, for the benefit of present and future law clerks and judges.

The reader already knows, from reading Chapter 4, my general philosophy governing the judge-clerk collaborative relationship. I do not delegate only technical, ministerial tasks such as checking citations. I do not attempt to dictate in advance the handling of every issue. I repose a great deal of discretion in my clerks, treating them as colleagues, something like junior partners in a small law firm. This creates the following apparent paradox: we operate on a basis of shared responsibility; but although all feel this responsibility, I retain the core responsibility, which has been well described by Judge Aldisert:

> It is the judge who must assume 100 percent of the responsibility. . . . To delegate some writing responsibilities to a law clerk is more than proper; it is an absolute necessity in this litigious age. This delegation, however, is legitimate only to the extent that the judge accepts the submitted language, understands what has been written, agrees with it and is willing to stake a professional reputation on it.[1]

This contemporary role requires the judge to immerse himself enough in the case not only to arrive at a correct disposition but to develop the best rationale; to convey these strategic decisions, with all their nuances, to a clerk; to monitor for accuracy and prevent superfluity in facts or law; and to ensure a writing style consonant with his own values and tastes. Given this guidance, the clerk's contribution is not a disembodied analysis of a discrete legal issue; it is a prototype or aspirant opinion that reflects a sifting and selection of the facts in the record, an ordering of priorities, and an organized discussion of the controlling law, logic, and policy as applied to the facts. When both judge and clerk have effectively performed their roles, the resulting opinion is in the deepest sense the judge's even though the clerk may have invested forty hours and the judge only two or three.

I add one vital caveat to this view of the judge as architect-editor. I think it important for the judge's own psyche and sense of self that he always have on hand some opinions to do entirely, except for checking and editing by clerks. Not only does this afford the judge an outlet for the creative urge that made him want to be a judge in the first instance, but continual activity as a writer helps make him a better architect, general contractor, and editor.

Achieving the right kind of delegation to law clerks in order to realize both maximum intellectual exchange and collegiality and minimum need to seek overt direction and instructions does not come naturally. It takes forethought and conscious effort by both judges and clerks. A reciprocity of responsibilities, thoroughly understood and faithfully carried out by both parties to the contract, is the key.

Let us now turn to the cardinal responsibilities of the judge and the clerk, as my experience has identified them.

II. Cardinal Responsibilities of the Judge

A. Threshold Indoctrination

In Chapter 4 I have described very generally what I look for in a clerk as an intimate member for a year or more in our chambers community. The ability to write well and clearly was one of my criteria. Even more important than a writing awareness in choosing a new clerk, however, is making good use of the first weeks of a new clerk's tenure in conveying standards and expectations and in carefully critiquing early work products. "As the twig is bent . . ." It is much easier to start off on the right foot than to attempt corrective measures in midterm.

I have been fortunate in having the superb services of a career law clerk for a number of years. When a new clerk comes aboard, she is able to conduct a one-on-one course on our chambers practices. But even if a judge does not have such a person with institutional memory, the course should be given. Its rewards greatly exceed the investment of time.

The course consists of these ingredients;

1. A list of Basic Do's and Don't's. These reflect the judge's accumulated preferences as to organization, style, and certain substantive matters. How courts and judicial personnel are referred to, what an opening paragraph should cover, length of paragraphs and frequency of captions, footnote policy, selectivity in case citations and in stating facts—these are the kinds of items where early teaching can save later work.

2. Selected Model Documents. An invaluable tool is a carefully selected packet of opinions, good and bad; of bench memos (if required) submitted to the judge; of memos sent in response to opinion drafts from other chambers. To the extent the new clerk understands what is deemed "good" and what "bad," very substantial progress has been made in a time-saving way.

3. Assignment of a Simple Opinion. If the new clerk arrives some weeks before a term of court, I have found it useful to assign her a draft opinion on a run-of-the-mill case. I call upon our central staff attorney's office to choose one of the cases that have already been screened out for disposition upon briefs without oral argument. The clerk then plunges in, does what little research is necessary, and concentrates on organizing and writing; the judge then discusses in detail the good and bad points of the draft. The result is that the clerk approaches her first post-argument assignment with some confidence and some seasoning.

4. Critiquing. Everything the new clerk writes should undergo an organized critiquing: the draft opinion just mentioned, the first bench memo, the first cover letter transmitting an opinion to other chambers, the first memo advising the judge about ways to improve a colleague's draft opinion. At this point weaknesses, if there are any, can be clearly sensed. The clerk may be "perfectionist" on legal analysis but skimpy on digging out facts; he may view each case as deserving equal time. Through all of the "course" the aim is to help the clerk do good work in every case, but also to make hard priority judgments, so that extraordinary effort can be invested and exceptional work done in the most difficult, important, and complex ones.

B. Easy Clerk-Judge Communication

Although many judges find bench memos helpful before and during oral argument, and the exchange of memos helpful in resolving specific problems encountered in working up opinions, I am a strong believer in keeping communications oral where possible and access to my own inner sanctum unrestricted and informal. When I see a neat and well-organized bench memo of, say, eight or ten pages, I wince. I think to myself, "There goes a day or more that could have been spent on an opinion or scrutinizing a draft opinion of mine or a colleague." This doesn't mean that I am against a clerk's preparing a memo for his own future use, including helping the clerk prepare the judge for oral argument. Such a memo need not be edited, rewritten, and polished—fine-tuning activities that eat up time. Nor am I opposed to memos focused on specific targets, such as a chronology of events, a chart of interlocking corporate relationships, or a summary of relevant legislative history.

As we have noted in Chapter 2, we differ from the British in the dominant form of communication between bench and bar: theirs is an oral tradition, whether we look at what barristers do or what judges do, while our appellate courts rely heavily on detailed briefs from lawyers and issue the most carefully prepared written opinions. I prefer the balance we have struck. But not in chambers. Not only does talking save time, but it enables clerks and judge to get to the heart of a matter, without any need for a series of "clarifying" memos.

C. Responsibility and Feedback

To give a great deal of responsibility to a law clerk is, as we have seen, a generally unavoidable consequence of today's demands upon an appellate judge. But a corollary proposition, just as crucial but sometimes unrecognized, is that there should be constant feedback from the judge so that the responsibility can be carried out with increasing effectiveness. Feedback includes both commendation and criticism. Where possible, I tell my clerk what my problem is and leave it to her to make the adjustment.

Of course, there are times when I feel that the change I want is something I should draft myself, for reasons of sensitivity to a judge we are reversing, or a deeper awareness of the feelings of my colleagues. Even here, however, it is worth trying to explain why I felt a change was indicated. In short, feedback is a potent instrument of learning.

D. Broad-Brush Editing

The generally accepted wisdom on the subject of editing a law clerk's draft is summed up in the Federal Judicial Center's *Judicial Writing Manual:*

> It is the unusual law clerk who has perfected a writing style that makes for a satisfactory opinion. Law clerks' fact statements, analysis, and conclusions may require major revisions. Judges should not simply be editors—no matter how capable the clerk, the opinion must always be the judge's work.[2]

I accept this teaching . . . for the first month of a clerk's service. After that, if I have chosen my clerk wisely, if I have used the early weeks in a deliberate teaching mode, if I know that one clerk has reviewed another's draft before I see it, the need for detailed editing ought to have disappeared. If I have been an effective architect and general contractor, I will have diminished my role as editor.

Nothing seems to me more counterproductive than to go through the routines I have mentioned and then sit down with a clerk's draft and go through it with a hyperactive red pencil, as if I were a professional copy editor. Not only have I canceled out much of the saving of time I should have realized, but I have gone far to destroy the clerk's own self-confidence. As for me, if I needed to show heavy revisions on page after page to prove to myself that I was doing my job, I am in a pretty sorry state. So I aim for a review process in which I don't have to worry about questions of organization, analysis, and general writing style, but can concentrate on key passages, the general tone and feel of the opinion. As I read, I do not constantly ask myself, "Would I have said this in these exact words?" Probably, after nearly three decades, I have an internal monitor that alerts me to constructions or words I would not use. So if, as I read, I feel comfortable with the language, I will resist any temptation to edit in detail. And if I find very little to change in a draft that may have taken my clerk several weeks to prepare, I will be thankful that the judge-clerk collaboration is working as it should.

E. Memos to Colleagues

In addition to reviewing opinions that I have initially drafted and to preparing their own drafts, I expect my clerks to contribute to memoranda to my colleagues. There are three principal kinds. The first is the letter transmitting an opinion from my chambers to other chambers. This is usually a very simple and pretty standard affair. But occasionally we will want to alert colleagues to a problem we have found difficult, to ask for their views on certain issues, or to explain why the approach taken differs from the tentative decision of our conference. I want my clerks, therefore, to be thinking about sending any such signals.

The second and main kind of communication is my responses to colleagues' drafts and reactions to comments and suggestions they may have made to my drafts. Many judges keep this function entirely to themselves, feeling that collegial response is something quite personal, involving a wide tolerance for the idiosyncrasies of colleagues. I prefer to bring my clerks into the reviewing process as it concerns other judges' drafts, because their sharp eyes can find many minute points where improvement can be made. Obviously "nit-picking," as we call it on our court, can be overdone. I try to instill a sizable tolerance for ultratechnical and minor derelictions, stylistic mannerisms, and "fielder's choices," and then check every suggestion, using my own judgment about what is worthy to go forward. Then I will usually redraft the initial and more substantive paragraphs, trying to find what I hope will be an acceptable mode of expression.

The final kind of memorandum is a response to my colleagues when a petition for rehearing or rehearing *en banc* has been filed. As the writing judge, with a more detailed grasp of the case, I am in a position to help others, particularly—in an *en banc* petition—those who have not sat on the case. This is a very brief summary of my major reactions to the petition.

In all of these tasks, what I seek to convey is how best to communicate with my various colleagues on a wide range of matters. To the extent that a clerk's draft of a memo resonates with the same tone I would bring to it, I have saved valuable time, time that is better spent on opinions.

F. Impasse

There is one exception to my general approach of reposing responsibility on my clerks for opinion drafts. That is the case where the panel of judges has agreed upon a rationale and a result with which my clerk has no sympathy whatsoever. Indeed, he may feel so deeply about the issue that it is unwise on my part to expect a top-quality draft. Most of the time, a clerk's differences with a panel decision pose no problem. Like a good professional, a clerk is usually able to turn in a fine piece of work, just as a lawyer can advocate for a client whose position he may dislike intensely. Sometimes I can be persuaded to change my position, and in such a case I am usually able to persuade my two panel members. But there are issues and cases that provoke the strongest of feelings, and in these I have learned that the course of wisdom is to take on the opinion myself. If, even in the opening paragraph and statement of issues, a writer is thoroughly unsympathetic with the end result, nothing will be said as well as it should be. I would rather not try to remove one sauce and substitute another after the salad is made.

III. Cardinal Responsibilities of Law Clerks

A. Scheduling Work

Just as the judge must develop a sense of priorities, of what is more and what is less important, governing the overall workload of chambers, so must the clerk.

Almost no case reaching an appellate court is intrinsically

dull. One can always find some unasked question to raise or discern some fascinating theory to test. The beguiling temptation, particularly for a clerk new at the job, is to tackle an appeal, giving it one's best, sparing no effort to produce a draft opinion that will treat every facet of the case in a way that will answer all questions, asked and unasked, with encyclopedic thoroughness.

If a clerk follows this route on the first assignment, another session of court will have rolled around before she has even touched a second assignment, which may involve a much more novel, profound, or controversial issue. So the clerk falls farther and farther behind as the causes, great and small, remorselessly flood into chambers. And we should not overlook all of the unplanned tasks—to study incoming opinions from other chambers, to help defend, explain, or change one's chambers' drafts in the face of comments from other chambers, to help fight off a facially persuasive petition for rehearing.

The ability to sift out the more important from the less important, to prioritize, to set internal deadlines—this ability, though conventionally rated lower than intellectual brilliance, would win in any poll of experienced judges. It involves a discipline on the clerk's part to set a timed work schedule, to try to meet it, and to revise it as some cases prove easier and some harder. A schedule set by the judge is bound to be more arbitrary and less realistic than this continual monitoring by the clerk.

B. Respect for the Record

If responsibility number one is respect for time, a close number two is respect for fact. A new law clerk must keep in mind that this is something beyond most law school experience. Law schools, even those with strong clinical programs, must perforce stress legal reasoning, principles, and the exacting use of case authorities. In casebooks and moot court exercises, the facts are preselected for the student.

A law clerk or a judge, however, cannot accept the selection or description of facts as given them in the briefs of adversaries.

The precise words said by witness, counsel, or judge *and* the context in which they were said determine the outcome of contested rulings. I have experienced new clerks drafting opinions, immediately after reading the briefs, on an intriguing issue of law presented by the appellant. When I have gone back to the transcript, I have found that the issue was never raised below, a fact which appellee failed to note in his brief.

I would advise a new clerk to seize the first opportunity to become acquainted with a record of an appeal, whether or not the particular opinion requires such knowledge. Browsing through docket entries, perusing exhibits, reading direct and cross examinations as well as instructions to a jury, and sensing the tenor of motions and pleadings can open one's eyes to the endless possibilities of enlightenment that can be found. The record can be a clerk's best friend.

C. Due Regard for the Judgment Below

A new clerk, fresh out of law school, is charged with energy, is eager to see justice done, and is a little impatient with those who have not reached the empyrean heights of analysis to which he or she has been recently exposed. So I try to inculcate an awareness that a great deal has happened in the court or agency below, involving presumably competent and aggressive advocates and a trained and experienced judge or administrative official, all subject to definite rules of procedure and evidence, and the evidence itself, testimonial and documentary. What I am aiming for is not a decisive attitude regarding the decision below, but a slight beginning presumption, in view of the considerable investment in pleadings, discovery, pre-trial conferences, and trial, that the decision being reviewed was not clearly erroneous in its factual findings, or mistaken in its legal reasoning, or an abuse of discretion. This does not, of course, mean that the presumption cannot quickly dissolve in the face of obstinate facts or contrary law.

D. Outlining

What I have said in Chapter 9 about the necessity of outlining for a judge applies equally to a clerk doing a draft opinion.

There may be clerks who, staring at a computer screen, have clearly in their mind's eye the exact sequence of their thoughts. But I doubt it. Even simple-looking cases can throw out problems of selection, priority, emphasis, and sequence, which, if not resolved in advance by some sort of an outline, result in an overwritten, repetitive, cumbersome opinion. I stress the words "some sort" because I do not mean that the outline stage is very formal or standardized. Nor is it necessarily a single document. One begins with a large-scale map, a bird's-eye view of the course of the entire opinion. Then as the writer approaches each discrete unit, he or she constructs a mini-outline for that section. Nothing is graven in stone; the desired order and depth of treatment of an issue may change as one writes. The key objective is to know where one wants to go.

E. Brevity

The brighter and the more analytically gifted a recent law graduate may be, the more perfectionist she may wish her drafting to be. But perfectionism is the enemy not only of productivity but of brevity. And overwritten, needlessly encyclopedic opinions are no credit to a judge, a court, or the law, and most certainly of no help to lawyers.

Outlining helps a clerk, as well as a judge, to obey this commandment. The process highlights things that interrupt the flow of narrative or of reasoning. To the extent judges or clerks feel confident in their grasp of the facts and their handling of the issues, they are likely to achieve brevity. To the extent that they are uncertain, they feel the need to explain ad nauseam, to grapple with straws, to devote precious space to utterly worthless arguments.

In addition to lack of organization and lack of assurance in approach, reluctance to jettison learning is an enemy of brevity. After probing some vexing question and finding the answer only after much thought and research, and then eventually deciding that the probe was a wild goose chase and really has very little bearing on the opinion, one must be superbly disciplined to be able to discard the bootless product. While the judge may well excise such nuggets of learning

as she reviews the clerk's draft, the really helpful clerk does
his own painful surgery.

F. Cross-fertilization with Co-clerks

In a chambers boasting more than one law clerk, opportunity to gain the benefit of cross-fertilization of good minds
blends with the hazard of wasting time in excessive conversation. I know that clerks in some chambers work in splendid solitude in separate rooms. I have found it, however,
worth the risk of unprofitable chatter to have my clerks
work in the same room. The fact is that they strongly resist
using a quiet study down the hall, unless they are in the
middle of intensive composition. There is the obvious danger of too much talk, but my clerks' sense of the pressure of
time seems a sufficient safeguard.

When a clerk comes to a point where a theory should be
tested or a choice made between alternative reasons, a focused discussion between clerks is invaluable. And after a
clerk has completed a draft opinion, I expect him to submit
it to a co-clerk for comment. I do not expect the commentator clerk to spend time duplicating the work of the writer
clerk. But the more distanced editing judgment of a co-clerk
helps produce a document that need claim but minimum
time of the judge in making formal corrections. In short, I
do not get a rough draft but quite a polished document. I can
concentrate on substance.

G. Consultations with the Judge

When a clerk begins work on a draft, she has had the
benefit of not only her own reading and research, but pre-
argument conference with the judge and co-clerks, the oral
argument (which has revealed concerns of the individual
judges), her judge's report of the tentative post-argument
decision by the judges, and her own judge's instructions. But
there will be many decisions, mostly minor but some major,
that lie ahead. They will include decisions in selecting the
significant facts and procedural history to relate, choice of

the proper standard of review and the applicable law, and the sequence in which the issues should be discussed. Moreover, there may some issues in regard to which the judges' conference gave no guidance. As to most of these issues, the clerk in the kind of collegial chambers I have described will have confidence that her tentative resolution will be acceptable to the judge. She will not seek guidance before drafting.

But the sensitive clerk will always have antennae out for issues that do need the judge's immediate attention. Further study of the record may reveal facts that have not been taken into account, further reading may reveal case authority opposing the tentative decision, and further reflection may lead to doubt of the rightness of the court's approach and/or result. Perhaps the tentative decision stands free from doubt but alternative routes have appeared, as to which there has been no guidance. Or the facts or the law may be in such equilibrium that the judge's sense and experience must be called on as tiebreaker.

At such junctures, it is vital that the clerk bring the problem or the opportunity to the judge. Usually it is wise to supplement discussion by giving the judge marked passages of the transcript, relevant cases to read, or a sharply focused memorandum. Perhaps the problem can be quickly resolved, as when the judge knows some prior history of law or practice in his jurisdiction. Sometimes as much as a day or so is required to sort things out. But in any event, the clerk and the judge end up on the same wavelength. I remember a few awkward instances where a clerk failed to approach me at a critical turning point, the result being a draft that either could not be accepted or had to be substantially reworked.

H. Revising

I have noted that the ease and speed with which a computer spews out words are a threat to brevity. I add that a computer printout of a draft opinion, fully spell-checked and margin-justified, easily beguiles a writer into thinking that the job is done. At this point the law clerk must summon up willpower to review everything caustically, cut away all that is not necessary, and make clear what is opaque, crisp what meanders, and sharp what is blunt. Only when a clerk gains an appreciation of what a good copy editor can do to even a highly presentable first draft can rewriting come into its own.

I. Awareness of Judge's Tone and Style

The good clerk has his antennae out from his first day on the job to absorb the nuances of the judge's manner of communicating with colleagues. The clerk's aim should be to be able to draft memoranda to be sent from chambers with as little need for extensive rewriting as possible. Style of writing is, of course, basic. But equally important are the sense of deference manifested by the judge and the judge's restraint, willingness to compromise, and tact.

For example, I like my clerks to receive criticisms or suggested changes in a positive frame of mind, being willing to make concessions which do not affect our basic approach and to think of ways to accommodate the suggested changes in the least disruptive way. If we are critical of another judge's draft, I want a clerk to suggest specific word changes that will make it easier for the other judge. And I want my clerks to exercise some restraint in making technical but minor criticisms (even though I stand ready with my blue pencil to double-check) as well as to be alert to very good work that deserves a word of commendation.

IV. Judge-Clerk Collaboration

A. Judge's Draft

When a clerk reviews an opinion that I have drafted, her comments generally fall into one or more of three categories. To begin, there always are minor technical corrections in citations. Then there are criticisms, indicating that something should be deleted or that some view expressed is wrong. Finally, there are constructive suggestions; these add thoughts that strengthen the opinion.

An example of a negative comment occurred when I too quickly disposed of an issue on the ground that a prior proceeding had given the appellant full opportunity to litigate the issue but that he had failed to take advantage of it. I therefore proposed to apply the legal doctrine of collateral estoppel and to refuse to reconsider the issue. But my clerk, who had read the briefs more carefully, pointed out that somewhat different issues and parties had been involved in the prior proceeding. I had been saved from an embarrassing misapplication of law.

A more positive suggestion was made in an opinion where, though I proposed holding that appellant had waived a cause of action by not pressing it, I went on to discuss what statute of limitations period would apply if the cause had been preserved. My clerk challenged this second step, which was unnecessary to the holding of the case, being pure dictum. Nevertheless, I felt that if we said nothing after our holding of waiver, we would be interpreted as implying that appellant's argument for a longer limitations period would have prevailed but for the waiver. Since the issue was an important, lively one in the field of labor-management relations, I thought we should indicate our views favoring a shorter period in cases like this. The result of our exchange was that I modified our dictum language to indicate doubts but not to make a flat statement of views. By holding my feet to the fire and making me justify going farther than strictly necessary, my clerk had caused me, while signaling some doubt on the merit, to moderate my language and leave flexibility for a future case squarely presenting the issue.

B. Clerk's Draft

Here is a not-too-typical example of my reactions to a clerk's draft. It illustrates the kinds of weaknesses I look for. In a multi-defendant criminal appeal, involving ten different issues, my clerk worked for almost three weeks before producing his draft. I then went over the briefs, read parts of the record, and discussed close issues with my clerk. At the end of our collaboration, when we were both satisfied that we had done our best, I had made the following contributions:

—My clerk's opening paragraph was melodramatic. He had been carried away by the intensely human drama. I rewrote this paragraph to set the tone that I thought was appropriate.

—My oral argument notes revealed that a few additional significant facts had been conceded. We added these.

—My clerk had worked so closely with all issues that he tended to see each as finely balanced. But after research and discussion, most of the difficulties had evaporated. So I toned down some of the agonizing introductions to various issues.

—Surgery was called for on some footnotes. For example, one footnote made a sound response to a very sophisticated argument that might have been, but was not, made. Another distinguished a case that could have been, but was not, cited.

—I did some reparagraphing (into shorter paragraphs), repositioned "only" a few times, inserted a few "road sign" captions, and caught some misspellings and typographical errors.

—My major substantive contribution was to eliminate discussion of three issues. One had been briefed by both prosecution and defense, but had not been preserved at trial. The other two simply did not deserve discussion. I did not blame my clerk for giving them full treatment; this kind of decision should be the judge's.

C. Division of Labor

Some opinions lend themselves to a planned division of labor, the judge doing some parts and the clerk doing others. One example was an attorney's fee case at the end of an important litigation. The attorney was claiming a very large fee. I left to my clerk the statement of the factual and procedural background and the setting forth of the legal authorities relevant to the standard of review and factors to be considered in fee allowances. My job was to dig into the details of the time spent, the work done, and the amounts claimed for each segment. This was a case where I knew my clerk could find the appropriate law but felt that I should develop my own "feel" for the work done by the lawyer.

Sometimes a chambers is saddled with a case of high importance and fearsome dimensions. An example is the type of school desegregation case common in the late 1970s and 1980s. Not only did such cases include a number of hotly contested trial court rulings and involve a vast and complex record, but often there was a need for fairly prompt decision, if school authorities were to be able to prepare for the next school year. In these circumstances, the entire chamber might be mobilized, with judge and all clerks participating in the original drafting. Indeed, on occasion the chambers of all judges on the panel pitched in, with responsibility for drafting discrete parts. In such a rare kind of collaboration, it is critical that the "writing judge" be recognized as having the prime responsibility for accepting, rejecting, and modifying contributions, so that the final result will not resemble a horse produced by a committee—that is, a camel.

D. Creative Symbiosis

Sometimes the clerk-judge collaboration results in something more than suggesting a wise deletion or a strengthening addition. There are happy occasions when one suggestion leads to another, which in turn suggests still another—an experience in shared creativity.

Here is an example of how the chemistry can work. An advocacy and support organization for mental inmates of a state mental institution brought charges against the officials in charge of the institution, claiming that practices and procedures required by a long-standing consent decree had been ignored. The trial court ruled that the procedures were no longer required, the decree having expired.

The judges at conference all agree that the interests of both patients and the institution require resolution of the issue. But the law clerk, as she digs into the case, soon comes up against a roadblock. Hidden away in the appellee institution's brief is a claim that the appellant organization lacked "standing" to bring suit. That is, the organization, under Supreme Court precedent, was said to lack the intimate and direct concern with the institution's practice that entitled it to status as a party.

To the judge, this is a bombshell. He knows that even though this issue has not been part of the case up to now, and even though it might be thought unfair to raise it now, the claimed defect is jurisdictional, can be raised at any time, and could sound the death knell of the case . . . on a "technicality." Moreover, to analyze the issue and thread a way through often obscure if not contradictory case law would be a formidable task. Whatever might be the result, new law would be made for the court.

The judge and the clerk confer. They first discuss whether, despite the jurisdictional nature of the issue, it could be deemed waived by failure to raise it earlier. No. This is not likely. Then they discuss whether the issue can be avoided by a view of the merits. If the judges agree with the trial judge, they could easily affirm, because whether appellant has standing or not, the result would be the same. But the discussion at conference has shown that it is doubtful that the judges will affirm on the merits. This "easy" way out is blocked.

Finally, either the judge or the clerk suggests going back in the record to the very beginning to read the original complaint and see who were named as parties. Eureka! In addition to the patient advocacy organization, several individual mental inmates were named. *They* clearly have standing. The road to the merits is now cleared. A technical discovery has removed a technicality as a roadblock.

In the example just mentioned, the end result was to enable a decision on the merits to be made. Sometimes, however, it can be just as valuable a contribution to leave such a decision to a future case. Such a situation developed in the course of preparing an opinion on a complex appeal involving a multitude of issues. Almost hidden was an issue raising the questions whether and when a worker, uninjured physically, could recover damages for purely emotional harm arising from a negligent act of an employer.

Although some commentators have made the logical case for treating damages to the emotions the same as damages to the body, and some courts were inching in this direction, so to rule would create a significant precedent.

The law clerk began the process by submitting a draft

favoring the novel position, carefully distinguishing cases cited by the employer as not constituting any absolute bar to recovery. The judge, being moved not so much by logic as by such prudential factors as apprehension of a great influx of new emotional injury cases and the difficulty of winnowing out the fraudulent or frivolous cases from the genuine, drafted an opposite argument. Then, as the judge and the clerk dug deeply in discussing the merits and weaknesses of each approach, it gradually became clear to both that whatever the merits of the new position, the claims made and the evidence introduced in this case as to the alleged negligent conduct, the foreseeability of harm, and the extent of harm suffered were such as to preclude any reasonably justified and limited decision. The issue had been injected into the case almost as an afterthought. An attempt to make significant new law on such a record could not be justified.

And so the lengthy drafts of both judge and clerk were jettisoned in favor of a short explanation of why the issue would not be addressed. The merits of the issue were left for another day. Perhaps no good law was made by this result of symbiosis, but possibly bad law in either direction was avoided.

So far we have discussed the construction of appellate opinions at two levels. If I may use a phrase from the world of practicing lawyers, Chapter 9, on "doing an opinion," depicted the judge as solo practitioner; this chapter viewed a judge's chambers as a small law firm. But neither the judge nor her chambers works in isolation. They are, in a sense, a branch office of a much larger firm, consisting of all the judges and their chambers. It is to the workings and interrelationships of this larger group that we now turn.

11

Opinions III: The Workings of Collegiality

I. Appellate Collegiality: Its Characteristics

"Collegiality" descends from the Latin word *collegium*, meaning a body of colleagues or coworkers. The term fits appellate courts with exactness, for the judges on such a court are a small band of brothers and sisters. They are all peers, having no real superior, their chief judge or chief justice bearing heavy administrative responsibilities but having no more than one vote in any case. Their association with each other is long-lasting, often for the duration of their professional lives. They have differing values and philosophies, but they share the common discipline of the law and fidelity to their court.

I can think of no other contemporary institution that brings to every decision this degree of intimate, equal, permanent, independent, and single-minded collegiality. A law firm or a doctors' group practice relies on the individual achievements of its diverse specialists. The members of a legislative committee, though required to act collectively, cannot forget their primary allegiance to their constituents and their parties. Coworkers in an executive branch agency or a large corporation are ranked within a well-recognized hierarchy. And although trial judges in a multi-judge court may lunch together, share experiences with each other, and govern their court in a collegial manner, each is alone in carrying out his or her judicial duties. All of these modes of collegiality are, I think, transcended by that of appellate judges.

Collegiality at its best has several qualities. One is intimacy—intimacy beyond affection, resulting in a deep if selective knowledge of one another. Nobody knows one's societal values, biases, and thought ways better than a colleague. This intimacy is fed from the spring of our common enterprise and manifests itself in an abiding concern for each other and, above all, for the court. There is no instinct for competition; at oral argument there is no desire to appear to outperform colleagues. There is no envy and no sense of inferiority or insecurity. Openness characterizes the relationship. By openness I mean an absence of dissimulation, maneuvering, or exploitation. We say what we mean, and though much of our energy is spent in trying to persuade each other, we rely on the words that clothe the thought. On the whole, there is as little pettiness and enmity as one can expect among strong-minded people working together.

All this is not to say that there are no costs or burdens in the collegial life. Appellate judges lack the autonomy of trial judges, who preside with undivided authority over their own courtrooms. Not only must appellate judges be prepared to live with a certain restraint on their style, but they must compromise on many matters of substance. They write for not just themselves but others also. In doing so, they may chafe under the constraint of consensus. And occasionally they may be outvoted on a significant issue on which they feel strongly. It is during these dark moments that they muse over the paradox of collegiality. They know that they enjoy the respect of all their colleagues. But it is a generalized respect. In any given case, there is no such thing as a respect for one's specific opinion that will carry any weight whatsoever with another judge who has invested enough effort to develop and feel deeply about contrary views. There is absolutely nothing one can do to convince a colleague of the error of his or her ways. And the only way to survive with serenity is to don and wear proudly the sheltering cloak of civility that we call collegiality.

I therefore would describe appellate judicial collegiality in hornbook fashion:

> The deliberately cultivated attitude among judges of equal status and sometimes widely differing views
>
> working in intimate, continuing, open, and noncompetitive relationship with each other,
>
> which manifests respect for the strengths of the others,
>
> restrains one's pride of authorship, while respecting one's own deepest convictions,
>
> values patience in understanding and compromise in nonessentials,
>
> and seeks as much excellence in the court's decision as the combined talents, experience, insight, and energy of the judges permit.

II. An Endangered Quality

For my first fifteen years on the appellate bench, I was a member of a court with only three judges—the same size as when it was created in 1891. We sat with the same colleagues from forty to fifty times a year. There was no precedent created in which all of us did not participate. Because of this judicial Garden of Eden, one judge in reviewing some of my earlier preachments on collegiality charged me with "optimism bordering on innocence."

This was fair comment. My own court of appeals for the First Circuit now consists of six active and four senior judges, and all the other twelve federal courts of appeal have ten or more active judges and up to ten senior judges. When one considers that in a court of ten judges who sit in panels of three there are no fewer than thirty-six different panels on which any individual judge can sit, one begins to grasp the difficulty of maintaining a collegial atmosphere. While it is possible for a judge on such a court to sit with every colleague at least once a year, it is not likely. A federal appellate judge ends up sitting several times a year with the same colleagues, once a year with some, and not at all with others.

The difference in the collegial atmosphere between sitting with all of one's colleagues each month and sitting with each only once or twice or even three times a year is enormous. How much knowledge, conscious and unconscious, of each other's strengths, biases, and foibles is present in the first situation and how little in the second. How much motivation is present to establish the most harmonious relationships, to cater to particular habits and tastes, to minimize differences in the first situation and how little in the second. If we have to deal with someone all the time, unadulterated self-interest leads us to try to make the experience enjoyable. But if we sit with another judge only once or twice a year, there is less incentive to try to forge an open, relaxed, and trustful relationship. In such event, each sitting of a court approaches the convening of a panel of polite strangers.

The threatened dilution of collegiality in federal courts has led some to propose capping the numbers of appellate and trial judges. The Federal Courts Study Committee, in its 1990 report, speculated:

> It has been suggested that 1,000 is the practical ceiling on the number of judges if the Article III judiciary is to remain capable of performing its essential functions without significant degradation of quality.[1]

Since then there has been increasing debate on this issue. Not only is the degradation of quality to be feared, but also the dilution of collegiality. Indeed, the two overlap. Collegiality enhances quality, as its absence diminishes quality.

As Chart 2 in Chapter 3 reveals, the number of active federal district and circuit judges already exceeds eight hundred, with senior judges increasing the total to more than eleven hundred. So some would say that the time for freezing the size of the federal judiciary has arrived. The same comment could be made about the judiciaries in the most populous states.

While, as I have urged in Chapter 3, the federal courts should not be required to devote so much of their resources to what should be state court business, I suspect that even if all efforts to confine federal and state judiciaries to court-worthy causes were completely successful, the need for additional judges would continue to rise. The capping solution might preserve quality and collegiality for those fortunate enough to gain access to courts, but for those excluded there would be no judicial process at all. Were only the federal judiciary to be capped, the nation's court system would be divided into an elitist federal forum, where the most "important" cases would be decided, and residual state courts, where every else would be adjudicated. No longer could we pretend to aspire to Hamilton's goal of ONE WHOLE.

What seems to me a more realistic course, in addition to confining federal and state courts to their rational jurisdictions and court-worthy causes, is, first, as I propose in Chapter 15, to determine the basic "mix, pace, and measure" of a judge's activities and the facilities and services that can best constitute a rewarding judicial vocation, and seek to achieve these standards in both federal and state courts; and, second, to realize that collegiality may no longer be taken for granted but must be pursued deliberately and self-consciously.

It is therefore with the objective of stimulating an awareness of the fragility of collegiality and of what might be done to strengthen it that we now turn to some don't's, some do's, and some examples.

III. Chilling Collegiality

Collegiality may be likened to a flower that can be helped to grow by someone blessed with a green thumb. The skillful gardener may decide to get a head start on the season by growing seedlings indoors. But he knows that a chilling temperature, like an unexpected frost, can destroy his efforts. So it is with judicial collegiality. There are some errors of commission or omission that can threaten the growth of collegiality.

A. Precipitate Pronouncements

A necessary virtue for a trial judge is the ability to be both prompt and decisive in her rulings. But in early exchanges among appellate colleagues, tentativeness, ambivalence, and uncertainty work better in advancing the dialogue that underlies a truly collegial decision. I have found that more often than not, the wisest of judges are not ashamed to leave conference saying, "I don't know. I'm not sure." On the other hand, nothing is more disheartening than to hear a colleague, in opening discussions, say, "Nothing's going to change my mind."

B. Delay in Responding

Keeping an open mind does not mean absence of communication. When one receives a draft opinion from a colleague, both civility and efficiency strongly indicate a reply within a day or so. If the draft suggests problems that require some research, an interim "I'm working on it" reply tells the writer that his work is not being ignored. If, however, a judge who has labored hard on a draft is greeted with silence for days and weeks, collegiality has been chilled not only by the discourtesy but by a gratuitous infusion of inefficiency. For when the ultimate response is eventually received, the writer, if not also the responding colleague, has to invest extra time to refresh a memory blunted by the passage of time. Revision that might have taken a few minutes now requires hours.

C. Corrosive Language

One corrupter of written or oral discourse is the unthinking use of words that are, in the mind of the reader or listener, so imbued with irritating or pejorative meaning that rational discussion is likely to be derailed. Examples include attacking an argument as explicable only because of a colleague's prior experience or associations—an ad hominem insult; referring to a colleague's position as "unprincipled" or "boorish" (if the term is at all justified, there are far better ways of making the point); or even terming a colleague's reasoning "wooden." Sometimes I find myself changing language in a draft opinion or memorandum without conscious thought. I just know that it would have sent the wrong vibrations to a colleague. This is something like what a musician must experience when she adjusts her instrument to be in tune with the rest of the orchestra.

D. Lobbying

Sometimes a judge will feel so deeply about an opinion he has drafted that he will cross the thin line separating the judge from the advocate. To attempt to persuade colleagues by one's written reasoning is of course the business of an appellate judge. But to seek a colleague's support by saying "I hope you'll join my opinion. I feel very strongly about this" is to violate one of collegiality's unwritten rules, that against seeking favors in judicial matters.

E. Critical Overkill

One of the most delicate collegial judgments is deciding when a suggested deletion or addition to a colleague's draft is just a bit much. This is a decision that should always be made by a judge, even if a diligent clerk has done a thoroughly professional job of checking for citations, style, and substance. The responding judge, in matters of substance, does well to ask: "Does this really matter? If neither result nor approach is affected, should I worry if a harmless dictum or an unnecessary paragraph remains in the opinion?" In matters of style, the responding judge does well to remember that individuals differ and their styles differ. Though a court desires to speak with a single voice, that voice has—and I think should have—varying accents. In addition to unnecessary and irritating suggestions as to both style and substance, an unhelpful mode of response to a draft is a general suggestion to telescope a lengthy discussion, soften or limit a conclusion, or reorganize the order of discussion, without proffering concrete suggestions for specific changes.

IV. Encouraging Collegiality

While collegiality can be nourished by conscious effort, it must spring from the soil of sincere appreciation of one's colleagues. Given that, a judge should be aware of the special opportunities to foster collegiality that exist at each stage of the opinion creation process—when the draft is first written and circulated, when a judge responds to the writer, and when the writer reacts to a suggestion.

A. Awareness of Strengths

A Golden Rule of collegiality, if not *the* Golden Rule, is that just as one wishes to be valued for one's strengths, so should one be aware of and appreciate the strengths of colleagues. It is extremely unlikely that one judge on a multijudge court would be superior in all relevant respects to his or her colleagues. The whole idea behind appellate courts is that a collection of different minds is better able to perceive error and to guide the development of the law than is one mind. So the sometimes uncomfortable fact that others are not clones of oneself is to be cherished, not regretted.

One judge may shine in scintillating analysis and penetrating questioning at oral argument. Another may prepare cases prodigiously and spotlight weaknesses not apparent from the briefs. One may have a reliable reservoir of practical common sense—or just plain courage. Another may show his strength best in painstaking commentaries on drafts of opinions. One may have just the needed touch in suggesting ways to compose differences. And sometimes a judge, just by his character as reflected in his personality, may raise the level of deliberation to bring out the best in all. A solidly collegial court is one in which each judge's qualities are valued, and each judge knows they are valued.

B. Anticipatory Collegiality

This is by all odds the most effective kind of collegiality and is practiced by judges who know each other very well. It is the instinctive and unself-conscious sensitivity to one's colleague's sensibilities exhibited by a judge as she talks with or writes to her fellow judges. In writing an opinion she has a sixth sense of the way her colleagues are likely to react to an argument. She recalls not only the questions asked by her colleagues during argument and their comments during case conferences, but their values and philosophies as years of service together have revealed them to her. Sometimes the same instinct will lead a writing judge to signal in advance to her colleagues that she has run into trouble in trying to draft an opinion in the manner originally agreed upon and to focus their attention on her problem. A court in which anticipatory collegiality forms the normal mode of communication reaps an unseen harvest in a vastly reduced number of hotly debated issues.

C. Responsive Collegiality

Seldom is it wise or necessary to declare, on receipt of a colleague's draft opinion, that one's views are irreconcilable to it. At this stage, usually, the door is still open to change, sometimes very basic change. I recall that on a significant number of occasions, responding judges have been able to present a new way of looking at a case, or a hitherto overlooked case authority, or some undervalued fact or procedural point, and that a writing judge has gracefully changed course. So one is well advised to frame a difficulty as a question or a tentative problem. This leaves the door open to a continuing dialogue and the chance of accommodation, whereas a declaration of disagreement or the firing off of a dissent closes the door.

It is also fruitful to submit alternative language that would enable the responder to live with the decision; more often than not, the writing judge will willingly accept the substitute language. And sometimes the discipline of trying to fix something reveals that nothing is broken after all. And there are occasions when the responding judge may help avoid an unnecessary split decision by suggesting a viable middle ground, as by avoiding a sharp disagreement on the merits by remanding a case for further fact-finding, clarification of a judge's reasoning, or reconsideration. Finally, if a colleague has done something exceedingly well, a discriminating word of commendation is not out of place. Appellate judges have a largely distant, unseen, and silent audience; their best audience is their immediate peers, whose favorable reactions are prized.

D. Reactive Collegiality

Just as the two kinds of collegiality I have discussed require some conscious thought, so does the reaction one undergoes on receiving criticism and suggestions from a colleague. The first requirement is to suppress the irritation—and sometimes the anguish and even resentment—one feels on being told that one's work is less than perfect. The passage of time serves as a very effective suppressant. One then is able to think constructively, avoiding both an attitude of haughty rejection and one of servile acceptance. What is likely to emerge could include acceptance of some thoughts, with others rejected or questioned, thus continuing the dialogue; accommodation through devising new language that avoids the issue or disposing of the case on an entirely different ground; or concession, accepting the superiority of a colleague's idea and redrafting a good part of the opinion. The final stage is reached when the writer realizes that the opinion has been much improved by the exchange and expresses appreciation.

V. Collegiality in Action

A. The Responding Judge

The easiest kind of response to a colleague's draft occurs when one has no difficulty in concurring. This is an occasion for discriminating praise, accompanied by a few minor "nit-pick" suggestions. Almost as easy is the response when one agrees generally but has a few substantive suggestions that some language be dropped and some be added. More difficult is the task of responding when one detects more basic problems. At this juncture, the responding judge may well write, "I would like to concur but am troubled about one problem. Would you think about this and see if I have a point?" Chances are that the point is a good one.

Sometimes the issue is so clear that the responding judge, if there is a truly collegial atmosphere, will write, "I regret to say that I am so troubled by your conclusion to issue A that I enclose new proposed pages 8A to 13A to replace your pages 8 to 15." Often the writer accepts the substitution with gratitude. And, of course, the ultimate adverse response: "I appreciate the consideration you have given my views, but I am not persuaded. I am sorry to say, particularly in light of all the work you have done, that I am in basic disagreement with your approach. I enclose a brief dissent." Or the memorandum may say, "While I can go along with the result, I find I cannot accept your reasoning. I enclose a separate concurring opinion."

B. The Writing Judge

On one hard-fought case, a responding judge, who previously had been opposed to the writer's draft opinion, had become convinced by it and had commended the writing judge. The writing judge answered: "I am most grateful for your memo, the more particularly as you had abandoned your earlier position. My opinion was the work of others as well as myself, including your own suggestions." And quite often we see a memorandum from the writing judge to this effect: "I want to thank both of you for your memoranda. I appreciate the time and trouble which you so obviously took. Many of your recommendations are helpful; they will strengthen the opinion and improve its tone."

Here is another example of a collegial tempering of tone. Oral argument had changed our minds from affirming to reversing. The writing judge duly wrote a strong opinion reversing. So converted had he been that he castigated the trial judge rather forcefully. One of his brethren tactfully pointed out that after all, we would probably have acted the same way if we had not had the luxury of hindsight and a strong oral argument that had helped us see the error of our ways. The writing judge replied:

> You are absolutely correct about the excessive tone of this opinion. When I swung myself over, I thoughtlessly swung too far.
>
> Reminds me of the judge who was asked how he was getting along on a case, and who said he'd not been able to make up his mind, but when he did he was going to feel very strongly.

This, I submit, is collegiality in action at its best.

VI. The Role of Separate Opinions

A. General Considerations

Why should dissenting and concurring opinions be discussed in a chapter on collegiality? Because they are ruptures in the cloak of consensus ordinarily worn by collegiality. To the extent that separate opinions are deemed necessary by the writers, to that extent is collegiality diluted. It is therefore the obligation of each member of an appellate court to give serious thought to when, why, and how to indulge one-self in a separate opinion in order to minimize any corrosive effect on underlying collegiality. In over a quarter of a century I have authored some 2300 opinions; in that period I have written only twenty-seven dissents and twenty-one concurrences. That may signal a craven yielding to a majority, but I prefer to think it is rather a testament to the efficacy of real collegial interaction in reaching a result all can accept.

Nevertheless, even in the most collegial of courts, just because they consist of different individuals with different perspectives and values, there will be occasions for the recording of separate views. The values of consensus and independence are in constant tension. Chief Justice Hughes made the classic statement:

> When unanimity can be obtained without sacrifice of conviction, it strongly commends the decision to public confidence. But unanimity which is merely formal, which is recorded at the expense of strong, conflicting views, is not desirable in a court of last resort, whatever may be the effect upon public opinion at the time. This is so because what must ultimately sustain the court in public confidence is the character and independence of the judges. . . .[2]

Although Chief Justice Hughes was writing about all appellate courts, including his own, his statement, as of the late twentieth century, is more pertinent to the "inferior" appellate courts. For the United States Supreme Court is, after all, a unique institution. Some refer to it as part judicial and part political. I think of it as part expounder, part advocate, and part prophet. Chief Justice Rehnquist has pointed out that the task of error correction has been left to the state and federal appellate courts while the Supreme Court "[tries] to do what we ought to do—in the words of Chief Justice Taft, pronounc[e] 'the last word on every important issue under the Constitution and the statutes of the United States.'. . ."[3]

Faced with such vital issues in lengthily litigated cases, on which reasonable persons can disagree, it is no wonder that separate views are deemed eminently worth preserving. Chief Justice Rehnquist candidly acknowledges this fact of life:

> [T]here is virtually no institutional pressure to [alter one's views along the lines of the thinking of the majority]; dissent from the views of the majority is in no way discouraged, and one only need read the opinions of the Court to see that it is practiced by all of us.[4]

For the rest of us, in the state and federal appellate courts, there are several general propositions that can safely be advanced about separate opinions—concurring, dissenting, and "dubitante" (a very gentle way of dissenting). The first is: consider a separate opinion only after making efforts to persuade colleagues or concluding, after deep thought, that such efforts would be futile. The second is: before forging ahead, weigh the time involved and decide whether a separate opinion is worth the sacrifice to your regular opinion load. Third, if a separate opinion still seems worthwhile, be brief; a dissenter can usually make his point without assembling a massive scholarly apparatus. And the final caution is: after writing, let the product simmer, then eliminate all the unflattering innuendoes and pejorative words.

What follows is a brief listing of subordinate propositions for concurring and dissenting opinions that would generally be accepted by the judicial-legal community.

B. Concurring Opinions

They are justified

1. When a judge strongly prefers *a different theory or ground* to support the result, e.g., the judge would not reach the merits because of a procedural bar.

2. When a judge wishes to *limit the holding*, e.g., the judge concurs in this case involving the interstate transfer of prisoners but would not extend this to apply to an intrastate transfer.

3. When a judge wishes to *expand a holding*, e.g., the

judge points out that the instant case by its reasoning and holding effectively overrules a precedent.

4. When a judge wishes to *expand the majority's reasoning* on a particular point, e.g., the judge wishes to drive home a point to the bar or the trial courts, or to address a dissenter's argument in a more thorough manner than would fit the court's opinion.

A judge should never merely declare that she concurs. This is no more illuminating, and less quotable, than two examples collected for a judges' seminar by Judge Walter Gewin:

> I concur in the result and so much of the opinion as supports the result.

And this gem, delivered by an Irish chief justice, after hearing the view of his two colleagues:

> I agree with the decision of my brother on the right for the reasons stated by my brother on the left.[5]

C. Dissenting Opinions

A concurrence is like a fencing foil; it elegantly makes its usually bloodless points. A dissent, on the other hand, is more like a broadsword. It takes more resolution and commitment to wield it and there is the expectation of drawing at least a little blood. In any event, there is a feeling of unjudicial glee as one shucks off the normal restraints of writing for a panel and proceeds to thrust and parry with gay abandon. For this very reason, we judges are well advised to resist the temptation unless we find a compelling interest and no more effective alternative. Sometimes, however, a dissent is the precise instrument that should be used. This occurs

1. When the dissenter feels that a *serious mistake of law* has been made *on a significant issue* that is *likely to recur*. I have noted three prerequisites: a mistake that is serious, not minor; an issue that is significant, not trivial; and an

issue that is likely to recur, not one relating to a law that has just been repealed. The dissent in such a case alerts the non-panel members of the court of a likely petition for rehearing *en banc* and serves also as a flag to the Supreme Court if further review is sought.

2. When all the judges on the panel feel that the *issue is close* and that a dissent will sharpen the focus and reflect the closeness. In such a case the dissenter is acting with his colleagues' blessing.

3. When the dissenter feels that her panel colleagues have *erred as to the facts*, e.g., in finding a sufficiency or insufficiency of evidence to support a verdict, or *erred as to procedure*, e.g., in considering the merits of an issue in the absence of an adequate objection or request. In such cases, the dissenter's motive may be solely to keep her colleagues honest or at least deter their transgressions.

4. When the dissenter feels strongly enough about the *injustice of a rule* or precedent that he wishes to send a signal to bench and bar, the state courts, the legislature, the law schools, and commentators underscoring the inequity, anomaly, or inconsistency and calling for change.

5. When the dissenter feels strongly enough about the *conduct of the judges or lawyers* involved in the case to issue her own warning to the prosecutor, plaintiff's or defense counsel, or trial court. Even though the majority may not have found reversible error in the proceedings, the unvarnished indignation of a dissenter may serve a useful purpose.

A skeptical reader, after reading what I have said about collegiality and conscious efforts to nourish it, may ask whether the endeavor is justified. I think I have said enough to indicate that the opinions of a truly collegial court are bound to be better in substance, style, and tone than the effusions of one judge supporting a result commanding the votes of a majority without any effort to harmonize nuanced differences of view.

What has so far been unsaid is that collegiality is not only a guaranty of top judicial work; it is also a cherished source of joy in the life of an appellate judge. Even though judges may disagree on basic issues, they still—in a collegial court—relish the company of their colleagues and look forward to sitting on another case with them. But the pressures of the times—the escalating caseload, the emotional overtones of some of the issues, the occasional reporting of internal disagreements by the press—threaten collegiality. It can no longer be taken for granted. It may someday be regarded as a quaint relic of simpler times. If so, we shall surely be the poorer. In the meantime, the paradox of collegiality among independent peers is eminently worth thinking about, planning for, and struggling to maintain.

12

On Judging Appeals I: The Quest for Legitimacy

In this chapter I depart from describing what happens during the several stages of the appellate process. I look inward and ask myself, "What are my best thoughts about judging appeals? What kinds of questioning and reasoning do I find helpful in arriving at what I can comfortably call a principled decision?" In a sense this is a much-delayed response to the challenge of a great judge and good friend, the late Alvin B. Rubin, who served on the United States Court of Appeals for the Fifth Circuit. In a review of this work's predecessor, *The Ways of a Judge*, Judge Rubin commented that I had offered "no insight into the formula for judging, saying only that it remains 'unrevealed.' " He added, "I would have welcomed some suggestion, however tentative, of Judge Coffin's personal thoughts about how to decide [difficult] cases."[1] Here, then, are my suggestions concerning both routine and difficult cases. They are, and will always remain, I surmise, tentative.

Unlike most if not all other professionals, judges, like knights of old, engage in a never-ending quest for a Grail—

the Grail of Legitimacy. They yearn for the magic formula which could persuade everyone to accept it as right that they possess the power they do, to find them trustworthy, and, to use today's parlance, to believe they can make "judicially correct" decisions. Legitimacy, as I use the term, has three faces. The first is a satisfying explanation of the "anomaly" of the unelected judge in a democracy. The second is an acceptable assurance of accountability. And the third is defensible decision-making. These are the goals we seek.

I. The Role of Judge in Our Democracy: A Reconciliation

A. The "Anomaly" Problem

The question debated in every generation is: isn't it an anomaly that the decisions of unelected judges sometimes prevail in a democratic society, even though they may differ from the decisions, legislation, and policies of elected officials and the views of a majority of the citizenry? I need not, as a practical matter, restrict this question to unelected judges, for certainly judges running for nonpartisan reelection under a Missouri-like plan, without an opponent, cannot hope to secure any kind of public mandate to "legitimate" future decisions. And even judges who have survived partisan elections are generally so invisible that their election gives them little guidance in decision-making. So the "anomaly" theorem applies not only to all federal judges but to the overwhelming majority of state judges.

This basic challenge to legitimacy, the anomaly theorem that posits a lack of fit between our kind of judiciary and our kind of democracy, is my starting point as I try to chart my own internal buoys and beacons. One might ask why I bother with such a hoary question, which in any event has been answered by two centuries of adjudication, if not by logic. But the question naggingly persists and each generation has to face it, achieving either peace or uneasiness of mind. For me as a practicing judge, wrestling with the anomaly question is my first step in developing a concept of my role, its restraints and freedoms.

I think that the question of anomaly and the suggestion of improper deviation from the normal that it implies suffer from two shortcomings. One is that those who take seriously the theorem lack a full awareness of the extent to which the concept of judicial power to void statutes for constitutional reasons was a peculiarly American development in the decades preceding our nationhood. The other is that the assumption that such power is inconsistent with our democratic form of government misperceives precisely what kind of a democracy we have.

B. An American Heritage

In briefly reviewing the public record relating to judicial power to overturn legislative acts, I do not wish to be understood as claiming that this issue was extensively debated and clearly and explicitly decided by our Founding Fathers. The most that the Constitution yields is an implication that such power exists. And not until John Marshall's tour de force in *Marbury* v. *Madison* in 1803[2] was the doctrine firmly enshrined in our jurisprudence. But the burden of my message is a light one. It is to document the fact that the idea, a shy and long-forgotten plant in England, took on new life in the colonies and flourished as a hardy perennial. Its scent was very much in the air as the new states began their lives, as the Constitution was being drafted, and as the states debated its ratification.

1. Colonial Revisionism. Strangely, the lineal ancestor of "the anomaly" was the early-seventeenth-century English lawyer, reporter of decisions, and judge Sir Edward Coke. As reporter, he reported several cases in which, as an attorney, he had argued that "repugnant" laws could be invalidated by a court.[3] Then he reported his own opinion as chief justice of the Court of Common Pleas in *Dr. Bonham's Case:*

> And it appears in our books, that in many cases, the common
> law will controul Acts of Parliament, and sometimes adjudge
> them to be utterly void: for when an Act of Parliament is against
> common right and reason, or repugnant, or impossible to be
> performed, the common law will controul it and adjudge such
> Act to be void.[5]

This made little splash at the time and was, a century and a
half later, flatly contradicted by Blackstone, but the significant fact for our present inquiry is that Coke's Reports commanded "almost biblical veneration" in the colonies[6] and
that *Bonham's Case*, as Professor Goebel concluded in his
masterful Holmes Devise study, "began a new life in
America in the context of the constitutional principles that
had been in process of formulation" and became an "ingredient in the complex corpus of ideas and usages from which
a distinctively native doctrine of control over legislation
eventually emerged."[7]

In the years preceding the Revolution, the American colonists became accustomed to the Privy Council subjecting colonial legislation to judicial review. Then, after passage, between
1763 and 1774, of five "Intolerable Acts," the colonists, leaning
on the Tory Bolingbroke's belief in the fixity of the constitution, developed the concept of an "imperial" constitution (as
distinguished from the English constitution), under which Parliament, though all-powerful at home, was powerless to legislate for the colonies except in matters of imperial trade.[8]
Goebel sums up our pre-independence experience:

> The principle that government must be conducted in conformity
> with the terms of the constitution became a fundamental politi-
> cal conviction. What was not fully established was where the
> ultimate decision on conformity or repugnancy was to be lodged.
> Everything in the experience of the American lawyers, intellec-
> tual and practical, had prepared the way for committing this
> power to the judicial.[9]

2. Insemination in the States. With independence came
statehood and the resort by all the states to something they

had, as colonies, lived with for generations—a written instrument setting forth the structure of government and "the metes and bounds of the fundamental law."[10] In six of the states, constitutions specifically proscribed enactments of the legislature which would be repugnant to the constitution.[11] In six *other* states, court decisions recognized, explicitly or implicitly, the power of courts to invalidate legislation.[12] In at least three of these states, the decisions were highly controversial and, in all likelihood, widely known and discussed.[13] And in South Carolina, the thirteenth state, a court decision was shortly, in 1789, to adopt Coke's language in *Dr. Bonham's Case*, but avoid invalidating a statute by declaring that the legislature could not have intended the result urged by the statute's proponent.[14] So in all the states, after independence and before the Constitution, the seeds of judicial review of legislative acts had been planted.

3. The Constitutional Convention: Incubation. Shortly after the convening of the Constitutional Convention in Philadelphia in 1787, the proposal of a Council of Revision was debated. This was to be composed of the executive and a number of "the National Judiciary." It was to have the power of advance veto over congressional acts, subject only to override. The two principal interventions were those of Elbridge Gerry and Rufus King. Gerry said that the judges had "a sufficient check agst. encroachments on their own department by their exposition of the laws which involved a power of deciding on their constitutionality."[15] King supported this argument of the availability of judicial review, saying that the Justices of the Supreme Court "ought to be able to expound the law as it should come before them, free from the bias of having participated in its formation."[16]

Two and one half months later, toward the end of the Convention, the Supremacy Clause was unanimously approved, proclaiming that the Constitution, the laws of the United States, and treaties "shall be the supreme law of the several States . . . and the Judges in the several States shall

be bound thereby in their decisions. . . ." Professor Goebel
trenchantly comments:

> The command of the article was directed equally at any law-
> making body and at all judges, the ultimate arbiters of enforce-
> ment and of enforceability. That this was to be the role of the
> bench was plain from all that had been said about the judicial
> function; and that is why the judiciary, alone of the departments
> of government, was singled out for mention.[17]

4. The Ratification Debates: Foreshadowings. What remained of our incubation period was the stage of debating
and voting on ratification of the Constitution in the several
states. In the debating stage, No. 78 of *The Federalist*, authored by Alexander Hamilton, writing as "Publius," was
definitive. It faced head on the argument that judicial power
to void legislation would imply that the judiciary was superior to the legislature. It reasoned that statutes contrary to
the Constitution are void, but that a legislative body could
not be judge of its own powers, and that the courts are not
superior but are preserving the power of the people, declared
in the Constitution, in keeping the legislature within its
assigned limits.[18]

Publius not only made the case for judicial review for the
New York ratifying convention, but provided the intellectual basis for debates in other states. There were three significant presentations. The first was that of future Supreme
Court Justice James Wilson in the first state to ratify, Pennsylvania. In his speech, later published, he said, "[T]he legislature . . . may transgress the bounds assigned to it . . . but
when it comes to be discussed before the judges, when they
consider its principles, and find it to be incompatible with
the superior powers of the constitution, it is their duty to
pronounce it void. . . ."[19] In Connecticut, Oliver Ellsworth,
future Chief Justice, made the solitary reference to judicial
power, saying, "If [Congress makes] a law which the constitution does not authorise it is void; and the judicial power,
the national judges, who to secure their impartiality, are to
be made independent, will declare it to be void."[20]

The third pronouncement, fraught with portent for the future, was that of future Chief Justice John Marshall in the hotly contested Virginia convention. The debates in convention had been preceded by a most unusual action by the Court of Appeals, which, being subjected to a new law loading new tasks upon it and other courts without additional compensation, saw an assault on the independence of the judiciary and sent to the legislature a *Remonstrance* proclaiming that "the constitution and the statute are in opposition and cannot exist together; and that the former must control the operation of the latter."[21] On the eve of the legislature's grappling with this, Marshall reasserted that if the United States "were to make a law not warranted by any of the powers enumerated, it would be considered by the judges as an infringement of the Constitution which they are to guard."[22] Fifteen years later, Marshall was to write the opinion in *Marbury* v. *Madison*, formally embracing the doctrine in constitutional jurisprudence.

Far from being an anomaly, therefore, this right of judges to monitor the fit between legislation and the Constitution evolved as a distinctly American contribution to government.

C. Our Kind of Democracy

A second misunderstanding on the part of those who decry the powers of the unelected judge in a democracy concerns the key word "democracy." To the extent that this means rule by the majority on every issue, there can be no denying the anomalous nature of judges with power to contradict the majority. But democracy has many variants.

The first thing to note is that we are not a pure or unalloyed democracy in the old Athenian or New England town meeting sense. We are a representative democracy. I lived this principle when serving as a member of the United States House of Representatives. While I sought the votes of my constituents on the hustings in an exercise that was purely democratic—an election—I knew that after the election those constituents could not vote on specific legislation that came before the Congress but would have to rely on my judgment. I carried in my wallet part of Edmund Burke's address to the Electors of Bristol: "Your representative owes you, not his industry only, but his judgement, and he betrays, instead of serving you, if he sacrifices it to your opinion." I knew, of course, that if I differed from my constituents on too many issues, or on one transcendent issue, I would forfeit their fealty. But I still possessed a wide latitude of discretion.

This, however, is only the start of scrutiny. For the Founding Fathers, men of experience and wide reading, distrusted absolute power in any person or institution. The form of government they created was not borrowed from any one model. It was not even a representative democracy in the English and continental sense in which parliament is supreme. It defies a generic label and claims no simple pedigree. Scholars have to settle on the phrase "mixed government" or "limited republic."

In terms of the franchise, the President may be said to be elected by all the people. But the votes of the electoral college are not proportionate to population, and our present "winner-take-all" system makes it possible to win the electoral vote while losing the popular vote. And should no majority of electoral college votes be obtained and the election be thrown into the House of Representatives, each state would cast one vote, in defiance of "democracy." Members of the House of Representatives are chosen on the basis of population, but a state would presumably be entitled to one member even though its population were below the number meriting representation. And, of course, the Senate, with Rhode Island and Texas each having two Senators, is not even remotely "democratic."

In terms of powers, the President, by virtue of the veto override requirement, has a vote equal to one third of both houses of Congress plus one. Indeed, if Congress adjourns and the President, by refusing to sign a bill, executes a pocket veto, his vote can outweigh 535. The Senate, so disproportionate to population, alone possesses the power to advise and consent to treaties and to the appointment of judges and justices and other officials. And should the majority of people wish the Constitution to be amended, their wish would go for naught unless two thirds of both houses of Congress or two thirds of the state legislatures should call for an amendment, and three fourths of the states approve.

As the Library of Congress scholar Louis Fisher sums up:

> To call judicial review antidemocratic is tempting, but misleading. The Constitution establishes a limited republic, not a direct or pure democracy. Popular sentiment is filtered through a system of representation. Majority vote is limited by various restrictions in the Constitution: candidates must be a certain age, Presidents may not serve a third term—regardless of what the people want. Although states range in population from less than a million to more than twenty million, each state receives the same number of Senators. Filibusters conducted by a minority of Senators can prevent the Senate from acting. Majority rule is further constrained by checks and balances, separation of powers, federalism, a bicameral legislature, and the Bill of Rights.
>
> To the extent that the judiciary protects constitutional principles, including minority rights, it upholds the values of the people who drafted and ratified the Constitution.[23]

II. Accountability in the Three Branches

In addition to reconciling our kind of judiciary's possessing power to void laws and curb officials with our kind of democracy, a second step in the quest for legitimacy is to satisfy the demands of accountability. Conventional wisdom has it that in both the federal and many state systems of government the judiciary is the least accountable branch because it alone is insulated from elections. Not only does this fact infuriate many legislators, who must live under the Damoclean sword of perpetual campaigns, but it is a lightning rod for citizens who are angered by a court decision.

My view is that such conventional wisdom is flawed both by a failure to appreciate the fact that different accountability mechanisms apply to each branch of government, state or federal, and by a failure to recognize the extent to which accountability is built into our judicial systems. And to apply to the judiciary an accountability device that is suitable for the legislature and the executive—the electoral process—is to misapprehend and undermine the core concept of an independent judiciary pledged to uphold constitutions.

The concept of accountability, most naturally, sprang from the world of business, where profit generally serves as an adequate measure of performance. Even here, however, there is widespread concern that management's accountability to shareholders is often more theoretical than actual. Moreover, it is increasingly recognized that broader social and environmental factors must be taken into account in measuring a company's performance. And holding public officials to account is yet more complex and elusive.

I write with the perspective of one who has spent three fourths of his adult life in the three branches of the federal government. I began by serving two terms in the House of Representatives, then spent the next six years, first, as managing director of one foreign aid agency (the Development Loan Fund), second, as deputy administrator of the Agency for International Development, and, third, as the delegate of that agency to an international organization (the Organization for Economic Cooperation and Development). For the ensuing period of almost three decades I have served on the United States Court of Appeals for the First Circuit. In the course of these years I have seen and lived under the three systems of accountability.

A. The Congress

As a member of Congress, I soon found that such an apparently indisputable measure of performance as one's "voting record" was more like an onion, from which layer after layer could be peeled off. One voted at many different stages in the progress of a bill: in subcommittee, in full committee, on amendments, on motions to recommit (kill) the bill, on final passage, on motions to reconsider, on the conference report, and on motions to overturn a presidential veto. And the votes could be an unrecorded voice, standing, or teller vote, or a recorded vote.

In more recent times, accountability has been made even more difficult by the changing nature of much of the legislation. I have described the change as one "from freestanding, single-subject measures to complex, omnibus, multiple-subject, vast-scale authorizations; continuing appropriation resolutions; and budget reconciliation bills. New ideas of members are likely to appear (or be hidden) in such vehicles."[24] The by-products of this omnibus approach to legislation have been a reversion of power to leaders, a shifting of power from authorizing committees to the financial committees (budget, tax, and appropriations), and what I have called "a haven of blame avoidance for members."[25] Another significant change has been not only a quadrupling of staff since the 1960s, but an immense increase in their responsibilities and power. Because of the nature of the new legislation, "[n]egotiations are between staffs, who alone have hopes of mastering the details of huge committee reports and compendious bills."[26]

Finally, the ability of incumbents to attract a lion's share of campaign contributions, permitting almost unlimited access to the media, has drastically changed the meaning of accountability. We live in a television era when "image" may well have pushed "accountability" into the wings.

B. The Executive Branch

The President, while in a sense the most accountable of all officials, is subject to only a very rough kind of accounting. Such macro factors as prosperity or recession, peace or war, international humiliation or triumph, the image of the President as leader or good fellow—these are the ingredients of accountability.

As a senior official in the executive branch, I knew that I was accountable to the President. But I also realized that very seldom did accountability at that level go beyond an assessment of loyalty. Very few cabinet and sub-cabinet officials have been removed for reasons of poor performance. Accountability in the top ranks of the executive branch has been critically summarized by the National Commission on the Public Service, chaired by Paul A. Volcker:

> Presidents today are further away from the top career layers of government with 3,000 appointees—approximately 573 presidential appointees subject to Senate confirmation, 670 non-career members of the Senior Executive Service, 110 presidential appointees not subject to Senate confirmation, and approximately 1,700 personal and confidential assistants (Schedule C)—than was Franklin Roosevelt 50 years ago with barely 200. . . .
>
> The real question is whether the proliferation has in fact made government more effective and more responsive to presidential leadership. The Commission concludes that the answer is "no."[27]

As for the great ranks of the civil service, the commission's report was equally scathing. It gave the following example of the absence of a consistent and understandable performance recognition system:

> Seventy percent of the senior executives at the Internal Revenue Service recently said their bonus system did not provide an incentive to meet job objectives, 69 percent said the system is not administered fairly, and 76 percent said there was no direct linkage between their performance and the likelihood of receiving a bonus. Similar perceptions appear to exist across government.[28]

The report added the doleful comment "[C]areer public servants often become managers more by fiat and automatic promotion than by experience and skills."[29] The result has been an erosion of public trust, an inability to recruit and retain a top-quality work force, and "[c]rippled nuclear weapons plants, defense procurement scandals, leaking hazardous waste dumps, near-misses in air traffic control, and the costly collapse of so many savings and loans."[30]

Paul C. Light in his study of the office of Inspector General in the various federal departments and agencies distinguishes among "compliance accountability" (precise rules and punishment), "performance accountability" (positive incentives and rewards), and "capacity-based accountability" (investing enough in people, systems, and structures to create the conditions of success).[31] His melancholy finding is that while compliance accountability is popular with Congress and Presidents, yielding highly visible results in volume,

> [n]ot only does compliance accountability often reward short-term gains in lieu of long-term capacity building, it may distract Congress and the President from addressing the hard questions about how to design institutions and programs to work better from the very beginning.[32]

His conclusion: "After all the statistical accomplishments are totaled and all the staff and budget increases reviewed, government appears to be no more accountable today than before the [Inspector General] Act."[33]

C. The Judiciary

As for the judiciary, trial judges, though they may seem to be the sovereign of their courtrooms, are subject to review of their every final decision by three or more of their appellate colleagues. Their conduct beyond the purely judicial is also subject to scrutiny by the judicial council of their state or circuit. Appellate judges are subject to a formidable threshold restraint; they must persuade a majority of their colleagues before any opinion can issue with their court's imprimatur. A second, highly efficient engine of accountability is the tradition that in all but the most frivolous of cases, the opinion must be in writing. A third is the case law written by other courts, for a court does not lightly embark on a course foreclosed by its peers. A fourth is the possibility, if not the probability, of review by the United States Supreme Court. A fifth, admittedly effective only in the long run, is the critical reception of the legal academic community in the journals of the law schools. And a sixth is the check that may be administered by the Congress or a state legislature in amending or passing a law that effectively overrules the court's decision.

Beyond this kind of accountability relating to specific decisions, appellate judges, as well as trial judges, are closely monitored in their extrajudicial lives. Their lives are lived subject to a "Caesar's wife's" code of ethics; their associations, communications, and activities are monastically confined; their investments and extrajudicial earning activities are strictly regulated, reported, and examined. Complaints against them are processed within a formal structure. State supreme courts, state and federal judicial councils, and, in the case of federal judges, the Judicial Conference of the United States exercise governance over all judges. And the Congress and state legislatures engage increasingly in carrying out oversight functions.

This brief *tour d'horizon* shows that when rhetoric is put aside, the judiciary is, in its own matrix of mechanisms, at least as accountable as its sister branches. It also shows that more effective accountability remains an unrealized goal for all branches. Elections test roughly for acceptable stands on a few dominant issues, but do not test for insight into the national interest, legislative skills, and leadership ability. Civil service procedures may reward the brilliant and identify gross incompetence but not root out the sluggard, the timeserver, the official who plans badly or fails to follow through, the insensitive field worker who infuriates state and city representatives who must deal with him. Judicial review can correct the most egregious errors and judicial self-government can exorcise flagrant misconduct, but there will remain some bench bullying in the courtroom, inefficient case management, and unpardonable delay.

In his 1992 Oliver Wendell Holmes Lecture at Harvard Law School, Chief Judge Stephen Breyer of my own court, in speaking of the problem facing health regulatory agencies in gaining public respect for hard decisions, gave voice to another approach to legitimacy:

> [I]t seems to me that public respect depends not only upon the perception of public participation but also, in part, upon an orga-

nization's successful accomplishment of a mission that satisfies an important societal need. . . .

Insofar as a systematic solution produces technically better results, the decision will become somewhat more legitimate, and thereby earn the regulator a small additional amount of prestige, which may mean an added small amount of public confidence.[34]

To apply this thought to the appellate judiciary, sound decision-making and decision-making perceived as sound will, in the long run, contribute to a widely shared sense of legitimacy. So—with humility but without excessive apology—we push on to see how appellate judges can better account for the area of freedom in decision-making that is permitted them. We look not to external guardians but to the internal ways of thinking that can guide them.

III. Lure of the One Right Answer

The reader might agree with me that the power of the unelected judge to frustrate majority wishes on occasion is far from an anomaly in our unique, history-driven form of democracy, but was an inevitable, if not formally purposed, development. One might also accept my conclusion that, in its own way, the judiciary is just as "accountable" as are the legislative and executive branches of our national and state governments. But, on the part of judges and lay citizens alike, there remains a hunger for assurance that in deciding cases, including the hardest ones, judges draw on objective truth, not their own moral and philosophic values.

An observer of the contemporary scene may be more sympathetic with a skeptical attitude about the existence of "the one right answer" when she contemplates such issues as those raised by abortion, capital punishment, hate speech, the uses of genetic research, and "the right to die." Long ago, Karl Llewellyn referred to "the single right answer" as "the illusion of dogmatics" and confessed the source of his enlightenment: "Square roots shook me out of this, with the $+/-$ answer."[35] Recently the pragmatist scholar-judge Richard Posner, in his wide-ranging *The Problems of Jurisprudence*, sounded the same note:

> Without social, cultural, and political homogeneity, a legal system is not able to generate demonstrably right, or even professionally compelling, answers to difficult legal questions, whether from within the legal culture or by reference to moral or other extralegal norms—the traditional province of natural law.[36]

But for this statement he was taken to task in a review by Professor Eric Rakowski, who wrote:

> For the last twenty years, many scholars (led by Ronald Dworkin) have maintained that to contend that no right answer exists to legal or moral questions because impartial judges, lawyers, or moralists disagree is typically to make an idle metaphysical claim, an assertion ... about the ontological [i.e., objectively real] status of moral or legal expressions.[37]

This is a debate at a stratospheric level which I, as a practicing judge, do not expect to reach in my lifetime. For Dworkin's paradigm philosopher-judge, Hercules ("a lawyer of superhuman skill, learning, patience, and acumen"),[38] in deciding a constitutional issue,

> must develop a theory of the constitution, in the shape of a complex set of principles and policies that justify that scheme of government, just as the chess referee is driven to develop a theory about the character of his game. He must develop that theory by referring alternately to political philosophy and institutional detail. He must generate possible theories justifying different aspects of the scheme and test the theories against the broader institution. When the discriminating power of that test is exhausted, he must elaborate the contested concepts that the successful theory employs.[39]

In stating that this kind of thinking is at a much higher altitude than that in which I work, I do not mean to denigrate it or the varied and possibly fertile acres of jurisprudence presently under lively cultivation. It may well be that at some future time, perhaps early in the next century, perhaps in another century or so, there will be such a consensus among moral philosophers and jurisprudential scholars on one, a few, or even more social issues that decisions of the United States Supreme Court and those of lesser courts may be based on them.

In the meantime, my own approach is unashamedly eclectic. There are cases where, for example, in interpreting a statute, my only concern derives from Legal Positivism— what has the majority decreed? There are other times when a Utilitarian calculus—greatest good for the greatest number—comes into play, as when the effect of a company's licensing policy on the competition is measured under the antitrust laws. Dean Langdell's Scientism ("Think like a lawyer") is still a lively stock in trade in many common law cases. Natural law and its Social Contract progeny may well inform decision in novel areas of conflict between the state and the individual. Some cases depend more on an accurate appreciation of the critical "facts of life" than on legal doctrine and thus draw sustenance from the Sociological School. Is *Roe* v. *Wade*'s trimester analysis of pregnancy an example?

What I have just alluded to are enclaves or "schools" dealing with the nature of, or sources of, law. Other groups marshal their adherents under the banner of method and analytical technique. Being a product of my times, I acknowledge a fealty to Legal Process, its emphasis on institutional appropriateness and neutral principles. I would, for example, hesitate before judicially imposing hard and fast deadlines on administrative agencies for holding hearings or taking other important actions. But I am also sensitive to the skeptical strains in Legal Realism, challenging conventional thinking about legal principles. If law enforcement officers have given *Miranda* warnings, must I assume that any statements thereafter made by a criminal suspect were made voluntarily, or is there still a possibility of official overreaching and manipulation? The thriving field of Law and Economics is relevant to market analysis, certain problems in damages calculation, and other issues. Linguistics is opening up new issues of interpretation. And probably a dozen other specialized disciplines are potential grist for the judge's mill.

In sum, I feel that I must "single out" (the root meaning of "eclectic") the conceptual framework or approach best suited to deal with a given issue, because, in my view, no one approach adequately covers all cases.

The reader will note that I have not identified as guides to decision the much-discussed bipolarities of judicial restraint and activism, loose and strict construction, and liberal and conservative values. This is because, for the most part, they are chameleon words. An activist judge, finding constitutional violations, proceeds to dictate significantly how a prison or school system shall be run. But when a judge or court essays to restrict what advice doctors can give their patients, in the interest of avoiding misuse of grant funds for family planning clinics, is this no less "activist"? As for approaches to construing statutes and constitutions, I suspect that most judges are both strict and loose, depending on the clause or provision they are construing. Some clauses are written with precision; others, like "due process" clauses, are expansive. Some are obviously dated in that they were devised for conditions no longer important in the light of demographic, scientific, technical, or societal change; others stand the test of time with unimpaired relevance.

I do not deny the existence of a difference between "liberal" and "conservative." After all, for well over a century, *Iolanthe* has stood for the proposition "How Nature always does contrive/ That every boy and every gal/ That's born into the world alive,/ Is either a little Liberal,/ Or else a little Conservative!" The difficulty arises in determining what people profess to be liberal and conservative about. Nevertheless, we can assume that judges, generally emerging from a background in or around partisan politics, reflect something of the dominant attitudes of the country's two major political parties. But the reflection is very seldom an intense one, and it fades with time. This is not to say that it disappears but that it plays a less significant role than is commonly supposed.

So I end this brief attempt at philosophizing about philoso-phy by saying that I cannot assure the reader that I can anchor my most difficult opinions in the closest cases in any objective "right" fount of jurisprudence. Benjamin Kaplan, former justice of the Massachusetts Supreme Judicial Court, in reviewing the predecessor of this volume, *The Ways of a Judge*, commented (after noting my brief sketch of legal and moral philosophy):

> But judges are indifferent philosophers and are rightly wary of subscribing to any single jurisprudential (or moral) scheme. When confronted with competing values represented by alterna-tive rules, they try to foresee the practical consequences of the choices (cruelly difficult exercises of the imagination) and then elect among them on some utilitarian basis, deviating from that course when it would invade unduly the integrity of the indi-vidual.[40]

Having followed the trail in pursuit of "the one right an-swer" and having not been able at this juncture to pursue it farther, I propose that we follow what is perhaps a less ambitious trail in the chapters to follow, one blazed with lowercase letters. In reviewing the last book written by the widely respected scholar the late Alexander Bickel, *The Mo-rality of Consent*, I described the approach in these words:

> In the absence of an all-purpose, generally accepted judicial phi-losophy, we shall have to settle for a bundle of discrete smaller philosophies—respect for procedural fairness, candor and rigor-ous craftsmanship, sensitivity to federalism, faithfulness to legis-lative purpose where such is discernible, and alertness to official arbitrariness. The development, for our time, of those middle distance values and the imperfect justice for which Bickel teaches us to settle may depend upon these smaller philosophies and upon the saving grace of pluralism—the appointment of judges not only of competence and integrity, but of varying val-ues, bents and philosophies.[41]

These will be the concerns of Chapter 13. In Chapter 14 I shall aim a little higher and try to address the demands of cases calling on judges to develop a sense of how this society can deal with its individual members under new conditions in a spirit most faithful to our origins and genius.

As we leave the high ground of jurisprudence, I can do no worse than offer this endnote from a talk on "Judges and Jurisprudence" I gave to my colleagues on the state courts in Maine some years ago:

> *Here is a matter of nomenclature*
>   *Having to do with judicial nature.*
>
> *There are several words in the hierarchy*
>   *Which roughly describe our esquirearchy.*
>
> *We begin at the bottom, down where the sludge is,*
>   *For that's where you'll find all of us judges.*
>
> *As learning in law becomes purer and purest,*
>   *We rightfully call the possessor a jurist.*
>
> *But only the most esoteric student*
>   *Deserves the title of jurisprudent.*
>
> *If ever together should come this trio,*
>   *We'd then see judges perform* con brio.

13

On Judging Appeals II: Familiar Waters

As we descend from Olympus and commence our search for trailmarkers at lower altitudes, it is useful, I think, to divide our more particularistic quest for legitimacy into two kinds of cases. The first is the generality of cases, occupying the attention of most appellate judges most of the time. They are not necessarily easily resolvable or "routine." But they are most often finally decided without disagreement among judges of even widely varied social, economic, and political backgrounds. And if there is disagreement, the issue dividing the judges is likely to be a technical or professional one, not one fraught with philosophical implications. To use a nautical metaphor, these cases are in coastal waters, which are well charted, with buoys, landmarks, and beacons guiding the pilot.

The second category of cases, though much smaller in quantity, is nevertheless today substantial and of large significance in the development of the law. These are cases presenting the conflicting claims of an individual and society. In addition to all the craft skills practiced in the first group, they involve a particular kind of tension between opposing values, a kind that calls upon judges to draw on their deepest views of civilized society and the right relationship, consonant with our Constitution, between the individual and the state in a specific situation.

To continue my nautical metaphor, these cases are in largely uncharted waters, where conventional guides are inadequate and one must seek the help of sextant or radio signals. Here the metaphor breaks down, for there is far more certainty in plotting position from a skillful "shooting of the sun" or, especially, from radio signals than in discerning, in a "hard case," the right balance between the individual and society. But the fact remains that something beyond conventional equipment is needed.

As to both types of cases, I seek for legitimacy, first, in the presence of guidelines of substance, attitudes, and process that effectively prevent or minimize aberrant judicial approaches. Where these are absent, I must be content with a full and open account of the basis on which I think the values I have relied upon are justified. If judges pursue both routes conscientiously, then it is my faith that whether or not specific decisions meet with the approval of the public, in the long run such judges will have earned the trust and confidence inherent in "legitimacy."

I. Idiosyncratic "Pre-judice"

In plumbing judicial thought processes, we first identify certain kinds of influences that must be cleared away if serious judging is to take place. These are the biases and the preconceptions that judges, as human beings, possess and against which they must inoculate themselves—prejudices in the root sense of the word, "before judgment."

A. Ad Hominems

These are thoughts and feelings that appeal "to the man," that is, to one's emotions rather than reason. I have alluded to them briefly in discussing the judges' post-argument conferences in Chapter 8 and threats to collegiality among judges in Chapter 11. Judges, no less than lay persons, are subject to instant responses to inflammatory stimuli. Such baggage includes repugnance to or liking for a party—for example, aversion to one convicted of a foul crime or to a troublemaker, or attraction to a respected community leader; antipathy to the events at issue, whether the case involves the vending of pornography or a squalid organized crime "enforcement" attempt; and preexisting views of the strengths or frailties of a notoriously "bureaucratic" government agency. Such reactions do not, in most judicial chambers, flourish under the light of intense study and discussion of the germane facts and law of the case. When the stone is lifted, letting in the sunlight, the slugs scurry away.

B. Judges' Backgrounds

Less venomous than the ad hominems are what we might call the "ad vocationems," the values inhering in the social, economic, and vocational background of the judge. Some may find it difficult to look with sympathy on the plight of the poor, or, conversely, to deal fairly with the rich. Others may take a dim view of all governmental regulatory activity or, conversely, believe that corporations are invested with original sin. Sometimes the kind of law practice a judge engaged in before her appointment to the bench casts a shadow. When one has been either a plaintiff's or a defendant's lawyer in personal injury or products liability cases, a prosecutor or defense lawyer in criminal cases, or a labor or management lawyer in labor relations cases, old adversarial values are hard to shake. A judge who comes from an academic background is tempted to become a self-appointed guardian of academic autonomy. These hidden "tilts" are not discussed; controlling and compensating for them are subtle challenges to a judge. An effective antidote is the variety of backgrounds usually represented on a multi-judge court; they tend to offset or at least minimize particular predispositions. And usually the passage of time saps their strength.

C. Policy Preferences

Several cuts above the background biases in respectability are the social policy likes and dislikes of judges, such as "liberal" and "conservative" attitudes mentioned near the end of Chapter 12. They cannot be exorcised, being probably part of the deepest values held by a judge. But they should not exercise their influence *sub silentio*; if invoked, they must be openly discussed, assayed, and justified insofar as the judge is able to do so. Leading the list are such hotly debated policies as abortion, school prayer, gay rights, and capital punishment. Closely following is litigation involving prisons, school boards, public housing and welfare organizations, and anti-discrimination, environmental, and consumer protection laws. Judges may vary widely in their predispositions, being pro-establishment in some kinds of cases and pro-individual in others.

D. Institutional Attitudes

A final set of values which I have termed idiosyncratic includes attitudes toward institutional factors—the tension between process and substance, the standards of conduct expected from trial judges, prosecutors, and other participants in the judicial process, and access to the courts.

A judge may venerate process or may prefer to subordinate process where injustice would result. Ideally, and frequently, process and substance trend toward the same end. But sometimes faithfulness to process results in the exclusion of a party or an issue from the litigation, in the countenancing of errors committed by the trial court, or in tolerating agency decisions that, while wrong from an appellate court's point of view, are not quite irrational. By the same token, faithfulness to substance may mean that a fair, wise, and legally sound decision is rendered at the expense of consistency with precedent. Justice may have been purchased at the expense of uncertainty.

Similarly, appellate judges differ over the appropriateness of exercising their supervisory power over trial judges, prosecutors, and members of the bar generally. Some feel that trial judges and prosecutors should be held to the punctilio of fairness; others feel that they are already overburdened with a confusing cargo of boilerplate commands and cautions from on high.

Finally, a judge may be deeply concerned over the danger of overburdening the courts and may take a restrictive view on allowing access to them or may be just as deeply concerned about the denial of such access by rulings that appear to be overtechnical.

These are all attitudes springing from a judge's concept of the roles of courts and judicial review. We can call them institutional attitudes. Each reflects a worthy consideration. The differences in these attitudes are here to stay. They ensure that even ordinary cases involving no great substantive issue will yield a certain amount of irreducible disagreement. But, as we shall see in the following section, there are powerful forces tending to produce consensus.

II. Centripetal Craft Forces

A caustic critic of contemporary judging, who could be either an uninformed but opinionated barfly or a learned philosopher decrying the failure of judges to agree on "the one right answer," would close the record at this point, after noting the sources of idiosyncratic preconceptions. In so doing, such a critic would be in good company with Rabelais, who wrote of the difficulty Judge Bridlegoose had gotten himself into by imposing a sentence that had been deemed inequitable. In defending himself to his superiors, he referred to his failing sight.

> For this reason, he said, he had not been able to read the points on the dice as he had in the past. . . .
>
> "What dice," asked Trinquamelle, the presiding justice, "do you mean, my friend?"
>
> "The dice of judgment," Bridlegoose answered, "the hazards of justice, the same dice that all your honors ordinarily use in

this honorable court, as all other judges do in the decision of a case, . . . who all observe that chance and hazard is exceedingly sound, honest, useful, and necessary in the disposition of cases and controversies at law."[1]

Such a view, unhappily one which has survived Rabelais, ignores the fact that a very large part of appellate judging involves the application of craft skills and professional disciplines which are held in common by all judges, of whatever backgrounds. They have bite in them, are not easily ignored, and serve to limit all centrifugal forces. A brief survey of these centripetal forces makes the point.

A. Five Constraints of the System

There are five fundamental features of our American appellate system that work to confine judicial discretion. They constitute most of the essential elements of appellate decision-making listed at the end of Chapter 1. The first is reliance to quite a considerable degree on the performance of adversaries. Judges, in the main, are bound by what the opposing counsel in a case have done. A second feature is our reliance on a heat-tested decision by a court or agency, an event that imposes a significant barrier to be surmounted if a reversal is to take place. A third constraint is the rigid requirement that only matters placed on the record below may be considered. A fourth is the demanding discipline that an appellate decision must be put in writing. And a fifth is the necessity of persuading a majority to join in any proposed decision. All of these elements combine to discourage if not foreclose individual aberrant decision-making.

B. Tickets of Admission

Almost as palpable as the basic features of the system are the judge-made doctrines that serve as the palace guards, carefully checking every case to see whether it has a proper ticket for admission to appellate consideration. To begin with, there are the requirements of subject matter jurisdiction and personal jurisdiction. The former involves such questions as whether a federal (or state law) question or diversity of citizenship is present; the latter, whether adequate service of process has been made on a party. Then there is a third ticket required: there must be appellate jurisdiction. That is, the appeal must be from an appealable judgment and filed in timely fashion.

Even with these demands satisfied, there must be "standing," i.e., sufficient direct, usually "pocketbook" interest in the outcome of a case to warrant court consideration. There is the allied question of whether there is a live "case or controversy."—that is, the case may be refused admission either because it presents a question prematurely (the matter is not "ripe") or too belatedly (the matter is "moot"). In similar manner, a case may be denied admittance because remedies have not been "exhausted" in agency proceedings or in those of a state court (where a claimant seeks federal habeas corpus relief). In some cases the subject matter itself will be considered out of bounds, most notably in cases involving "political questions."

On such issues, I think disagreement among appellate judges would be found only in the exceptional case.

C. Rules and Conventions

A multitude of less tightly controlled restraints are the practices, rules, and judge-made law which govern the conduct of trials and appeals. First on the list are the various trial and appellate rules of procedure; these range from the very specific and rigid (such as time limits governing appeals) to rules allowing a wide degree of discretion to the trial judge (such as allowing amendments to pleadings). Second are the rules of evidence and their accompanying judge-made doctrines regarding burdens of going forward and of persuasion, levels of scrutiny of statutes or other state conduct, and presumptions.

The third type of guidance directs judges in their efforts to find and apply legal standards and principles. Here, precise rules give way to well-entrenched conventions, such as the distinction between a holding and a dictum, the preemption of one law by another, the principle of *stare decisis* (or the relative sanctity of applicable precedent), and *res judicata* and collateral estoppel (the controlling effect of a prior decision involving the same parties or those closely related to them). The interpretation of statutes has given rise to a massive body of supposedly helpful canons of construction (many of which are mutually contradictory).[2]

D. The Pull of Deference

Like magnets, there are certain traditions of deference exercising an influence on appellate courts, attracting their attention, requiring their consideration, and sometimes compelling their submission. The concept of deference is admittedly fuzzy, embracing everything from a perfunctory nod to craven acquiescence. But it is nevertheless real and, in more cases than one might suppose, applied by judges in a similar manner.

The first is deference to the decider of first instance. Such a decider would include not only the administrative agency and the trial judge but also an arbitrator. Sometimes an appellate court is faced with the vexing task of reviewing a trial court (with proper deference) to see whether *it* has accorded proper deference to a hearing officer or administrative law judge.

Then there is the overarching deference owed to the decider of last instance, the United States Supreme Court. There is no disagreement among appellate judges on other courts when a Supreme Court opinion is directly applicable or casts a pretty definite shadow over the contours of a particular case. The disagreements arise when some judges like a specific opinion and wish to expand its application and when others dislike it and wish to confine it to its original bounds. There are other occasions when, although Supreme Court precedent may be clear, it may be old, widely criticized in many dissents of Justices and in law reviews, and thought to be contrary to the current views of a majority of the Court.

Even so, appellate judges may well hesitate before taking the bold step of declaring the demise of lofty precedent.

Deference to state or federal law is governed by different considerations. A state court is, of course, obliged to apply the federal constitution, where applicable and more protective of individual rights than a state constitution. And it is equally obliged to apply federal statutes where relevant. In so doing, it is not confined to any single court for its authority. It may pick and choose from federal court decisions or it may invent its own approach. But a federal court, in a case resting on diversity jurisdiction or in a federal question case where state law controls on a given point, has no such freedom. It must defer to the law of the appropriate state.

The decision of a court to defer to the law of another system in such cases is not likely to be a source of disagreement, although exactly what that law is may be. For example, a federal court, sitting in a diversity case, may find little guidance as to what state law may be. In such event, judges may wish to certify the question to the state court and request an authoritative answer. But other judges may feel that the answer is clear enough, that the certification process would further delay what has already been too lengthy a litigation, and that the state court would not wish to be burdened by the proceeding. Similarly, much law has grown up around various bases for a federal court abstaining while a state court proceeds to decide some or all of the questions involved. The criteria governing such decisions to abstain leave much to discretion in assessing the weight of various factors, providing ample room for disagreement despite an overall policy favoring deference.

Deference due other courts is yet another factor exercising its own pull. One state supreme court will hesitate before disavowing the precedent of another or, especially, of several. One federal court of appeals will similarly not lightly disagree with another circuit, especially of several. It does not desire to create a split among the circuits and thus add to the potential caseload of the Supreme Court. But even in this area, it makes a difference what kind of decision is being made. If the issue is one where unanimity and finality of decision are more important than theoretical correctness, deference is highly likely. If, however, the issue is one of substantive principle, as to which the court feels strongly, deference is likely not to be the ruling consideration.

In this section I have sketched a universe of skills, traditions, conventions, rules, and principles that link all judges, state and federal, as members of one profession. Although they differ in their precision, intensity, and authority, on the whole they are forces trending toward consensus. So far, I have spoken in general terms. While I share in all of these restraints, like all judges I have developed my own gloss, my own separate guides to the guidelines. Insofar as I am able to identify them, I shall now do so. Otherwise, the picture of my navigating in the coastal waters of the ordinary case would not be complete.

III. My Own Canon

The most resistant task I have faced in writing this book has been to try to identify anything particularly individualistic and interesting about how I go about my work in deciding appeals. What I am about to say is all that I can confidently claim. And I know that it is neither terribly original nor illuminating. But it is all I can offer.

A. The Justice Nerve

I place at the head of my list that which is the most important and the hardest to define—my justice nerve. Every judge possesses one. Just exactly where it comes from I cannot say. Probably from the whole mix of genetic inheritance, family upbringing, youthful role models, education, vocational and other experience, reading, associations, and the several thousand appeals in which one has written an opinion or cast a vote.

But, as Justice Potter Stewart said about pornography, "I know it when I see it." I feel the justice nerve tingling as I dig into briefs, read parts of the record, and sense deceit, trickery, or mere manipulation on the part of one party, a callous disregard of court procedure or etiquette on the part of counsel, a calculating disrespect for the court (as if to invite erroneous rulings), an overbearing or patronizing prosecutor, bland insensitivity on the part of an administrative agency, or persistent hostility to counsel on the part of the judge. Sometimes the nerve tingles as I read of extremely lengthy sentences to prison, stemming from mechanistic sentencing guidelines . . . but I seldom can do anything about them.

Indeed, there often being a gap between law and justice, there are limits, severe limits, on what can flow from an activated justice nerve. Sometimes, of course, when all judges share the same sense of outrage, it is likely that the result, whether affirmance or reversal, will reflect that sense. There are other times when one's own justice nerve is the only one that is flicked. In that event, one has the ultimate option of filing a separate opinion, dissenting or concurring. There are also lesser options. One may persuade one's colleagues, without changing the basic result, to narrow the opinion (e.g., rather than positive approval of the questionable conduct, a narrow affirmance based on the trial court's discretion in a very close case); to tailor the remedy (e.g., by granting more limited injunctive relief than sought); to impose costs or other sanctions (even on a successful appellee who may have needlessly obfuscated an issue); to express disapproval of certain conduct, even though in dicta; or to issue a warning of sanctions or a changed ruling if certain conduct is repeated.

Even though such actions fail to change the outcome of a particular case, the expression of a strongly felt sense of injustice by a judge or court often influences the future conduct of a prosecutor, defense counsel, judge, or agency.

B. Procedural Regularity

I count myself as one of those marching under the banner of process, even though on occasion this results in some hapless litigant not having her case heard on appeal. It seems to me that in the long run, where rules set forth precise requirements as to the making of objections, the filing of motions, other papers by the parties, and judgments by the court, and the fixing of time limits and deadlines, more good than harm is done by insisting on compliance than by making exceptions in particular cases, even though equitable considerations may exist. I would acknowledge, as do the cases, the propriety of making exceptions where a shocking miscarriage of justice would otherwise occur. But those are extremely rare cases. For the rest, we are, I think, well advised to rely on the competence of the bar. Otherwise, courts are likely to find themselves wading deeper and deeper into a swamp of judge-made law concerning permissible exceptions to the rules. When possible, however (which is frequently), I will indicate to the litigant who has lost out through some procedural default that his case on the merits was not likely to prevail in any event.

C. The "Material Fact"

As the reader knows, I value the record and the necessity of a rigorous reading of it to identify the key facts in a case. I also acknowledge my deference to the trial court's findings of fact. Such attitudes are hardly unique or worth including in my personal canon. What I mean by this section has reference to the highly useful device of summary judgment, which permits a judge to dispose of a civil case on the basis of affidavits and other papers if no "genuine" issue of "material fact" exists.

The virtue of this procedure is that it allows a case to be decided without a trial. No jury need be drawn nor long days spent with witnesses testifying. In these days of climbing caseloads, summary judgment is increasingly alluring to the harassed trial judge. But the danger is that the root requirement of summary judgment may be overlooked. That requirement is that the court must view not only facts favorably to the party opposing summary judgment but also the reasonable inferences from these facts that favor such opponent. What I fear and sense is a subtle tendency on the part of both trial and appellate courts to devote less and less energy and analytical thought to the second part of the requirement—identifying the favorable reasonable inferences. Ironically, the result of a precipitate granting of summary judgment is that while the lower court may be saving trial time, the appellate court is forced to spend a great deal of time plowing through a large record and agonizing over a very close issue, with the possibility that the cause will after all be remanded for trial.

D. The Decision Below

Deference to the decider of first instance, judge or agency, is, as we have noted, one of the basic attitudes held in common by all judges. I discussed in Chapter 10 my goal of persuading my clerks to indulge "a slight beginning presumption" of validity in the decision being reviewed. I mention it here to show how it plays a role in my own thought processes. Over time I have seen enough transcripts, trial records, and administrative agency case files to have a healthy respect for the effort and competence that have been invested at the first level of adjudication. This has in turn inculcated in me a habit of giving, as a preliminary reaction to a case, a tentative benefit of doubt to the decision below.

Before taking a position on an issue involving the conduct of a trial, I read the transcript of testimony in some depth to obtain a "feel" of what was foremost in the minds of counsel and the court when the ruling was made. Often the result is that I come to appreciate that what the judge said and ruled made sense in the context, although when divorced from context it seemed vulnerable. Similarly, I may develop what I think is a brilliant way of resolving a case. But I have learned through embarrassing experience to hold my fire and suspend judgment for a decent interval; the chances are that the idea occurred to the trial judge and was rejected for good and sufficient reason.

This conferring of the benefit of doubt on the trial judge or agency is only tentative. In three quarters or more of the appeals, the initial trust is confirmed. But in a significant minority of cases the appellate court will find a basis for disagreement, partial or total. I must admit also that this preliminary deference is considerably diluted if I know from other cases that the agency has been singularly stubborn in refusing to adhere to case law principles or that the trial judge is habitually captious to counsel, overly quick on the trigger, peremptory, or erratic. In like manner, preliminary deference is likely to be more durable if I know the agency has a reputation for competence and integrity or if the trial judge is known for her carefulness and deliberateness. Moreover, deference is inevitably enhanced if the trial judge has taken the trouble to explain the basis of rulings and final decision in some detail.

E. Abuse of Discretion

In Chapter 8, in discussing the judges' conference, I included in my spectrum of conferences that presenting an issue of abuse of discretion by the trial court. Here, I try to describe how I go about the task of decision in such cases—how I determine how bad must bad be before it is abuse.

First of all, I try to sop up the collective experience recorded in cases dealing with similar problems. This kind of research is frustrating, because the cases turn so on their facts. There is no such thing as a case on point. But as I read, I gradually develop a feel for what has been deemed within and beyond the pale of civil judging.

Then I try to read every scrap of the record. The briefs may overlook the hints of reality that can place even a cold record in a different light than first appeared. Immersing myself in the record helps me put myself in the position of the trial judge and see what has gone on before and after. Sometimes what appears as stupidity or insensitivity, or worse, taken out of context, will appear innocuous or only a minor slip once the tone of the trial is recreated.

My next step is to think of the future. This cuts both ways. I may think that what was done, if repeated or enlarged, would erode fairness so deeply that it must be nipped in the bud. Or I may conclude that a reversal in this case would so chill trial judges that they would shrink from exercising their own judgment in the future and mechanically bow to what the judge might feel was the appellate court's policy preference. Somehow I try to arrive at the point where I have full sympathy for the crisis-strewn path of the trial judge, while remaining attuned to the occasion when prejudice cannot be extenuated by the pressures of trial.

I know of no formula in this kind of case except to live with the record until one breathes it, to gain what one can from similar cases, to brood over the consequences, and, finally, if one's sense of rawness becomes blunted over time, affirm. But if the redness remains, after days and weeks, take a big breath and reverse.

F. Considering the Alternative

An oft-told tale tells of an ancient person who, on being asked what he thought of old age, replied that it was quite acceptable, "considering the alternative." I find the exercise helpful in testing decision. I have earlier written about my affinity for spelling out the policy implications of a decision, that is, showing that not only is the result in accord with governing law but it makes sense as well. I now stress the converse, the helpfulness of showing that a contrary result would not, in the generality of cases, make as much sense.

In criminal cases, a court may be reluctant to set a defendant free or, as more often is the case, to order a new trial. But when one contemplates the effect of a precedent allowing admission of the offending evidence, and foresees a chain of similar future rulings eroding long-settled standards, one is strengthened in one's court's decision to reverse a conviction. In civil cases, a court may not wish to deny a deserving

and sympathetic plaintiff coverage under a civil rights statute. But the prospect of opening up civil rights liability to a
broad group of putative plaintiffs never contemplated by the
legislature may prove the weightier factor in decision. And
I have already noted, in the immediately preceding section,
how useful it is in arriving at a decision on abuse of discretion to look down the road and consider the long-run implications.

G. Sensitivity to Parties, Counsel, and Judge

Sometimes an appellate judge, writing in the solitude of
chambers, may be under the illusion that he is writing for
the ages. This is seldom if ever true. Even if the importance
of the case and the decision augur for a life of some years, it is
nevertheless true that those most intimately involved have
been live human beings—the parties, the counsel, and the
trial judge. I think it important that an appellate judge, however lofty or abstract his analysis may be, not lose sight of
the realities enveloping the participants.

It is with this thought in mind that I seldom attempt
humor at the expense of the litigants. Certainly not in a
criminal case where liberty is at stake. And not in most civil
cases, where, whatever the stakes, individuals must feel very
deeply. Perhaps in a commercial case, where large corporations' battles with each other are a routine part of their life,
some witty observation may lighten the discourse with little
chance of offending sensibilities. But in general an appellate
decision spells significant loss to one of the parties and is
not an occasion for merriment.

Lawyers, too, have feelings. Just because their mission is
to exert all reasonable efforts on behalf of their clients, some
of their arguments may irritate or even infuriate appellate
judges. But responsibility lies with the process, not, generally, with the individual lawyer. While some lawyers' performances merit the most acid-tongued criticism, I think judges
are well advised to maintain a high irritation threshold.
There is some irony, for example, when, after an appellate
judge has labored for weeks in researching, analyzing, and

discussing a troublesome issue, she writes, "We find the argument entirely without merit." Sometimes a court will vent its irritation on a hapless prosecutor for some remarks made in closing argument. The reality may be, however, that defense counsel baited the prosecutor and in a sense invited the retort.

Not least deserving of the appellate court's sense of the realities is the trial judge. A new appellate judge may feel that the trial judge has nothing else to do but to keep in mind new rules and procedures as they may be discerned from appellate opinions. I recall that as a new judge, I thought I was being helpful to trial judges by suggesting how they might in the future handle situations similar to that in the instant case. The hard reality is that trial judges have to keep in mind hundreds of requirements imposed by statutes, procedural rules, rules of evidence, Supreme Court opinions, opinions of their own appellate courts, and local rules. I therefore hesitate long before suggesting new procedures.

Being sensitive to the perceptions and problems of the trial judge is not a challenge for new judges only. It demands eternal vigilance. After almost three decades of appellate judging, I was an uncomfortable member of an audience in one of our recent circuit judicial conferences, listening to a panel of trial judges hold forth on the subject "What's Wrong with the Court of Appeals?" One after another of the veteran judges, all good friends, ticked off the following list of complaints: the appellate court was misled by the parties, neither of whom presented the trial judge's reason for making a particular ruling; the appellate court, after writing a long opinion, should have provided the trial judge with a summary road map to indicate the actions desired, instead of a bland directive, "remanded for further action consistent with the foregoing"; the appellate opinion contained a statement unnecessary for the decision (an obiter dictum) which, however, caused considerable damage by inviting new litigation; the appellate court did not give needed support to the trial judge by backing up his imposition of sanctions on uncooperative counsel.

Not all such complaints are inevitably justified or curable, but the wise appellate judge, as she endeavors to craft workable advice and decision, will always try to imagine how the opinion would appear to the trial judge.

H. Concern for the Reader

Even though what I now have to say has nothing to do with either the result or the essential rationale of an appellate opinion, I think it important enough to have a place in my canon. For I view the appellate opinion as an instrument of communication that reaches beyond the legal profession. At its best it is a means of enhancing, through the media, citizen understanding of the way key issues are decided. I therefore have concerns about the way in which judges write their opinions.

My chief concern is over a tendency to refine the art of distinguishing one case from another to the point where the pyramiding of exception upon exception, or distinction upon distinction, creates an awesome structure of ratiocination that is medieval in its scholasticism. This is, I think, a contribution of the academy to judicial craftsmanship. Our law schools have devoted their very considerable talents to the most sophisticated analysis. Some of this is rigorous and helpful thinking; some is, in my opinion, overrefined hairsplitting.

The dangers are twofold. The first is that the true course of the law cannot be followed by ordinary people, or ordinary lawyers. One needs only to read Plato to realize the impossibility of pinning Socrates down to any final conclusion. The second is that academic brilliance can provide plausibility for almost any desired result. To the extent that this happens, basic trust in a rule of what can be considered "law" by ordinary people is diminished.

So my inner compass tells me to simplify when I can. This is not terribly difficult, since I do not see 20/20 when viewing overly nice distinctions, whether they are in a brief, an oral argument, a clerk's draft, or a colleague's circulated draft opinion.

Of lesser importance, I think sheer length and overpublication cheapen the currency of significant opinions. When I see opinions of over forty, fifty, and sixty typewritten pages, I shudder. Who, except for the lawyers in this case and a few other cases in the same area, will read it? And yet there may be wisdom hidden within it that has some lasting value. I venture to say that neither Justice Holmes nor Judge Learned Hand would today be revered for their opinions had they been of such length. Perhaps writing with pen in hand—and at a stand-up desk—was a guarantee of brevity. As to the quantity of appellate opinions that are published in permanent hardcover volumes, I can only quake. So many add not even a jot or tittle to law. Admittedly, the practicing bar feels that it gains something by psychoanalyzing even the most fact-bound and pedestrian opinion. But there is an end to available shelf space in law offices, and even computers reach a point of diminishing returns.

We have now traversed the domain of the not-too-difficult case. We have touched on the various forces that influence judges. Some, those which I call idiosyncratic, are likely to be suppressed by reflection and discussion, or in any event neutralized by the differing predispositions of other judges on the same court. Then there are the crafts skills, rules, conventions, and attitudes. While one can say that they constitute a professional stockpile held in common, their use varies from judge to judge. On the whole, they push toward consensus. Finally, each judge has his own canon—special approaches or points of emphasis. I have tried to identify mine. Judges necessarily differ as to these, just because they are separate human beings.

So, even in the bulk of ordinary cases, despite the centripetal forces, judges and courts will differ about such matters as whether counsel has done enough to preserve a point for appeal, whether there is sufficient evidence to support a verdict, whether an error in an evidentiary ruling was harmless, or which case law precedent should be followed. State supreme courts will differ among themselves, as will the federal circuits. Most of these differences are not in the constitutional realm and reflect very little about basic views about society and the individual. This large domain of difference is not what concerns the public, because the disagreement among judges is not on issues as to which citizens generally have an opinion, much less a conviction.

There should accordingly be no sense of surprise when we find courts and judges differing deeply in the smaller but highly significant area where a clear rule does not control and where deeply held value judgments are in contest. Perhaps the wonder is that there is as much consensus as does exist.

We now visit that area.

14

On Judging Appeals III: Uncharted Depths

I. Introduction

What we have been discussing in Chapter 13 and elsewhere are cases which end in consensus or, if not, a division of opinion based on different views of the facts or different weights given to the law. The dissents would be technically, not ideologically, driven. They constitute, quantitatively, by far the major part of the caseload of both federal and state appellate courts, perhaps 80 to 85 percent.

We address in this chapter a genre of cases much smaller in numbers but much more testing in their challenge to the sensitivity and wisdom of judges. They are "hard cases." These are cases whose outcomes, as agreed by most judges after careful analysis of the record facts and survey of the relevant statutory and case law, are not *clearly* determined by preexisting principles, rules, or precedents. The differences among judges are not merely technical but include differences in perception of the importance of the interests of the parties or in other values involved in the decision.

I do not attempt to discuss the universe of hard cases. Both common law and statutory law are rich in the lore of "hard cases make bad law." These are beyond our focus. So also are many constitutional cases, typically those relating to the great structural provisions of the original document, as distinguished from the Bill of Rights and later amendments. Such include cases presenting issues of separation of powers, federal-state relations, the powers of Congress under the Commerce Clause, and the powers of the President in foreign affairs.

The cases we deal with in this chapter are a significant part, though not all, of the hard cases confronting today's appellate courts. They are the cases presenting conflicts between the rights of individuals or groups of individuals and the interests of society or its surrogates, such as departments, units, or officials of the federal or state governments, or persons acting "under color of state law." They are found at the moving edge of constitutional analysis, wavelets on the beach evidencing (depending on the view of the beholder) either a rising or an ebbing tide.

It is, of course, a given that many cases of this genre are no longer "hard," because the United States Supreme Court has pronounced judgment, establishing the rule or principle to be applied. But there is little likelihood that constitutional analysis in this area will be frozen in crystalline form. Variations of the human predicament, as the individual and society interact, are infinite. New conditions, technology, and laws never cease to make their appearance. State courts are free to probe the meaning and reach of state constitutions. And the Supreme Court itself is subject to change over time.

In attempting to say something fresh and sensible about dealing with constitutional cases arising from confrontations between individuals and the state, I first aim a wide-angle lens at the dominant focus of constitutional analysis in the closing third of this century. I then sketch the relevant and foreseeable conditions of societal and individual life in the opening years of the new millennium. These reveal, as a situational imperative, the likely nature and intensity of the conflicting interests of individual and state in the years ahead. My search for an effective approach in dealing with this kind of hard case begins with identifying the values I see likely to be the most relevant. But values alone do not decide cases. So I continue my quest by outlining a more meticulous and sensitive balancing process than has generally characterized appellate courts. And I close by casting a long glance forward at what might be the next development in law affecting relations between the individual and society.

II. Changes in Constitutional Focus

With the benefit of hindsight, one can see the evidence of imperceptible change over great spans of time. Like the coming and going of glaciers or the grinding together of tectonic plates, the focus of constitutional analysis in various eras becomes discernible. During much of the nineteenth century, constitutional litigation centered on the structure of government, the distribution of power between state and nation and among the branches of the federal sovereign. Then came the conflict between the Constitution as interpreted by the Supreme Court and the Constitution as seen by the President and the people, the ensuing Civil War, and the final resolution of the Thirteenth, Fourteenth, and Fifteenth Amendments.

In the late nineteenth century and the early decades of the twentieth century, the emergence of great industries led to deepening debate over the power of government to regulate them. This led to a running battle over welfare legislation and the Supreme Court's view of the Contract Clause of the Constitution. With the Contract Clause finally tamed, the New Deal ushered in years of heady federal governmental activism and experimentation, when the Commerce Clause provided the basis for the most significant constitutional jurisprudence. I remember that when I was a law student in the 1940s, my course in constitutional law was almost wholly confined to this clause.

Now, after nearly three decades on the federal appellate bench, I can look back and see that they are almost exactly coterminous with an increasing concentration on questions of individual rights versus societal interests. Although great issues of school desegregation were being litigated in the 1950s, culminating in *Brown* v. *Board of Education of Topeka, Shawnee County, Kansas*, 349 U.S. 294 (1954), the caseloads of most state and federal appellate courts were not significantly changed until the 1960s. By the end of this decade, most of the rights guaranteed by the first eight amendments of the Bill of Rights (against encroachment by the federal government) had been selectively incorporated into the Fourteenth Amendment, and thus applied to state governments.[1] Also, resurrected from almost a century of desuetude, the Civil Rights Act of 1866 (42 U.S.C. §1983) became, within a very short time, the major vehicle for an individual wishing to vindicate his or her civil rights against a governmental agency.

During the 1970s and 1980s, civil rights actions, often brought on behalf of large classes of plaintiffs, sought injunctive relief, or damages, or both, from police, municipalities, prison officials, hospitals and mental institutions, social service departments, welfare agencies, subsidized housing developments, school boards, and universities. The bases for the suits included alleged deprivation of procedural due process in both civil and criminal cases, discrimination directed at gender or sexual preference, infringement on privacy or personal autonomy, and encroachment on freedom of religion, association, and speech.

The extent to which these cases have come to front and center in the nation's courts is evidenced by the fact that some seventeen hundred pages of tightly packed case annotations in two columns of small print per page in the United States Code Annotated are devoted to the jurisprudence of 42 U.S.C. §1983. Virtually all of these cases date from the late 1960s. A rough computer check of state and federal cases indicated that before 1950 there was no such case, before 1955, twenty, and before 1960, only 159. A check of all §1983 cases, state and federal, revealed that as of the end of 1991, there had been 44,148 such cases. Even though this figure is but a small fraction of the universe of reported cases, it

represents a novel, complex, and profoundly important segment of current constitutional adjudication. We may justi-
fiably say that the characteristic feature of constitutional
jurisprudence in the late twentieth century is its focus on
the tension between individual rights and societal interests.

III. Rising Societal Pressures

As we approach the new millennium, some facets of life are
reasonably predictable. Population, for instance. When
I entered the legal profession, we were a nation of
130,000,000; we are now double that figure. The increase
continues, and with the increase (not to mention the fright-
eningly larger increases in much of the rest of the world),
there are remorseless pressures on material resources—
energy, land, forest, air, and water. With correspondingly
greater interdependence and international competition,
there will be compelling demands to restructure our educational system to make access more real and results more
effective, to rebuild inner cities to upgrade the environment,
to develop a more comprehensive and adequate health care
system, to reverse the trends in crime and prison populations
. . . all of this while somehow managing to achieve budgetary
balance and bring the deficit under control.

It does not require much foresight to sense a future in
which social control devices, ranging from taxes, to ra-
tioning, to elaborate measures regulating the provision of
essential goods and services as well as amenities, will play
a much more prominent role than at present. In the mid-
1970s, Robert Heilbroner issued his pessimistic prophecy of
"a future in which the exercise of power must inevitably
increase and many areas of freedom, especially in economic
life, be curtailed."[2] While Cold War pressures have merci-
fully withered since his prophecy, environmental, resource,
and energy problems have become more apparent. We cannot
adjudge it unrealistic.

Against this backdrop of contracting horizons and ex-
panding social and economic constraints, we face the para-

dox of a stubborn insistence on individual liberty. At its most superficial level, it takes the form of unashamed consumerism, guided or misguided by the mass visual media. Even at this level we can say with assurance that people will increasingly aspire to "justice-determined" distribution of goods and services in short supply. This ever more acute justice nerve will lead them to expect access to the forums of decision, to demand fairness in decision-making, and to insist on equality of treatment.

Underneath consumerism, there is a deeper value assigned to personal liberty in the senses of privacy, autonomy, and life-style. With the end—for at least a time—of the Augustan Age of plenty, we can predict that access to government, including the courts, fairness in institutional proceedings, equality of consideration and treatment, and residual privacy in a crowded world will be increasingly cherished individual objectives. Their recognition will not be without institutional inconvenience, expense, and frustration, but protection of the smaller liberties in a shrinking world, and perhaps even some "safety net" guarantee of a realistic opportunity to participate in mainstream societal life, may be the prerequisites of a stable and cohesive national community.

In sum, the new conditions of human existence promise to be such as to elevate in new kinds of ways, with greater intensity and higher degrees of refinement, the age-old issue of the proper balance between the rights of the individual and the interests of the state. This state of affairs I call the situational imperative which, apart from any special theory of jurisprudence, should move us to examine and reaffirm our constitutional heritage, to consider institutional limits with a more realistic eye, to sensitize our process of balancing individual rights and society's interests, and to examine ways of preserving our essential social fabric from disintegration by the alienation of large sectors of society.

IV. My Cardinal Beacons

In this section my mission is to isolate and identify the cardinal beacons or values that I look to for direction in deciding constitutional cases posing a conflict between individual rights and state or societal interests, if and when I am not tightly confined by precedent. I try to take direction from my reading of the Constitution—the original document, the Bill of Rights, the Civil War and other amendments—as a profoundly rights-oriented charter. My first beacon, the oldest, has been prominent since its eighteenth-century beginning—liberty. The second, made explicit only in the nineteenth century, is equality. A third, resisting and checking the first two, is, in my lexicon, "workability," the capacity of reasonably well managed institutions of government to fulfill their missions while respecting individual rights. The fourth, discussed at the end of this chapter, signals a direction that, so far, only a handful of cases have taken. But the conditions of the times suggest increasing resort to it. I call the value "community."

A. Liberty

In choosing liberty as my first value, I recognize not only that I am not saying anything new or original but that I risk being enveloped in rhetoric. But I am also acutely aware that any fear of sounding trite must, pride notwithstanding, be put aside. For my deeper fear is that the centrality of liberty in our constitutional arrangements is today too often subordinated to administrative fiat and convenience. So my purpose here is simply to document, however briefly, that keystone value.

In the first place, our English forebears gave us, by both their action and their inaction, a rich libertarian heritage. Magna Carta's positive influence reached far beyond the original limited contract between a king and a few favored barons. And the negative experiences involving the Star

Chamber, the Court of High Commission, the rack, the gib-bet, and the Tower in the realms of Tudors and Stuarts were duly recorded in the ten-volume set of Emlyn's *State Trials*, well thumbed by our Founding Fathers at Philadelphia.

The result, as Irving Brant tells us, is that there are "twen-ty-four elements of a Bill of Rights in a Constitution that is said to contain none" and thirty additional rights in the first ten amendments. When we add the nine rights vouchsafed in the post–Civil War amendments, we reach a total of sixty-three specific freedom-protective provisions—to which we must add a sixty-fourth, the Twenty-sixth Amendment pro-tecting the right to vote of all citizens over age eighteen. As Brant summarizes the Constitution, with its amendments, "Seen as a connected whole, the spirit is the same through-out. It is a spirit of unqualified devotion to human rights, human dignity, the liberty and equality of free men."[3]

To this enumeration we must add those rights in the Bill of Rights which have now been selectively applied to the states through incorporation into the Fourteenth Amend-ment. And, finally, there are new rights or protections which time, society, and technology have identified as being within the essential spirit and intendment of the Constitution. Thus the old word "search" is applied to electronic surveil-lance. Freedom of association is recognized although "associ-ation" is not to be found in the First Amendment. Similarly, unreasonable burdens on one's right to travel are struck down, although "travel" is not mentioned in the Constitu-tion. And, most prominently, there has emerged a right of privacy or personal autonomy which now includes the right of a woman to have an abortion in early pregnancy.

B. Equality

In contrast to liberty, which so saturated both the Consti-tution and the Bill of Rights, equality, although given top billing in the Declaration of Independence, was not men-tioned. It was not mentioned because it was as circumambi-ent and pervasive—and thus seldom separately perceived or thought worth talking about—as the air . . . although we must add that some people were more equal than others. We can understand how James Madison could say both that equality was "the leading feature of the United States"[4] and initially resist suggestions for a Bill of Rights, saying that they would "do no more than state the perfect equality of mankind . . . an absolute truth, yet . . . not absolutely necessary to be inserted at the head of a Constitution."[5]

The Civil War and the abolition of slavery led to explicit recognition of the primacy of equality in the Thirteenth, Fourteenth, and Fifteenth Amendments. Equality, at first taken for granted, now took its place in the American pantheon of values. As Professor Samuel P. Huntington put it, "The eighteenth-century value of liberty was quickly joined by the nineteenth-century value of equality."[6]

It remained for the principle of equal protection (specifically mentioned in the Fourteenth Amendment) to be applied to the federal government through the Fifth Amendment (which contained no reference to equal protection). This step was taken in 1954 in *Bolling* v. *Sharpe*, in which the Supreme Court said, "[T]he concepts of equal protection and due process, both stemming from our American ideal of fairness are not mutually exclusive. . . . [D]iscrimination may be so unjustifiable as to be violative of due process."[7]

Today, as one approaches the marble-columned facade of the Supreme Court and looks up, the words one sees are "Equal Justice Under Law." And, for the memorable linkage of liberty and equality, we look not to a scholar or a judge but to a President, who began his remarks at Gettysburg by recalling "a new nation, conceived in liberty, and dedicated to the proposition that all men are created equal."

C. Workability

So far we have been discussing the attitudes toward individual rights which I believe inhere in the Constitution and its amendments. Complementing such attitudes is a judge's view of the institutions of government, for his assessment of institutional obligation and capacity to respect individual rights is always part of the balancing process.

In an early essay, in reflecting on the four forces influencing judicial decision that Justice Cardozo identified in *The Nature of the Judicial Process*[8]—logic, history, custom, and social justice—I felt impelled to add a fifth, the factor of workability. This I described as "the extent to which a rule protecting a right, enforcing a duty, or setting a standard of conduct—which is consistent with and in the interests of social justice—can be pronounced with reasonable expectation of effective observance without impairing the essential functioning of those to whom the rule applies."[9] I thought this factor was least confining on appellate courts when they were attempting to govern conduct within the immediate judicial family—the trial court, prosecutors, and, to a more limited extent, private counsel.[10] Having served in both the Congress and the executive branch of the national government, I had a healthy respect for the difficulties departments and agencies faced in carrying out official missions. I was concerned that courts might overstress institutional capacity, although equally concerned that deference to administrators and officials might be "a shield for solipsism, for unrestrained personal predilection."[11]

I now see the need for a more rigorous approach to workability. In the first place, it applies not merely to rules governing institutions, but also to any action taken or contemplated by a governmental unit or official impacting individual rights. In the second place, I have come to feel that courts cannot be faithful to the constitutional primacy of individual rights if they embrace a policy of blanket deference to officialdom.

The *American Heritage Dictionary* speaks of "workability" as being "used of proposed ideas or plans, the success of which is likely if properly managed."[12] This introduces the notion of something doable *if* approached with reasonable ability and commitment. It suggests to me that there should be some judicial monitoring of the adequacy of justification of governmental action adversely affecting an individual. Just as there are gradations in valuing individual rights, so must there be some gradation in deference accorded to governmental institutions and their representatives. In situations of emergency and crisis, near-absolute deference would be expectable. But in routine operations, it would not seem to be asking too much to require some showing of justification for governmental action that significantly and adversely affects individuals. That is, after over two centuries of national independence, "the people" are entitled to reasonably properly run institutions which ought to be able to justify their actions. Moreover, technological advances, particularly in the area of retrieving and using information, have significantly increased the potential for more efficient and sensitive operations.

In any event, whether the institution is a prison, a law enforcement agency, or a social welfare program, "workability" couples a sensitivity to individual rights with an equal sensitivity to administrative capability to carry out institutional missions while affording optimum respect for those rights. The latter sensitivity contains a modicum of healthy skepticism of undocumented administrative justification. Over time it may be expected that more, rather than less, may be expected from government officials and institutions in their actions burdening individual rights.

All that I have said in this section has related to cases arising under the rubric of due process, where the questions were whether an asserted individual right was deserving of any due process and, if so, what kind and how much. But the same concept of workability, it seems to me, applies to equal protection analysis. It is hornbook law that in dealing with state economic regulation, courts will uphold any state classification of its residents if they can conjure up any rational basis for the classification. But if an individual is adversely affected by legislation, more so than others, is it really faithful to our basic charter of rights to uphold the legislation if a court can hypothesize a possible rational basis or purpose of the legislation, even if such reasoning had played no part in its enactment? As Professor Tribe has demonstrated, courts, taking a dim view of some state classifications among residents, have covertly engaged in heightened scrutiny, resulting in "the manipulable discretion of judges operating with multiple standards of review all masquerading as 'minimum rationality.' "[13] Perhaps the time will soon arrive when our higher expectations of the capacity of government to respect individual rights will declare the concept of minimum rationality obsolete.

V. A Rights-Sensitive Balancing Process

Merely identifying one's basic values does not go very far in illuminating how one would deal with hard cases of the type we are considering. My responsibility, therefore, is to try to bring some concreteness out of abstraction. To fulfill this responsibility, I invite the reader to accompany me through the steps of the balancing process, pausing at some critical points to consider relevant cases. I shall draw upon my James Madison Lecture, given at New York University School of Law in 1987.[14] I shall discuss some of my own opinions. They have the merit of exemplifying my own approach to assessing and balancing interests in rights-sensitive cases. They have the disadvantage of not being law, each having been reversed by the Supreme Court. But one who writes for the future can always hope for deferred vindication.

To begin, I do not present the kind of balancing I advocate as a mechanistic marvel, eliminating subjectivity. Nor is it a jurisprudential theory or an all-purpose approach suitable for all kinds of cases. But if it is conscientiously done, I believe it not only will result in better decisions, more faithful to our constitutional mandates, but will elevate the dialogue among judges and increase the chances of understanding and consensus on the part of people generally.

Two prerequisite qualities are openness and carefulness. By openness I mean laying on the table the opinion writer's real reasons and thought processes, for without this there is little chance of meaningful dialogue or consensus. I realize that the ultimate work product of a court may, in order to gain a majority, be more opaque, but in the beginning there should be candor. By carefulness, I mean a self-conscious craftsmanship at every stage of the decision process, rejecting unspoken or facile assumptions and generalizations, and a fairness in stating issues, facts, and arguments.

A. Stating the Issue

Often an advocate is advised to frame an issue in a brief so that it becomes an argument in one's favor. Such an attitude augurs ill for a judicial opinion. If the court is unanimous, the words used may conceal the real issue decided. If the court is divided, the reader ends by feeling she has read two entirely different cases. The Supreme Court opinions in *Bowers* v. *Hardwick* are an example. In that case, a homosexual plaintiff challenged the constitutionality of the Georgia sodomy statute. The majority saw the issue as "whether the Federal Constitution confers a fundamental right upon homosexuals to engage in sodomy and hence invalidates the laws of the many states that still make such conduct illegal and have done so for a very long time."[15] The dissent took sharp issue with this statement of the issue and countered: "[T]his case is about 'the most comprehensive of rights and the right most valued by civilized men,' namely, 'the right to be let alone.' "[16] Such a divergence of views over the nature of the issue cannot fail to lessen the likelihood of persuasive balancing.

A generic issue-framing difficulty in rights-sensitive balancing cases is posed by an all too common failure to give society credit for having any interest in preserving individual rights. Hence the frequent reference (which I have consistently made so far in this chapter) to cases pitting the right of an individual against the interest of society. To put the question this way is to invite a court to engage in a merely utilitarian calculus, where the interest of the many is sure to outweigh that of the one. If a protectible individual right is at stake, society has a genuine interest in that right, as well as the individual; both interests must then be weighed against the countervailing institutional interest of society.

B. Level of Generality

Often, because of or in spite of arguments of counsel, an appellate court will not consciously decide the proper level of generality for decision of a case. Sometimes the initial decision as to scale will be so limited and fact-bound that it will have lost all utility as a precedent for other cases. But any harm done is equally limited. The greater danger lies in deciding a case at a very high level of generality, equating an individual plaintiff and his controversy with a much larger universe of people and problems. The dangers are that the factual basis for a broad decision may be lacking and that the decision may paint with far too broad a brush, with far-reaching damage.

In my James Madison lecture, I gave three examples, which fairly present the "level of generality" problem. In *Griffin* v. *Wisconsin*,[17] the Supreme Court had to decide the constitutionality of a Wisconsin regulation which permitted a probation officer to search a probationer's home without a warrant so long as there were reasonable grounds to believe contraband was on the premises. Although dealing with only one regulation, the decision has implications for over 3,300 federal probation officers serving some 86,000 federal probationers or parolees and over 12,000 local, county, and state officers having responsibility for some 2,000,000 probationers and parolees.[18] The decision recognized a "special need" for increased supervision based on one recent research paper, and concluded that a warrant requirement would reduce deterrence because of the delay and intervention of a magistrate. All assumptions may have been sound, but there were no factual data bearing on the variety and frequency of need-to-search occasions or the extent of frustration caused by use of warrants.

In *Turner* v. *Safley*,[19] the Court upheld Missouri prison regulations relating to inmate marriages and correspondence, announcing the broad rule: "[W]hen a prison regulation impinges on inmates' constitutional rights, the regulation is valid if it is reasonably related to legitimate penological interests."[20] This ruling affected something over 500,000 federal and state prisoners, and was based on the reasoning that a stricter scrutiny of prison officials' decisions would "seriously hamper their ability to anticipate security problems and adopt innovative solutions. . . ."[21] Again, this is decision on a very large scale, without any factual land-scape showing the variety of problems posed by prisoners in all kinds of correctional institutions, from county jail to maximum-security prison.

Finally, in *O'Connor* v. *Ortega*,[22] the Court reviewed the warrantless search of a doctor's desk by his state hospital superiors and upheld warrantless work-related searches, based on reasonable suspicion, of employees' offices, desks, and files. I estimate, on the basis of census figures, that this ruling applied to some 14,000,000 state and local employees and 3,000,000 federal employees. The basis for the ruling was that even though the doctor had a reasonable expectation of privacy, "the realities of the workplace . . . strongly suggest that a warrant requirement would be unworkable."[23] And "[i]t is simply unrealistic to expect supervisors in most government agencies to learn the subtleties of the probable cause standard."[24]

When one reflects upon the infinite variations in work environments, in the frequency, nature, and importance of work-related searches, and in the level of sophistication of superiors, one cannot help feeling that the Court took a considerable leap of faith in removing, in one sweeping opinion, the warrant requirement for the nation's public employees.

C. Interest Analysis

The heart of rights-conscious balancing is interest analysis. In weighing the interest of the individual, a court should not only identify the individual right at stake, but evaluate its centrality and importance, the extent to which it is likely to be infringed, and the frequency of infringement. In assessing governmental institutional considerations, a court should identify one or more interests at stake, define the nature of the problem posed by the individual's conduct or complaint, and attempt to isolate the immediate and remote effects on government employees' morale and efficiency and on the physical and financial resources of the institution.

1. Nontenured Teacher and School Authority. My first exhibit is a 1970 case, *Drown* v. *Portsmouth School District*,[25] in which a school district refused, without giving reasons, to renew a contract for a nontenured public-school teacher. She claimed that the district's failure to give reasons was a denial of due process. Our court's opinion first addressed the teacher's interest in a statement of reasons. We recognized that an unexplained refusal to rehire forecloses any effort at self-improvement, any correction of false rumors or impressions, any ability to expose an improper motive, or any possibility to minimize or even exploit the reason for the district's action.[26] Addressing the interest of the school board, we found that no significant administrative burden would be imposed by a requirement that it state its reasons for not rehiring; that this would not inhibit the board from rejecting incompetent teachers; and that several states had adopted a statutory requirement to the same effect.[27] We therefore held that the benefits to the teacher of a statement of reasons for nonretention were so substantial and the inconvenience to the school board so slight that due process required it.

The issue reached the Supreme Court in another case, *Board of Regents of State Colleges* v. *Roth*,[28] which involved a nontenured assistant professor of political science whose one-year contract was not renewed. Again, no reasons were given. The Court first looked to see if the interest was a protectible liberty interest. It noted that the state had made no criminal or moral charge against the professor and imposed no stigma.[29] It found no record support for an assumption that nonretention creates practical difficulties later in the professor's career; even were there such evidence, it "would hardly establish the kind of foreclosure of opportunities amounting to a deprivation of 'liberty.' "[30] The Court went on to hold that the terms of the professor's appointment created no "property" interest in reemployment. Finding no protectible "liberty" or "property" interest, the Court had no occasion to assess the interests of the Board of Regents.

2. Prisoner and Prison. Five years later, in 1975, our court decided *Fano* v. *Meachum*.[31] Several inmates of the medium-security Massachusetts Correctional Institution at Norfolk were suspected, because of confidential informants' evidence given officials in a closed session, of involvement in setting fires, possessing contraband, and trafficking in drugs. They were ordered to be transferred to the maximum-security prison at Walpole, but a district judge had enjoined the transfer, having found that the proposed transfers violated due process because of the absence of hearings.

We first addressed the question whether the detriment caused by a transfer, within a state, from a medium-security prison to a maximum-security prison was serious enough to trigger due process protections. The evidence indicated stricter security, fewer rehabilitative programs, more difficulty in obtaining furloughs, more adverse confinement conditions, disadvantages in breaking off educational and rehabilitative programs and in adjusting to a new setting and its regimen, and the characterization on one's institutional records as a troublemaker, a source of difficulty in future efforts to obtain parole, furlough, and work-release privileges.

In assessing the burden that the corrections officials would face in revealing the substance of the informants' statements, we, like the district court, relied on the fact that in Walpole, where security was more strict than in Norfolk, a regulation forbade taking testimony in the absence of an accused, unless there was a substantial risk to security. This fact seemed to us to establish that the prison system itself had decided that it could live with the requirement without difficulty. We affirmed the trial court's decision.

The Supreme Court first recalled its teaching in *Roth*, rejecting the notion that *"any* grievous loss" triggered due process. What mattered was "the nature of the interest involved rather than its weight."[32] It then observed that once a person is validly convicted, he or she is properly subject to a prison system's rules and may be confined in any prison, though "much more disagreeable." The possibility that a transfer might be based on erroneous allegations of misconduct is "too ephemeral and insubstantial to trigger due process protections."[33] To hold that any substantial deprivation would invoke them "would subject to judicial review a wide spectrum of discretionary actions that traditionally have been the business of prison administrators. . . ."[34] The Court then reversed our decision.

3. Suspect and Police. Ten years later, in 1985, our court decided *Burbine* v. *Moran*,[35] which was briefly described in Chapter 3 in connection with a discussion of state court initiatives in constitutional law. The police, after fully giving *Miranda* warnings to a criminal suspect, falsely told the suspect's attorney, who had offered in a telephone call to be available if any questioning was to take place, that they were "through with him for the night," did not tell the suspect of the call, and then proceeded to take three inculpatory statements. In determining whether the suspect had knowingly waived his right to have counsel present, we first noted that the call from the attorney was not a routine offer to be of service, but a mid-evening call offering to come to the station, and that the suspect's state of mind might well be affected by knowledge not only that the attorney had been willing to come, but also that the police were making an eleventh-hour change in the ground rules they had given the attorney. We then canvassed all possible scenarios that could explain the police misrepresentation and found no other explanation than "deliberate or reckless irresponsibility."[36] We then granted a writ of habeas corpus, conditioned on the failure of the state court to grant an early retrial.

The Supreme Court reversed in *Moran* v. *Burbine*.[37] In addressing whether the suspect had waived his right to have counsel present, the Court acknowledged that knowledge of the attorney's telephone call might have been useful and even "might have affected his decision to confess" but that the Constitution does not require "that the police supply a suspect with a flow of information to help him calibrate his self-interest in deciding whether to speak or stand by his rights."[38] As for police culpability, though "objectionable as a matter of ethics," it is irrelevant because "even deliberate deception of an attorney could not possibly affect a suspect's decision to waive his *Miranda* rights unless he were at least aware of the incident."[39] And to extend the reach of *Miranda* to require police to inform a suspect of an attorney's efforts to reach him or her would spawn questions about police knowledge, "muddying *Miranda*'s otherwise relatively clear waters" and upset "the subtle balance struck in that decision," for the "minimal benefit [in protecting the Fifth Amendment privilege] . . . would come at a substantial cost to society's legitimate and substantial interest in securing admissions of guilt."[40]

My purpose in setting forth these case histories is not to seek among readers the affirmance I was denied by the appellate process. The law today is what the Supreme Court held. But if my view of the future has merit, a more finely tuned and factually supported balancing of individual rights and institutional interests may yet come into its own. It may come to be seen that the Constitution requires more of a court than to pronounce that even grievous harm triggers no due process protections unless it is of a certain "nature." And more than a brief reference to the traditional prerogatives of administrators. And more than the assumption that preventing police from lying to attorneys and concealing their lies from suspects will seriously frustrate law enforcement.

VI. The Looming Importance of Community

In introducing my cardinal beacons, I alluded to a value that looms on the horizon. It is not yet a factor in federal or most state court adjudication. It is what I call a community interest. By that I mean the self-interest a society has in preserving itself against the instability, insecurity, and disintegration threatened by the emergence, enlargement, and perpetuation of a very substantial underclass of uneducated, job-unqualified, welfare-dependent, unhealthy, despairing people living in dysfunctional families, all too susceptible to drugs and crime, with no sense of participation in, access to, or fealty toward that society.

There are two ways to deal with these divisive and destructive forces in the interest of preserving community. One is a "circle the wagons" approach, based on the fear and the need for security on the part of the stable and integrated members of society. I use the words "community interest" in a second way to connote a sense of community aspiration, a felt mission to have society so act as to induce rather than coerce allegiance. Such an interest suggests not only "safety net" programs to stave off catastrophe for the most unfortunate, but ways and means to enable the grievously displaced and disadvantaged to make reentry into the mainstream of society. Reintegration, participation, mobility, and access are the ultimate goals if we are not to surrender to the prospect of a class-crystallized, elitist, antidemocratic, and dangerously divided society. Of course, to the extent that such goals are advanced and individuals in desperate need are helped, the values of liberty and equality are also served. But far more than fundamental fairness and fraternity are at stake.

A. The Legislatures

The primary engines in a democracy to achieve these goals are the state and national legislatures. Courts by their nature are not well equipped to determine flash points of need or amounts and kinds of goods and services to enable people to rejoin society, or the preconditions which should accompany such assistance. We are dangerously myopic if we look only to courts to give life to constitutional values. Congressional Research Service scholar Louis Fisher describes the only appropriate focus:

> Judges share with the Legislature and the Executive the duty of defining political values, resolving political conflict, and pro-

tecting the integrity and effectiveness of the political process. Constitutional law is a process that operates both inside and outside the judicial arena, challenging the judgment and conscience of all three political branches at the national level, the state governments, and the public at large.[41]

He cites the famous desegregation case *Brown* v. *Board of Education*[42] and subsequent history as a working of the process.

> In issuing the desegregation decision in 1954, the Court pushed the nation a giant step toward the establishment of civil rights
> . . . .
>   Although the Court insisted on judicial supremacy in 1958, there was little progress toward the integration of public schools. . . . What finally turned the tide were a series of legislative enactments: the Civil Rights Act of 1964; the Voting Rights Act of 1965; and the Fair Housing Act of 1968. The struggle against racial discrimination required the conscientious effort of all three branches.[43]

We can hope that the Congress and state legislatures sense the hazard of shutting off a large and growing underclass from any fealty to or sharing in community, and that they legislate accordingly. Even if they do not seize the initiative, there exists the possibility of constructive dialogue or interaction between court and legislature. To probe where such possibility might lie, we look at both federal and state courts, at both constitutional and common law.

B. The Supreme Court

The recent forays of the Supreme Court into the question of providing community access and opportunity to the neediest have been in the field of education. In 1973 in *San Antonio Independent School District* v. *Rodriguez*,[44] plaintiffs in a property-poor school district, unable to supplement a state grant substantially, contrasted their plight with a property-rich district which was able to provide a much higher standard of education for its children. They claimed a violation of equal protection. The Court refused to acknowledge education as a fundamental interest warranting strict scrutiny of the Texas school financing system. But it did hold open the possibilities that "absolute denial of educational opportunities" might violate equal protection,[45] and that "some identifiable quantum of education" might be a constitutionally required minimum."[46]

The first possibility came to pass in 1982 in *Plyler* v. *Doe*[47] when the Court invalidated a Texas statute denying admittance to public schools of undocumented (or illegally admitted) school-age children. While the decision rests on the combined effect of (1) an absolute denial of educational opportunity, which is (2) imposed on a suspect class, and thus has not signaled any major doctrinal change in the Court's hesitancy to enter the school financing field, the opinion does sound the note of community survival. After noting prior cases recognizing the role played by public schools in preserving democratic government and the primary vehicle for transmitting our society's values, the Court stated, "In sum, education has a fundamental role in maintaining the fabric of our society."[48]

The second possibility left open in *Rodriguez*, the idea of a constitutionally supported minimum quantum of education, was again broached in 1986 in *Papasan* v. *Allain*,[49] where the Court indicated that an unsettled question was whether "a minimally adequate education is a fundamental right" such that its discriminatory infringement by a state would trigger "heightened equal protection review."

At the most, therefore, we can characterize Supreme Court (and therefore all federal court) posture on societal access/ community fabric values as dominated by hesitancy and reservation, but possessing some intimations of possibility.

C. State Courts

1. Constitutional Law. As we have seen in Chapter 3, the fifty state supreme courts are increasingly widening their perspectives and drawing upon their own state constitutional heritages. In what I have termed the community value field, the New Jersey Supreme Court, in a groundbreaking opinion, has held that a community's failure to provide a fair share of a region's low-income-housing needs abuses the state's police power and violates its due process and equal protection clauses.[50]

Other states have extended the principle of providing minimal opportunity to the field of education, accomplishing what the Supreme Court resisted in *Rodriguez*. Indeed, Professor James S. Liebman sees a much greater possibility, in the foreseeable future, for eliminating egregious disparity among school districts in the state courts.[51] He observes that although there is very little assurance, even though indirect, in state constitutions of minimum levels of nutrition, shelter, or subsistence, all but three expressly require the state to provide free education and make the duty enforceable in some degree.[52] Moreover, nearly all have recently legislated minimum educational performance standards imposed on all students.[53] He concludes that enactment of such mandatory standards is "a basis for inferring and enforcing a democratically legitimated obligation" to furnish the education needed to meet the standards.[54]

Several possible courses thus can be taken by state courts. They could grant equal protection relief in educational financing under their own equal protection clause, finding that the state's minimum standards legislation had created a "fundamental" right. They could elect not to be bound by the stricture of *Rodriguez* in interpreting their equal protection clause. They could also rest decision on their own constitution's provisions requiring "free public schools" or a "thorough and efficient" educational system.[55]

Such state court constitutional initiatives have the twofold advantage of encouraging diverse experiments in the "laboratories" of the several states as well as avoiding premature constitutional fixity. Not only would state constitutional decisions stay within state boundaries but they are subject to a much less traumatic constitutional amendment process than is the federal government.

2. State Common Law. Scholars are now probing the possibilities of common law as a source of help for the most disadvantaged. Professors Charles M. Haar and Daniel Wm. Fessler, in their book *The Wrong Side of the Tracks*,[56] draw on a seven-century-old common law "duty to serve, as an avenue of appeal that predates the federal Constitution."[57] They concern themselves with the supply of municipal services such as water supply, sewer connections, and street lighting. Over the centuries, they conclude, four motifs have appeared in judicial opinions:

1. The imposition of a common right to access drawn from the doctrine of services as *a public calling*, essential to individual survival within the community;
2. The duty to serve all equally, inferred from and recognized as an essential part of *natural monopoly power*;
3. The duty to serve all parties alike, as a consequence of the *grant of the privileged power of eminent domain*; and, finally,
4. The duty to serve all equally, *flowing from consent*, expressed or (more frequently) implied.[58]

All of these have contributed to "the judicial aspiration that all persons in similar circumstances be accorded similar treatment at the hands of entities that render a public service."[59]

To the extent that remedies for those seeking access and minimum opportunity to participate rest on common law grounds, as the authors point out, the rigidity of constitutional decisions is avoided. The decisions can be modified or reversed by a state legislature. A less intense dialogue among the branches will have taken place.

Notwithstanding all these preferred vehicles for reflecting an adequate response to the core value of community, should there be prolonged failure to act in the face of disintegration of critical proportions, or should the Supreme Court and the inferior federal courts grasp the nettle? Professor Tribe has reflected on this ultimate question:

> The effort to identify the "indispensable conditions of an open society" . . . proves inseparable from the much larger enterprise of identifying the elements of being human—and deciding which of those elements are left entirely to politics to protect, and which are entrusted to protection by judicial decrees. . . . The day may indeed come when a general doctrine under the fifth and fourteenth amendments recognizes for each individual a constitutional right to a decent level of affirmative governmental protection in meeting the basic human needs of physical survival and security, health and housing, work and schooling. . . . But despite straws in the wind and strands of doctrine pointing in this general direction, that time has not yet come, and constitutional lawyers must continue to struggle with less sweeping solutions and more tentative doctrinal tools.[60]

And here is where we must leave the hard case of the future. But we leave it knowing that some of the depths are being explored.

15

On the Future

I. Introduction

What I attempt in this closing chapter is not so much a forecast of what will happen to our state-federal appellate tradition as a prophecy in the Old Testament sense, that is, an open declaration of values to be preserved and striven for and what must be done if they are to be preserved. What I say has equal applicability to both state and federal appellate courts, which, as I stress in Chapter 3, I consider "ONE WHOLE."

We shall first identify the essence of the appellate process that merits preservation. We then shall address goals as yet unachieved (a positive agenda) and threats to judicial independence meriting eternal vigilance (a defensive agenda). Finally, for assistance in accomplishing both sets of objectives, we head in an unfamiliar direction: we look outside the judiciary to what I call an external agenda.

II. Preserving the Essence

At this point the reader will have come to appreciate the unique core values of appellate judging that give it a special position among all forms of group decision-making, just as the values of proportion, size, texture, and color give the Taj Mahal and the Parthenon a special position among all forms of architecture.

These values include the integrity of individual, intellectually demanding work, shared with a very small staff, and pride in that work; the support and enrichment of a small number of peers; the ability, subject to a sense of priorities in the management of one's time, to invest as much time as necessary in novel, complex, or "hard" cases; the inducement to develop and nourish a broad range of interests; the quintessential internal climate of serenity and independence; and the concomitant external indicia of respect and prestige.

In commenting upon the dismal apprehension of the Federal Courts Study Committee's 1990 report that numbers of judgeships would inexorably increase, because of mounting caseloads, and that the quality of work would diminish, I pondered on the predicament of "the efficient judge":

> First, there are the pressures to which he or she seeks to respond: an inexorably rising caseload; the demand for expedition in disposing of appeals; the demand to publish all opinions; the demand for oral argument in a greater number of cases; the rising involvement in administration and committee work; the accelerating popularity of continuing education; the proliferation of congressional oversight inquiries and hearings often resulting in new obligations and reporting requirements; the impact of government-wide ethical restraints, limiting judges' recompense from teaching and barring any compensation for delivering a scholarly address or writing a solidly researched article for a periodical.[1]

Were such a judge, who has already multiplied her productivity six times since 1945, to attempt yet another quantum leap in output, I asked myself,

[w]ho would want to dedicate the rest of one's working life to such an occupation? With judicial salaries not only set at levels below those of most successful lawyers but also chronically prevented from keeping pace with increases in the cost of living, and with both working conditions and job satisfaction on a downward slope, it seems clear that many of the most competent, reflective, creative, and public spirited potential judicial candidates will never surface. Over time, the quality of the federal judiciary faces subtle but certain erosion.[2]

This conclusion applies even more forcefully to the state judiciaries. I accordingly urged the initiation of a program of research which would be aimed, not at increasing output, but at determining what mix, pace, and measure of a judge's activities would yield a "reliable profile of the reflective, creative, serene appellate judge of tomorrow, able and eager to do sustained work of high quality."[3] Just as the goal of such quality-oriented research would be "to preserve the core values of the judiciary that have always been cherished,"[4] so should any forward-looking agenda for appellate judging accord top position to preserving its essence.

III. Perfecting Appellate Justice: A Positive Agenda

In this section my effort is not to construct a lengthy "shopping list" of useful steps that should be taken to improve the processes of appellate adjudication. It is rather directed to thinking in broad categories, trying to identify goals in each category, and making some illustrative suggestions of ways to advance those goals.

A. Role Rationalization

After over two centuries of partly deliberate, partly fortuitous development, both state and federal court systems could profit from a knowledgeable look at what they should be doing, vis-à-vis each other and also as compared with other forms of dispute resolution.

It seems to me that three goals fit both state and federal court systems: (1) the system should not be forced to entertain inappropriate cases; (2) it should not be required to conduct unnecessary trials; and (3) it should not have to deal with unnecessary appeals.

The first goal would be most dramatically advanced, as I have argued in Chapter 3, by transferring, with transitional funding, state law diversity cases to state courts, thus freeing up a fourth or more of all federal trial judges to attend to federal matters.[5] Other steps would include greater congressional restraint in federalizing crimes which have traditionally been the major concern of state law enforcement authorities and more deliberate consideration of the likely impact on trial and appellate courts of proposed legislation. The intense preoccupation of the federal judiciary with the hair-splitting distinctions imposed by the sentencing guidelines is an example of a disproportionate use of judicial resources stemming from a detailed code pursuit of a laudable goal.

The goal of avoiding unnecessary trials would be served by devising other forms of dispute resolution and by leaving decision in some matters to deciders outside of the formal judiciary, such as truly independent administrative law judges and administrative agencies with well-developed and respected procedures. As this book was written, all federal administrative law judges—some eleven hundred—were assigned to and dependent upon thirty-one federal agencies and executive departments whose cases they were charged with deciding. Legislation was being considered which would make such judges truly independent in their judicial function.[6] Were this goal to be achieved, some kinds of litigation could be completely handled at the agency level. Other types of cases might receive Article III judicial review at only one level rather than two. In either event, appellate court review could be reserved, on a discretionary basis, for the exceptional case.

In the past, proposals to restrict access to courts at both trial and appellate levels have been directed to specific candidates for exclusion, such as social security cases in the federal system, without any systematic effort to determine what standards of judicial process should be met as a prerequisite for diminishing or eliminating full judicial review. The pressures on both state and federal court systems have reached the point where the most sensitive, balanced, and searching review for alternative procedures is called for. But any action toward this end is primarily the responsibility of the legislative branch. The judiciary could contribute its expertise and experience, but it is clearly in a junior position.

B. Procedural Improvements

A second group of objectives aims at improving the performance of appellate courts. Even though prodigious productivity has characterized appellate courts over the last two or more decades, improvements are still achievable.

Here, too, the goals are equally applicable to state and federal appellate systems. They are: (1) improved methods for processing appeals; (2) improved use of personnel; and (3) the optimum use of technology.

As Chapter 3 indicates, state intermediate courts of appeal are a fertile source of experiment in developing different tracks and procedures to deal with appeals. Federal courts have also adopted new techniques to screen appeals for oral argument or for summary disposition. A number have inaugurated pre-argument conference procedures to simplify issues or explore settlement. The most effective use of law clerks remains a goal, as do the conduct of top-quality research and the construction of the most appropriate opinions.

An objective long talked about but never thoroughly explored is distinguishing between appealed cases which involve only questions of commission of error by the trial court and those which involve decisions which will change, make, or enlarge the law. If ways could be found to make a fairly reliable determination in advance as to which category, error-correcting or lawmaking, fits a given case, those cases which solely involved findings of fact or pedestrian errors of law could be put on a fast track of abbreviated, unpublished opinions. Such a result would very significantly increase the productivity of state courts of last resort and the federal courts of appeal. State intermediate courts of appeal already are reaping the benefit of essentially this approach. But work must be done and experience gathered to see how the two types of cases may be identified, how reliable advance identifications are, how any misjudgments can be rectified, and whether results justify the effort.

In any effort to improve procedures and use of personnel, the judiciary itself is the prime mover. And judicial self-help, the willingness and ability of judges and courts possessing a special experience and capability to help others, is a prime resource.[7] When we come to the third type of improvement, the optimum use of technology, the need for sufficient legislative appropriation becomes obvious.

Perhaps in no other area of court organization and operation is there such movement as in the development of technology. As of 1991, state courts were apparently leading in innovative efforts, because they could experiment on a smaller scale.[8] But the federal court system has been far from idle, now boasting a Judicial Conference Committee on Automation and Technology, with increased staff resources. Although describing the uses of technology in the appellate courts is like aiming at a moving target, the lineaments of appeals of the future are already emerging from various experiments and pilot projects: increasing reliance on video records of depositions, testimony, or even a complete trial; access by attorneys to court opinions, argument calendars, rules, and notices through electronic bulletin boards; the holding of some arguments through closed-circuit television; the conferring of judges through telephone conference calls or closed-circuit television; the conduct of computer-assisted legal research; the composition of opinions on personal computers; the immediate circulation of drafts via electronic mail; and the prompt printing of approved drafts from the writer's floppy disks.

In stating the objective of utilizing technology, I have used the word "optimum." I do not mean "maximum." It seems to me that we face the subtle danger of being engulfed and trapped by technology. A judge may spend too much time replaying the videotape of a trial or may be tempted to second-guess the trial judge's credibility judgments. A televised argument or court conference may carry with it some chilling effect on questions or comments. Lexis or Westlaw may spew out far more precedent than needed to decide a case. The beguiling ease of composing on a computer may spell the demise of brevity. And instant circulation of drafts may subliminally stimulate hasty response at the expense of deliberateness. So, wholly apart from the legislature's role in equipping the courts, the judiciary has the inescapable responsibility of avoiding the fate of Dukas's Sorcerer's Apprentice, who commanded a broom to fetch water, but knew not how to stop the flood, lamenting

> *Would thou wert a broom once more!*
> *Streams renewed forever*
> *Quickly bringeth he;*
> *River after river*
> *Rusheth on poor me!*

C. Structural Manageability

Only after a serious effort has been made to rationalize the roles of federal and state courts and after sustained efforts to attain optimum effectiveness in techniques and procedures have been attempted should the formidable issue of adding to court structure be contemplated. This is probably less of a possibility for state court systems, which, so many having established intermediate appellate courts, seem structurally stable for the foreseeable future. In the federal court system, there has for at least two decades been recurring interest in establishing a national court of appeals just below the Supreme Court to resolve conflicts among the federal circuits. There is also spasmodic interest in creating specialized courts and in adding circuits to the existing thirteen.

My own prescription of goals for the federal system is: (1) no unnecessary layering of tiers; (2) no unnecessary proliferation of either circuits or specialized courts; and (3) no

unnecessary expansion of judicial personnel. The extent and
seriousness of conflicts among the circuits are once again
under study. Depending upon the results, I would counsel
recourse in the following sequence: first, encourage circuits
to follow guidelines for attempting to avoid significant kinds
of conflict; second, if these efforts are unavailing, convene an
ad hoc tribunal composed of circuit judges from the various
circuits to clean up the accumulated backlog; third, should
a sizable annual increment of significant conflicts still be
foreseen, call upon the Supreme Court itself to explore
whether it can improve its selection of cases to be heard and
do an even better job of winnowing nationally important
wheat from parochial or particularistic chaff; and finally, all
else failing, then and only then contemplate creating a new
national appellate court to deal with nonconstitutional conflicts.

Finally, we must recognize that structural change, although informed by judicial opinion and expertise, will inevitably and properly be the concern of Congress.

D. Quality of Judicial Life

In accordance with my emphasis on preserving the essence
of the appellate tradition as it has developed, I include the
quality of life of an appellate judge as a key objective on the
positive agenda.

In my view, again, with equal reference to state and federal
systems, there are three targets: (1) adequate space, equipment, and personnel support; (2) compensation and benefits sufficient to attract and retain top-quality judges; and
(3) a combined workload of cases, administrative duties, and
continuing education consistent with the possibility of a
sustained output of high quality. As younger men and
women are being appointed to the state and federal benches,
the provision for some sort of periodic refreshment-education
respite, akin to academia's sabbatical leave, will become a
vital ingredient.

In all of these matters, the legislature will have the final
word. In summary, of the four broad areas of aspiration and

positive effort we have identified, either Congress or a state legislature will be the critically important factor in three. The only exception is the initiation of procedural improvements; even here, improvements involving the use of new technology will require the legislative blessing in the form of funding.

IV. Threats to Judicial Independence: A Defensive Agenda

We come now to an agenda that is set not by positive ideas of what we want our courts and judges to do but by forces and attitudes that together constitute a threat to the continued independence of both state and federal judiciaries, a threat that is both many-faceted and subtle. It is not that a power such as George III has decided to reduce judges to impotence. Our federal and state constitutions all proclaim the independence of their judges. It is at the core of our governmental credo.

The threat, rather, springs from a variety of well-intentioned programs, policies, and laws. Each of the components of the aggregate threat has a justification, a reason for being. The hostile influences are not all outside the judiciary; we sometimes have a human proclivity to inflict injuries on ourselves. Together they bid fair to accomplish over time an eroding of satisfaction in work, an accumulation of burdens quite separate from judicial work, and, indeed, barriers to the ability to do good work that can sap the excellence that our centuries of colonial and independent existence have built into our tradition. And in referring to our tradition, I refer to our total court system, state and federal, trial and appellate.

A. Administrative Overburden

The first extrajudicial pressure is that from within the system, the claim made on a judge's time by his service on a committee or subcommittee of his court, judicial council, judicial conference, or group planning a workshop, retreat, or seminar. As of March 1992, 229 federal district and circuit judges served on some twenty-seven committees of the United States Judicial Conference. I think it is conservative to say that judges now spend from one fourth to one third of their time preparing for meetings, conducting studies, attending meetings, and reporting on them to their own courts.

As a system matures and grows larger, it develops a built-in engine to increase administrative overburden. An idea is suggested at the level of court, council, or conference. A committee is asked or created to look into it. Predictably, the problem proves to be more serious and widespread than originally thought. Alternative approaches must be studied. Contracts are made with consultants or academic experts; questionnaires are circulated; reports are submitted and, finally, approved. And another set of procedures, criteria, standards, guidelines, and reporting requirements has come into being.

My point is not to protest the professionalism of such approaches to real problems, but rather to caution against the impulse to fix things that still work, because every new administrative or non-case-related chore or function carries with it a cost, measured by judges' diminished availability to reflect on cases. Eternal busyness is a virus, draining serenity.

B. Legislative Excess

Occasionally both Congress and state legislatures veer away from their normal legislative approach of setting policy objectives and standards serving those objectives and, instead, attempt to anticipate every contingency by legislating minute provisions. Or they may, with every good intention, enact legislation the unforeseen effect of which is to impose an unplanned and substantial additional burden on the court system. I would call the former aberration micromanagement and the latter myopia, or, simply, shortsightedness. In either event, the effect on the judiciary is lamentable.

1. Micromanagement. When legislatures attempt to micromanage, the results often are the opposite of the laudable legislative aims. When Congress, for example, enacted the Speedy Trial Act, setting precise time limits within which criminal defendants must be brought to trial, the effect was not only to create an abundance of litigation concerning what periods of time should be counted and what should not, but, in many districts, to delay civil trials to an extent tantamount to denial of any trial. I have referred to the 1984 Sentencing Reform Act resulting in the issuance of extraordinarily minute sentencing guidelines, which have led to an enormous increase in litigation at both the trial and appellate levels. Other results brought about by the act's requirement of mandatory minimum sentences have been the virtual disappearance of guilty pleas and the trial of the most frivolous cases.

Another piece of legislation, drafted without any judicial participation, threatened to strip trial judges of much of their discretion at every critical stage in managing cases; only extensive negotiation with committee staff prior to enactment of the Civil Justice Reform Act of 1990 staved off what could have been a classic case of micromanagement. State legislatures have acted similarly in not merely reducing state court budgets but specifying just where the budget cuts should be applied, depriving state courts of all discretion in setting their own priorities.

2. Myopia. The second brand of legislative excess, what I have unkindly called myopia, occurs when lawmakers seek to advance a worthy goal which necessarily will involve litigation and courts. In connection with most such legislation, court activity is both appropriate and expected—without undue strain. Examples are acts protecting consumers, occupational safety, the environment, and freedom of information. Still other enactments threaten to involve federal courts disproportionately, as when lawmakers propose to curb hate crimes, failure to pay child support, the spousal abuse of women, or crimes of violence by making every such event that involves a firearm and/or interstate commerce a federal crime.

One narrow escape occurred when, in the waning days of a legislative session, Congress tacked onto a childhood vaccine protection law a provision that charged judges to decide whether claimants for compensation were eligible because their illness or death resulted from vaccination. Not only would this have required some three hundred or four hundred special masters at the trial level but it would have created a flood of appeals. The judiciary was never consulted about this legislation. Finally, after a year's desperate negotiations, the danger was averted.[9]

I do not mean to say that either micromanagement or myopia is as yet customary. But the prospect of more of the same is a source of increasing concern as we reflect on the pressures and the erosion of institutional memory in both state legislatures and the national Congress. In the former, not only is permanent staff often thin but turnover of staff and members is substantial. Moreover, the number of lawyer members of state legislatures is at an exceedingly low point, so low that there are often not enough lawyers to fill leadership positions in the committees dealing with courts.[10] In the Congress, staff turnover is high, retirements of members have sharply increased, and committee responsibilities are spread thin. A consequence is that many details in compendious reports and bills are settled through negotiation among staffs.[11]

The danger inherent in the erosion of institutional memory is a kind of institutional insensitivity that results in violating the spirit, if not the letter, of separation of powers.

C. Monitoring of Judicial Conduct: Overkill?

Another threat to judicial independence lies in the prospect of a surfeit of surveillance of judges' conduct. Of course, conduct involved in managing and deciding cases is necessarily subject to judicial review. And extrajudicial conduct is properly subject to governance under rigorous codes of conduct. But, in view of the scope and intensity of restraints imposed on the state and federal judiciaries since the early 1970s, one views with some alarm proposals to establish additional disciplinary mechanisms.

1. State Systems. First addressing the state systems, we note that some forty-seven states and the District of Columbia have adopted, in substance, the Model Code of Judicial Conduct, while the remaining three states have enacted their own rules.[12] This set of standards, governing judges' conduct during judicial proceedings as well as relating to speech, business activities, civic and charitable involvement, and political and other associations, came into being shortly after 1972. In 1990 the American Bar Association adopted a new Model Code. This code is now in the process of consideration and adoption by the states, but, because of two decades of substantial case law on judicial conduct, the process is expected to take considerable time.[13]

Enforcement machinery exists in all states and the District of Columbia. Beginning with California in 1960, states have created judicial conduct agencies, all of them having a substantial, if not majority, membership of lawyers and lay citizens. In Hawaii, there are no judge members. During this two-decade period of growth of judicial conduct codes, policing instrumentalities, and case law, the National Judicial College has brought out four editions of a textbook on ethics for judges—in 1973, 1975, 1982, and 1992. And the American Judicature Society has published the *Judicial Conduct Reporter*, containing articles, case notes, and reviews of publications, since 1978.

While there is unease in some quarters about the threat to judicial independence posed by the state commissions, I sense a generally stable situation, with little widespread demand for additional machinery. The real threat to independence of state judiciaries, dwarfing any judicial disciplinary mechanisms, remains their compelled involvement in funding and mounting initial or retention election campaigns, particularly partisan ones.

2. The Federal System. In the federal system there is a similar chronology, with perhaps an even more extensive resort to legislation:

—In 1970 the United States Judicial Conference created an Advisory Committee on Judicial Activities, to give advice to judges concerning the ethical nuances of any conduct. Initially chaired by Elbert Parr Tuttle, the revered former chief judge of the Fifth Circuit, it was dubbed the "Dear Abby" committee. I had the honor of serving on that committee. It and its successor, the Committee on the Codes of Conduct, have rendered nearly ninety published opinions and hundreds of unpublished memoranda of advice.

—In 1973 the long-standing federal code of judicial conduct was updated, drawing upon the then new American Bar Association Model Code.

—In 1978 the Ethics in Government Act was passed, requiring judges, along with top officials in the other two branches, to submit annual reports of their financial status and transactions. A Committee on Judicial Ethics was established to review reports from judges and other personnel within the judicial branch, now numbering well over two thousand. The instructions for filling out the report occupy some forty-eight pages.

—In 1980 Congress passed the Judicial Councils Reform and Judicial Conduct and Disability Act, setting up procedures for processing complaints against judges. Some complaints, if frivolous—as most of them have proved to be—can be disposed of by the chief judge of the circuit; others must be examined by a special investigating committee and reviewed by the judicial council of a circuit. Further appeals may be taken to the Judicial Conference Committee to Review Circuit Council Conduct and Disability Orders. And, in cases where impeachment would be warranted, the matter is referred by the Judicial Conference to the United States

House of Representatives. All circuits have adopted rules to carry out the statutory mandate, all but one having adopted a uniform set of rules. In 1990 Congress reviewed the operation of this system, noted findings of a task force of the Twentieth Century Fund that the Act was working well but that there was room for improvement, and made several curative amendments. A major finding was that there was a need for public awareness of this system.[14]

—The Ethics Reform Act of 1989 set ceilings on outside income that could be earned by judges and forbade the receipt of remuneration for speeches and articles. Extensive regulations have been issued to implement this statute.

—In 1990 the Judicial Conference Committee on the Codes of Conduct reviewed the Code of Conduct for United States Judges, in light of the new 1990 Model Code of the ABA, and has submitted proposed changes for formal enactment by the Judicial Conference. At present, the corpus of judicial conduct restraints consists of not only the Judges' Code, revised, but separate codes for clerks of court and deputy clerks, probation and pretrial services officers, circuit executives and other administrative officials, staff attorneys, federal public defenders, and law clerks; 231 pages of published advisory opinions; ten separate statutes relating to judicial conduct; eleven separate resolutions of the Judicial Conference of the United States; and numerous regulations.

It is against this background of continuing accretion of laws, regulations, reports, and enforcement mechanisms that judges view the 1990 legislation establishing the National Commission on Judicial Discipline and Removal. After half a century (1936–86) in which there had been no impeachment of a federal judge, three such removals occurred within three years, and two other judges have been convicted of criminal charges. The three impeachment proceedings had imposed heavily on the time and energies of both House and Senate. Accordingly, the late 1980s saw a number of legislative proposals calling for constitutional amendments to create a fast track for impeachment, to make removal automatic on conviction for a felony, to substitute term appointments for life tenure, and even to make judges subject to recall and to provide for removal by either a body within the judiciary or an independent commission.

In lieu of proceeding along any of these lines, the Congress opted for a thirteen-member commission, with members appointed by the President, the Speaker of the House, the President of the Senate, the Chief Justice, and the Conference of Chief Justices of the States. After a year and a half of accumulating data, commissioning studies, conducting hearings, and deliberating, the Commission issued its report on August 2, 1993.

It first concluded that any alternative to impeachment resulting in the removal of judges or suspension of their compensation would require a constitutional amendment.[15] It also found that existing complaint and discipline arrangements under the 1980 Act, including its "most important benefit . . . the impetus it has given to informal resolutions of problems of judicial misconduct and disability," were "working reasonably well" and that "[n]o alternative system of discipline of which the Commission is aware has similar potential for effective informal resolutions." It felt that the basic objective, well served by existing procedures, was to "walk the tightrope between judicial independence and accountability." It therefore concluded that proposals "which would replace not only the current impeachment process but the 1980 Act, were unnecessary and unwise."[16]

Although the Commission rejected radical actions, it did proffer recommendations for improved procedures on the part of the House, the Senate, and the Department of Justice to facilitate their labors, increase their efficiency, and provide periodic legislative oversight of the judiciary. For the judiciary, it recommended more disclosure of complaint proceedings and dispositions, more sharing of information within the judiciary, with state and federal prosecutors, and with appropriate congressional committees, more public education about complaint procedures, and more statistical reporting.

So the federal judiciary has apparently emerged from

this latest probing without suffering any serious threat to its independence. But the level of administrative burden and congressional governance has once again been ratcheted up.

D. Chronic Underfunding of State Courts

We have seen, in Chapter 3, the deep and wide effect on state court systems of years of traumatic deficits and the resulting spending cuts calculated and imposed on the judicial branch of state government as if that independent branch were simply another dependent department or agency of the executive branch. The effect has been a threat to an independent judiciary not as yet shared by the federal system.

What does all this signify? In my view, we have entered an era of changing relations among the branches of government, compelling us to seek new ways of coping with change while preserving the independence and integrity of each branch. It is an era of institutional vulnerability. State legislatures bear increased responsibilities and constituent demands in the face of inadequate staff support, escalating campaign costs, remorseless single-issue and special-interest lobbying, and the distorting effects of media coverage. State executives have the awesome initial burden of dealing with a universal budget crunch, heightened by the withdrawal of federal funding across a wide spectrum of social services.

But state judiciaries are uniquely vulnerable. They face, in addition to the strains of the electoral process, ever-increasing caseloads with accompanying stress, a frequently stark disparity between judicial compensation and that of lawyers generally, and inadequate support staff, equipment, and space. State court systems generate in fees, fines, and penalties a lion's share of their total costs. Their impact on state budgets is minimal. They have responded to repeated across-the-board cuts in the manner of an agency of the executive branch. They have now reached the point where their very independence and the quality of justice are at stake.

Malcolm M. Lucas, California's chief justice, describes the threat in these words:

We cannot wait for news from the governor or the legislature that we must cut back "just like every other state agency." If we do so, we not only risk losing the money we need, but we also risk undermining the stature of the courts as an independent branch of government and our basic ability to perform the very functions for which we are designed.[17]

The American Bar Association's Special Committee on Funding the Justice System concluded from its recent national survey of state courts that "the American justice system is under siege and its very existence is threatened as never before."[18] Its report features "A Call to Action" in the form of a bar-initiated, broad-based citizen "Coalition for Justice." Such a recommendation from such a body leads us into our final topic.

V. New Directions: An External Agenda

Traditionally, state and federal judiciaries have looked inward for ways to improve their operations. Of course, they had their own ways of dealing with legislative appropriations and judiciary committees, and judges have frequently participated in bar association activities. But basically their agenda was an internal one. What we have seen in this chapter, however, are problems largely beyond the control of the judiciaries. Virtually every item on both the "positive" and the "defensive" agendas—with the major exception of procedural improvements—calls for favorable action by the other two branches. And such action is not likely to occur without effective and focused support from the citizenry, which in turn presupposes a deeper understanding by people of the needs and problems of their court systems. Hence the need to look in new directions, all of them being beyond the judiciary itself.

A. State-Federal Amity

Much of this book has stressed the need for all concerned with the administration of justice to be inclusive in their concern, to be just as interested in improving and strengthening state court systems as they are in protecting and improving the federal court system. The external agenda begins with a sharing of concerns, aspirations, and strategy between the two sets of systems.

A beginning has been made with the creation of the National Judicial Council of State and Federal Courts, which serves as a national coordinator to encourage and strengthen local state-federal judicial councils and engages in educational projects of common interest to state and federal courts. On the state side there are the State Justice Institute, the National Center for State Courts, and the Conference of Chief Justices. On the federal side the Administrative Office of United States Courts has established a Coordinating Council of Federal-State Judicial Relations, staffed by a Federal-State Judicial Relations Office; the Federal Judicial Center has created an Office of Interjudicial Affairs; and the Judicial Conference of the United States has a standing Federal-State Jurisdiction Committee.

But beyond organizational bridges, there must be a change in the mind-set of judges, lawyers, law schools, colleges and universities, public interest groups, civic associations, the media, Congress, governors, and state legislators. The concept that we have a two-tier court system consisting of a first and second class must be eradicated. We must get back to Hamilton's concept of ONE WHOLE.

B. Judicial-Legislative Communication

As this chapter has demonstrated, most of the positive things that can be done for court systems and most of the threats to independence that should be eliminated depend upon Congress and the state legislatures. The problems and pressures facing both the judicial and the legislative branches call for fresh thinking and the willingness to try new approaches in dealing with each other.

In 1986 I tried to put myself in the position of the distinguished authors of the eighty-five essays constituting *The Federalist*, Messrs. Madison, Jay, and Hamilton. I imagined what they might say if they tried their hands at an eighty-sixth essay on the relations between the judiciary and the Congress. This is how they began:

> The Judiciary and Congress not only do not communicate with each other on their most basic concerns; they do not know how they may properly do so. Legislators enact laws without considering either their burden on the courts or how they might be interpreted. The paradox is that when the Judiciary exercises the powers Congress has thrust upon it, it is reviled as power hungry. Legislators, required to stand periodically for reelection, are suspicious of, antagonistic to, and ever ready to restrain and humble their secure, life-tenured colleagues.
>
> The judges, for their part, facing increasing responsibilities along with criticism for exercising them, and sensitive to ever accreting restrictions and diminishing standards affecting their life and work, are in danger of losing the respect, serenity, and independence that the Constitution sought to vouchsafe. The condition we describe, if not an acute crisis, is that of a chronic, debilitating fever.[19]

Hans A. Linde, former justice of the Oregon Supreme Court, has pointed out that "active participation of state judges in the policy process is much more taken for granted and much less controversial" than that of federal judges.[20] Nevertheless, proper communication remains a problem. The National Center for State Courts and the National Conference of State Legislators have collaborated in holding a 1989 conference and follow-up workshops on legislative-judicial relationships, underscoring the need for a "New Partnership." In 1991 the American Judicature Society devoted part of its annual meeting to a panel discussion on the subject among federal and state judges and federal and state legislative leaders.[21] And the Governance Institute, of which I am a director, is deeply involved in working with state bar associations on building bridges between courts and legislatures and with congressional leaders and federal courts in conducting pilot projects toward the same end.[22]

The range of subjects where joint exploration is likely to be useful includes proper and improper methods of communication, how to have timely communication to forestall problems, how to determine what impact legislation is likely to have upon a court system, how to bring to the attention of committee staffs statutory problems revealed in reported court opinions, how to signal a clearer legislative history, how to improve the "advise and consent" process in judicial nominations, and how to develop the most useful relations with legislative leaders, members, and staffs. This very range, though only a partial list of topics, indicates the vast potential for improving the functioning of both the legislative and the judicial branches without compromising the integrity of either.

C. Judicial-Executive Relationships

Relations between the judicial and the executive branches have received much less attention than those between the judicial and the legislative branches. This may reflect a sense that the fate of the judiciary depends much more heavily on the source of appropriations, laws, and court-oriented legislation. But it would be a mistake to ignore the necessity for establishing better channels of communication with the executive.

On the federal level, the Department of Justice can be an important source of information about the foreseeable impact of proposed legislation and a spokesman for the needs of the courts as a whole. The federal government and its agencies account for at least a third of the business of the federal courts in volume and even more in importance. Referring to the extent of this involvement, Professor Maurice Rosenberg has pointed out, "[It makes] a lot of sense for the U.S. government executive branch, Department of Justice, to take an interest in how the courts . . . [are] working."[23]

While the Department of Justice may, in its prosecutorial role, be suspected of giving partial advice, the creation of an office concerned with the overall functioning of the administration of justice, such as the Office for Improvements and the Administration of Justice that existed in the Carter administration, under the leadership of Professor Daniel Meador, might be free of any such taint. Such a vehicle currently exists—the Office for Policy Development—in the Clinton administration.

On the state side of the ledger, it is transparently clear that executive-judicial relations are extremely important. What we have noted about the impact of governors' responses to the budgetary crisis proves the point. The devising of channels of timely communication with the governor's office and, with key budgetary, justice, and corrections officials is likely to prove far more effective than cries of pain and the initiation of lawsuits.

D. Citizen Surrogates

Even though state and federal judiciaries pursue common goals and do their best to improve communication and relations with their legislative and executive branches, they will ultimately, on some issues, meet with intransigence, hostility, prejudiced attitudes, or overwhelming competition from some powerful interest group. When this occurs, the judiciary will find itself powerless. And even if it could find a way of wielding power, it would be inappropriate for it to do so.

It seems to me that the time has come when the pressures on Congress, on legislatures, and on governors are so great and the threats to the preservation of an independent judiciary of high quality are so real that the federal and state judiciaries need citizen surrogates. By this I mean a nonpartisan watchdog citizen group, respected by the media and the citizenry generally, which would therefore be able to have its voice heard on the most vital issues affecting the courts.

In a May 1991 address to a New Hampshire Bar–sponsored

conference on relations among the three branches, reported in *Judicature*,[24] I suggested that the organized bar adopt the role of "catalyst, stimulator, coordinator, and leader" rather than the exclusive intermediary between the courts and the legislative and executive branches. It would help create and work with a much broader group representing education, chambers of commerce and industry, organized labor and farm groups, the media, the clergy, public interest groups, ethnic and other minorities, and even the poor, the homeless, and those otherwise disadvantaged. Perhaps not all would lend their voice on a given issue, but they would be a resource to be drawn on, appropriate to the issue.

Now the prestigious American Bar Association Special Committee on Funding the Justice System has endorsed this concept, calling on state and local bar associations to form "action committees" to "serve as catalysts to lead" a broad-based "Coalition for Justice" to secure "adequate and balanced funding for the entire justice system."[25] If such a movement should materialize, I suspect that its concerns would encompass court problems beyond adequate funding.

On the federal scene, it seems to me that the best hope for an effective surrogate lies with organizations such as the American Bar Association, the American College of Trial Lawyers, the Association of American Law Schools, the Federal Judges Association, the Business Roundtable, the AFL-CIO and other unions, and Common Cause forming a network which, on occasion, could be mobilized on critical issues.

E. Educational Outreach

The final link in the external agenda chain has the longest-range goal with the broadest reach—the need to educate the citizenry in general about the value, the needs, and the problems of courts. We are already a justice-sensitized society in the sense that citizens are aware that the courts are open to them for enforcement of a large catalogue of rights. But we are not justice-system-sensitized in the sense that citizens can appreciate the dangers of case or administrative overload, excessive monitoring, micromanagement, partisan elections, or sustained underfunding.

In this area judges can make their own vital contribution. Granted, judges must always act consistently with the dignity and independence of their office. But they know best the values they serve and the threats to those values. They also know best what are problems and what are not. A concrete example of the need for educational outreach activity by the judiciary was cited by the Committee on the Judiciary of the U.S. House of Representatives in its report reviewing performance under the 1980 Judicial Councils Reform and Judicial Conduct and Disability Act. The committee was concerned about lack of public awareness, but recognized that "[a]s a legislative proposition, it would be difficult to require the judiciary to engage in outreach efforts." It did the next-best thing: the subcommittee chair and ranking minority member wrote the circuit chief judges, suggesting they address the problem through "a public and bar awareness program."[26]

If every judge in the country could spend part of his or her time each year speaking to schools, colleges, organizations of workers and of employers, and service clubs and on television and radio, a reservoir of understanding and respect would be built up over the years. Others are part of the educational mission. Secondary schools, colleges, and law schools can all contribute. Reporters for newspapers, magazines, radio, and television can themselves be educated and sensitized, for there is all too little really knowledgeable reporting of court system issues or even of cases.

The important point is that state and federal courts must make room in their own crowded agenda for educational outreach, must obtain expert advice, and must devise a program for carrying their cause to the people, because, in the last analysis, it is the people's cause also.

As we stare into our crystal ball and try to discern the contours of the future of not only the appellate tradition but the entire state-federal court system as it has developed over more than two centuries, we see several areas of change. First, as we look at other systems of law, we realize that we live in a shrinking and interdependent world and that developments in other systems, and particularly in the newly emerging regional international tribunals, will have some impact on us. Second, we can predict increasing interaction between state and federal systems, as each reaps the benefit of successful innovation. Third, we know that the accelerating efforts within the state and federal judiciaries and their support institutions to improve the process of adjudication will yield a substantial harvest. The potential of judicial self-help is immense.

Finally, however, we have seen the dependence of both state and federal courts on the legislative and executive branches of government and the looming need to assume a more activist role in preserving and improving the conditions which allow an independent judiciary to survive and flourish. In carrying out this mission the assistance of wider and deeper understanding by the citizenry in general and the more focused efforts of citizens' groups acting as concerned surrogates for the third branch are of vital importance. As we approach the millennium, perhaps the crucial question for us is whether the citizen majority and its least representative institution can work together to safeguard our unique and time-tested tradition.

The Appellate Idea in History

My personal view is that our own appellate system in its involvement of both lawyers and judges provides the most comprehensive and deliberate "second chance" of any in the world. But we stood on the shoulders of our ancestors.

We learn several lessons from a look at the ancestry of appeals. We learn, first, appellate justice is not only an ancient but a fragile institution. There is no guarantee of permanency. It is not to be taken for granted. Highly developed systems with easy access to professional judges and recorded proceedings have developed only to disappear. Ages pass in which appeal is almost unknown or is at most a plea for mercy from the sovereign. Yet, slowly the idea regerminates in several forms and over another millennium leads to the systems we have today. We realize that what we have has been dearly bought.

Second, we learn that seldom is there anything really new under the sun. The current interest in alternative dispute resolution, for example, revives an idea which first surfaced some three and a half millennia ago. Knowledge of the past may help us not only to avoid the errors but also to repeat the successes of the past.

And finally, the slow movement of the institutions and processes of justice over time prepares us for the fact of movement in our time, for the development of new institutions and processes in Europe and elsewhere—all with portentous implications for our own citizens and corporations. Communication among countries and increasing interdependence have visibly eroded old boundaries. Ancient traditions are softening, crisp distinctions are blurring, and radically new traditions and institutions are emerging.

I. Ancient Civilizations

The appellate tradition dates back some four thousand to six thousand years to several highly developed civilizations in that fecund area of the world we call the Near East.[1] The earliest concept of a judge is perhaps that of a tribal leader, such as the feisty characters depicted in the Book of Judges in the Old Testament. They could and did make war, love, and laws as the need arose. That judging was not a male monopoly is revealed in the story of Deborah, the prophetess and judge, whose custom was to sit under her palm tree and dispense justice[2] and whose song of victory over the Canaanites has been called "the oldest piece of literature in the Old Testament."[3] More typically, the judge was not the supreme ruler but a key minister of state, in whom were combined both judicial and high-level administrative duties. The course of appeal was to the monarch in the most rudimentary appellate systems.

Egypt

By the Fourth Dynasty in Egypt (2900–2750 B.C.), the chief judge was also the chief minister of the pharaoh, from whose divine authority all law and justice came. He wore the image of Maat, the goddess of justice, on a gold collar. We know that there was a structured appellate system, because administrative officials acted as local judges and the chief judge presided over a group of top officials who served as a supreme central court, the pharaoh himself being the final recourse on appeal. Further, there is a record of an appeal in a land title case dating from the reign of Ramses II, around 1300 B.C. One Mes sued Khay for wrongfully obtaining a title through fraudulent documents. Papyrus records preserve the written arguments, or briefs, of the parties and a summary of the testimony—an uncannily close approximation to the record on appeal of a contemporary land title case.

Mesopotamia

Meanwhile, in this ancient land between the Tigris and Euphrates rivers lived Sumerians, Babylonians, and Persians. Sumeria was living out its long span, enjoying the first extensive code of laws in history, that of Ur-Engur (ca. 2450 B.C.), precursor of Hammurabi. In that society priests sat as judges in the temples, but professional judges presided over a superior appellate court.[4] One feature foreshadowed the current interest in "alternative dispute resolution": every case was first submitted to a public arbitrator, who tried to bring about an amicable settlement. This very idea—requiring the parties, as a precondition to trial, to submit their dispute to mediation—is one of the "new" approaches state and federal courts are employing in their efforts to manage caseloads.

By 2100 B.C., the youthful Hammurabi had vanquished Sumeria and brought it within the Babylonian hegemony. Under his leadership, the administration of justice passed from the priestly class to professional secular judges, clerks, and notaries. The Code of Hammurabi itself, well preserved on a diorite cylinder, consists of some 285 laws organized by subject matter and ranging from the barbaric to the enlightened. The appellate process was advanced. In towns and villages, the mayor and a court of elders decided cases and the proceedings were summarized on clay tablets. In Babylon, a chief magistrate presided over a court of appeals staffed by "the King's Judges." A final appeal might in some cases be taken to the king himself.[5]

Pausing to survey the vast domain that was briefly Persia, we note again that the king was *the* supreme court. Below him was a seven-member High Court of Justice, and then local courts, with priests gradually yielding to laymen and even laywomen as judges. According to Herodotus, Cambyses (529–522 B.C.) devised a unique means to assure the integrity of courts. An unjust judge would be flayed alive and his skin would be used to upholster the judicial bench—to which the late judge's son would be appointed.[6]

The Hebrews

Although our view of appellate apparatus in the ancient Egyptian, Sumerian, Babylonian, and Persian civilizations resembles that of a snapshot, capturing one moment in time, we are able to trace more of an evolution in the Hebraic legal system. Delegation of the justice function from tribal leader to a hierarchy of local courts took place early in the Mosaic period, around 1200 B.C. The process is encapsulated and perhaps telescoped in Exodus. Moses had been fully occupied settling arguments among his people, hearing their plaints from dawn to dusk. His father-in-law, Jethro, came to visit him, and, sizing up the situation, told Moses that he was wearing out both himself and everyone else. "You must," said Jethro, "instruct them in the statutes and laws, and teach them how they must behave. . . . But you must search for capable, God-fearing men among all the people . . . and appoint them over the people. They shall sit as a permanent court for the people; they must refer difficult cases to you but decide simple cases themselves."[7]

As specialization of function took place, the Hebrew judicial system developed into a three-tiered structure. In every village, faithful to the mandate recorded in Deuteronomy 16:18, courts of three elders were appointed, their traditional locus being the city gate. By perhaps 300 B.C., there had developed the finely orchestrated network of sanhedrins ("sitting within council"). The larger cities had Little Sanhedrins of twenty-three members, and Josaphat (or Jehoshaphat) had created in Jerusalem a court of priests, Levites (a tribe that supplied the court officers), and heads of families. This Great Sanhedrin, of seventy or seventy-two, the court of first instance for the inhabitants of Jerusalem, was the court of appeal for all others and appointed the lesser tribunals. With the passage of time, there were professional secular judges at all levels, the lineal descendants of those first appointed by Moses. Large schools of religious law furnished recruits, each of whom served an apprenticeship as one of a judge's several juniors and ultimately succeeded to any vacancy. If a judge proved capable, he would move up, eventually to the supreme court.[8]

China

Two other venerable civilizations, those of the Chinese and the Hindus, do not seem to have made room for a layered justice-dispensing process. Confucius (551–479 B.C.), a judge among his many other roles, placed his stamp ineradicably on Chinese life up to modern times—a span of some two and a half millennia. His concept was that of the wise ruler who, taking all human particulars into account, would arbitrate a face-saving compromise acceptable to all. In a deep and benevolent sense he envisaged a government of men, not of laws. His key official for each province or village was a magistrate or governor in whom was vested all authority—executive, legislative, and judicial—with the emperor in Peking holding over him an appellate power in the form of the fatal silken cord, which, in case of bad judgment or misfortune, commanded suicide.

Lao-tze, traditionally considered Confucius's teacher, had distrusted intellectuals and professed a yearning for as little regulation by law as possible, trusting in spontaneity and simplicity. This proved to be a durable theme in Chinese thought. Law was to play a minor role. Differences were settled not by disputants standing on rights but by their seeking to reestablish harmony. Self-blame was a common response and solvent to a conflict. Mediation was far to be preferred to a lawsuit. And supporting these deep-seated attitudes was a traditionally maladroit organization of judicial administration—an untrained judge from another province, corrupt clerks, vexing delay, and humiliation. The seventh-century emperor K'ang Hsi is said to have articulated a doctrinal defense for this state of affairs, saying, "Lawsuits would tend to increase to a frightful amount, if people were not afraid of the tribunals, and if they felt confident of always finding in them ready and perfect justice. . . . I desire, therefore, that those who have recourse to the tribunals should be treated without any pity, and in such a manner that they shall be disgusted with law, and tremble to appear before a magistrate."[9]

India

The early development of the Hindu legal system is largely lost in the mists of time, at least to me. But I pick up the trail shortly after Alexander's retreat and death, late in the fourth century B.C., when India came into the skilled and fortunate hands of Chandragupta. Justice was meted out by village headmen or councils (panchayats). An inferior and superior court system served districts and provinces, with a royal council at the capital as a supreme court. The king himself, as we have noted elsewhere, was the court of last appeal.[10] By 270 B.C. the personal involvement of the monarch was brought to a high level by Chandragupta's grandson Ashoka, whose Rock Edict VI, inscribed on stone, proclaimed: "Complainants may report to me the concerns of the people at any time, whether I am at dinner or in the harem or in my carriage or in my garden . . . and any dispute or fraud shall be brought forthwith to my notice." Here again is, apparently, the ruler-judge of first and last resort.

Ashoka, if not too good to be true, was too good—or too unrealistic—for neither his philosophy of suppressing tensions in the interests of general harmony, of nonviolence, and of attacking "useless ceremonies and sacrifices" (Dhamma) nor his judicial practices survived him.[11]

At this juncture, where ancient civilization left off and modern civilization began, we might expect the appellate systems of these great civilizations to have continued on their way to perfection, or at least to have bequeathed their institutions to others. But with the demise of the Egyptian and Mesopotamian societies, much of their depositories and rich libraries disappeared, and their processes and institutions proved to be without progeny. As for Hebraic jurisprudence, it did not disappear. It followed every Jewish community throughout the Diaspora, the courts being allowed great sway by civil authorities to the extent that the Middle Ages saw Jewish judicial influence rival that of the original Palestinian courts.[12] But this tradition was internal, not associated with any centralized nation-state.

II. Greece and Rome

All of the ancient systems we have surveyed, either in the first instance or after one or more layers of courts, placed final appellate power in the monarch.

Greece

A more extreme contrast to this kind of autocratic justice cannot be imagined than that of the Greeks in their golden years. Innovative in art, architecture, philosophy, and drama, they also launched the first thoroughgoing democratic experiment in government. They left no room for any complaint about an elitist or undemocratic judiciary. As early as 594 B.C., Solon began cutting back on the adjudicative powers of the archons, the principal magistrates, allowing appeal to the people's courts.[13] Moreover, it was said, Solon was deliberately so obscure in wording his laws that litigants were forced to seek the aid of the popular courts in interpreting those laws.[14]

By Pericles' time, beginning in 462 B.C., the conservative Senate of the Areopagus, which had sought to make itself supreme, was stripped of many of its powers and restricted to trying cases of arson and homicide. As for other types of cases, public arbitrators were first resorted to in an effort to relieve the overcrowded dockets, but, failing satisfaction, the losing party could appeal to fellow citizens assembled as a court.[15]

The popular courts, several of them in session every day, constituted the *heliaea*, or supreme court. They were manned from a jury list of some six thousand, approximately a seventh of Attica's enfranchised citizenry. The juries in specific cases varied from 201 to 2,500 and decided all questions, whether of law or of fact. Almost any issue of politics or administration, as well as private justice, was fodder for decision. The parties would be allotted time by the water clock, witness statements would be read, and arguments would be made. (Demosthenes, during his arguments, would often ask that the flow of water be stopped while he read from a law or deposition.)[16] And, without further ado, the jury of hundreds or thousands would vote. There being no higher source of justice than the people, there was no appeal, even though a Socrates could be condemned to death by a plurality of only sixty in a jury of 501.

Every citizen's turn to serve on a jury came around about every three years. By the time of Pericles, jurors received sizable compensation; jury duty therefore must have been a major industry. While this was a day of the common man, the common man at the apogee of Athenian civilization was, compared with other times and places, uncommon. For a couple of centuries this system apparently worked well, with this remarkable, extroverted, theatergoing, market-shopping-and-talking, assembly-filling, jury-serving populace. The secret may have been that all shared a common stock of experience, values, and aspirations. Gradually, however, the lack of juridical memory, the inability of unguided and untrained juries to decide like cases by the same principles, and the absence of any sense of the importance of precedents so eroded respect for the law that even a man of such social consciousness as Plato despaired of a career in public service.[17]

Rome

So precipitate was the exit of Greece from stage center that in 338 B.C., only nine years after Plato's death, Greece yielded to Philip of Macedon, beginning 2,100 years of subjugation. Two hundred years after Plato's death, both Greece and Macedonia became provinces of Rome, at the very beginning of Rome's signal contributions to the concept of government by laws. In the days of the Roman Republic, the Roman legal apparatus was something of a carbon copy of that of Greece. There were no professional magistrates or principles of judicial direction. Juries, sometimes numbering in the thousands of citizens, were entrusted with deciding both facts and law, intermingling popular feeling and clemency as they saw fit; there was no right of appeal. The key role was that of the orator, whose knowledge of law was far less important than his efficacy in appealing to the jurors.

In the early days of the Roman Empire, at the beginning of our era, under Augustus, the lineaments of a professional legal system began to appear. The office of praetor was created—a full-time secular adjudicator, divorced from any duties of administration. Jurisconsults, who had been mere soothsayers or augurs, became skilled legal counselors, so much so that Augustus decreed that the written opinions of some jurisconsults were to carry the authority of his office—a significant step across the threshold toward the development of legal doctrine. Schools sprang up to train advocates; celebrated professors attracted students from all the empire and the provinces. Under Vespasian, the first endowed law chair in history was established. In Chapter 7 we have quoted the enduring advice of its first occupant, Quintilian, in his "Education of the Advocate."

Jurists began to think and write systematically; they were the first in history to approach law as a rigorous intellectual discipline. A century after Augustus, the emperor Hadrian gathered a cadre of jurists about him and commissioned them to replace the annual pronouncements of praetors with a Perpetual Edict to guide all future judges.

During the ensuing century, scholars brought Roman ju-

risprudence to its height—ironically, just as Roman administration and civilization were deteriorating. The Goths
besieged Rome, leaving Justinian in Byzantium as the heritor
of Roman law. He more than adequately lived up to the
challenge, commissioning seventeen Byzantine Greeks to
gather, organize, and condense all juristic writings into a
permanent, usable digest. All of this enriched both church or
canon law and later civil law systems, and even, ultimately,
English law. The right of appeal became the prized right of
any Roman citizen. We know from Paul that any Roman
citizen, anywhere in the empire, if charged with any offense
meriting death or imprisonment, could claim an appeal to
the emperor.[18]

III. The Dark Ages

Then came that crepuscular era in the western world known
as the Dark Ages. Because of the fragmentation and uncertainty of authority, the reign of law disappeared. The environment posed no incentive for study or teaching of law.
Such law as existed was in the nature of "rules of social
behavior" applicable to certain regions. A competent court
would have been hard to find. Even if such were to be found,
there would have been no will or capacity to enforce a decree.
The goal of dispute settlement was to restore a community
to peaceful coexistence rather than to achieve a "just" solution. The means were supernatural and nonrational.[19]

The Druids administered the Celtic legal system, such as
it was, with absolute power, even to designating human
sacrifices. The only approximation to appellate review was
the legendary gold collar, which the Irish judge Morann
wore. When his judgment was just, it would expand; when
it was not, it would contract and choke him. In Scandinavia,
as in Greece and republican Rome, early justice was unalloyed democracy. At a given phase of the moon, all the free
men, the Al-ting, met near the Hill of Laws. One man, old
or clever or both, a "law-speaker," would propose and expound a decision, and the multitude would shout approval

or disapproval. Montesquieu writes revealingly of such methods of dispute resolution in medieval France as trial by boiling water[20] and judicial combat, in which a litigant might choose a champion to fight for him, the champion's diligence heightened by the threat of having his hand cut off if he lost the battle.[21]

The resolution achieved by judicial combat being likely to be final (that is, resulting in the death of one party), said Montesquieu, "an appeal, such as is established by the Roman and Canon laws, that is, to a superior court in order to rejudge the proceedings of an inferior, was a thing unknown in France."[22] Indeed, the notion of an appeal, like other decision processes, was a challenge to arms, and what came to be called the appeal of false judgment required a vassal who felt himself aggrieved by a judgment to challenge the sentence as unjust and malicious and to fight the peers constituting the court convoked by the lord.[23] Even in those benighted days the principle was accepted that "justice delayed is justice denied." And so if a vassal simply could not obtain any decision, he would, with some risk to himself or his property if he lost, bring the appeal of default of justice before a lord paramount, whose court might then deal with the case.[24] Strangely enough, England observed the same practices in this era. "Appeal" also meant a criminal prosecution, to be resolved through trial by battle, based on the belief that Providence would give victory to the deserving. By the thirteenth century, appeal meant a way of getting a review, but, as in France, only at the price of accusing a judge of malfeasance or a jury of perjury.

These comments about "the Dark Ages" deserve a caveat. For "Dark Ages" is a western rubric; it refers to the period between the decline of "classical" civilization to the revival of learning in "the west." But the origin and flowering of Islam paralleled the Dark Ages. Muhammad died in 632. By the tenth century there had developed a "vast corpus" of legal doctrine.[25]

According to David S. Powers, who reviewed earlier conclusions of scholars that there were no appellate structures in Islamic law, there is substantial evidence of a system of "successor review in which a judge might reconsider and overturn a [predecessor's] judgment" for lack of jurisdiction or conflict with Islamic law. In addition, evidence suggests that the court of the chief judge of a capital city could review decisions of local and provincial judges. And all judges were subject to the head of the caliph's top "mazalim" tribunal. Powers adds that "the distinctive characteristic of Islamic judicial review is its relative *informality*" (emphasis in original), which left much room for "negotiation" with judicial authorities.[26]

Perhaps the most interesting feature revealed by this historical research is the concept of latitudinal rather than vertical appeal embodied in successor review.

We have seen the early civilizations of the Near East develop a structured appellate system, with secular professional judges, a permanent record of proceedings, and the possibility of a final appeal to the sovereign's clemency, which the world was not to enjoy again for two thousand years. Farther east, in China, and in India in Ashoka's time, the goal was not justice for litigants but peace and harmony for the community. In classical Greece, there was no appeal from the popular courts; the people could do no wrong. Imperial Rome gradually restored the appellate idea. It was nourished and sustained for centuries within the church during the Dark Ages, when appeals elsewhere in Europe were exercises in supplicating the supernatural or demonstrating the truth-serving function of brute force or blind chance.

Our story continues in Chapter 2, where we trace the course of the civil and common law traditions that bestride much of today's world.

Notes

2. THE APPELLATE WORLD TODAY

1. Arthur T. von Mehren, "The Comparative Study of Law," 6/7 *Tulane Civil Law Forum* 43, 47 (1991–92).

2. Herman Schwartz, "Constitutional Developments in East Central Europe," 45 *Journal of International Affairs* 71, 78 (1991).

3. *Id.* at 71.

4. Although I give specific page citations to quoted material, I acknowledge a general indebtedness for background on the history and practices of the civil law tradition to Professor John Henry Merryman's *The Civil Law Tradition*, 2nd ed. (Palo Alto: Stanford University Press, 1985).

5. *Id.* at 15.

6. *Id.* at 28.

7. John H. Wigmore, *A Panorama of the World's Legal Systems* (Washington, D.C.: Washington Law Book Company, 1936), pp. 1027, 1031.

8. Merryman, *supra*, note 4, at 29.

9. I am indebted to L. Kinvin Wroth, professor of law and, *inter alia*, legal historian, University of Maine School of Law, for this happy phrase. Letter to author, July 17, 1992.

10. Merryman, *supra*, note 4, at 38.

11. Martin Shapiro, "Appeal," 14 *Law & Society Review* 629, 647 (Spring 1980).

12. Merryman, *supra*, note 4, at 40.

13. *Id.* at 41.

14. Shapiro, *supra*, note 11, at 653.

15. Merryman, *supra*, note 4, at 140.

16. *Id.* at 84.

17. In using the term "English Tradition" in the context of the appellate process, I refer to the institutions and practices applying to appeals from Wales and England. I do not mean "Great Britain," which includes Scotland, which has quite a different legal system. Nor do I, generally, refer to the United Kingdom (except in its relationship with European organizations), which would also embrace Northern Ireland, whose appeals go to the Privy Council.

18. Von Mehren, *supra*, note 1, at 44.

19. D.C.M. Yardley, *Introduction to British Constitutional Law*, 6th ed. (London: Butterworths, 1984), p. 3.

20. *Id.* at 4.

21. Sir Douglas Wass, Foreword, in Ian Harden and Norman Lewis, *The Noble Lie: The British Constitution and the Rule of Law* (London: Hutchinson, 1986), p. ix.

22. Patrick McAuslan and John E. McEldowney, eds., *Law, Legitimacy and the Constitution* (London: Sweet & Maxwell, 1985), p. 59 (comment of Professor McEldowney).

23. Patrick S. Atiyah, "Judicial-Legislative Relations in England," in Robert A. Katzmann, ed., *Judges and Legislators: Toward Institutional Comity* (Brookings Institution: Washington, D.C., 1988), pp. 129, 134.

24. *Id.* at 135.

25. *Id.* at 156.

26. Barton Atkins, "Interventions and Power in Judicial Hierarchies: Appellate Courts in England and the United States," 24 *Law & Society Review* 71, 81 (1990).

27. See Chart 2 in Chapter 3.

28. *Id.*

29. *Id.*

30. Delmar Karlen, *Appellate Courts in the United States and England* (New York: New York University Press, 1963), p. 140.

31. Robert J. Martineau, *Appellate Justice in England and the United States: A Comparative Analysis* (New York: William S. Hein, 1990), p. 43.

32. *Id.* at 101.

33. *Id.* at 192.

34. *Id.* at 67.

35. *Id.* at 128–30.

36. *Id.* at 325.

37. *Id.* at 63.

38. *Id.* at 190.

39. Review on Top Salaries, *Report No. 22—Eighth Report on Top Salaries*, vol. 2, 1985, p. 34.

40. Burton M. Atkins, "Selective Reporting and the Communication of Legal Rights in England," 76 *Judicature* 58, 64 (August–September 1992).

41. Martineau, *supra*, note 31, at 107.

42. *Id.* at 11.

43. Julius Goebel, Jr., *Antecedents and Beginnings to 1801*, vol. 1 of

The *Oliver Wendell Holmes Devise History of the Supreme Court of the United States* (New York: Macmillan, 1971), p. 1.

44. Merryman, *supra*, note 4, at 16.

45. The story is told by Catherine Drinker Bowen in *John Adams and the American Revolution* (Boston: Little, Brown, 1950), pp. 424–39.

46. Wroth, *supra* note 9.

47. Goebel, *supra*, note 43, at 96.

48. Mauro Cappelletti and William Cohen, *Comparative Constitutional Law* (Indianapolis: Bobbs-Merrill, 1979), pp. 9–11.

49. *Id.* at 13.

50. Goebel, *supra* note 43, at 14–15.

51. *Id.* at 19–25.

52. *Id.* at 47 and 18.

53. Lawrence M. Friedman, *A History of American Law*, 2nd ed. (New York: Simon & Schuster, 1985), p. 168.

54. *Id.* at 392.

55. *Id.* at 397.

56. *Id.* at 405.

57. *Id.* at 406.

58. *Id.*

59. Merryman, *supra*, note 4, at 32.

60. Martineau, *supra*, note 31, at 7–8.

61. Karlen, *supra*, note 30, at 157–58.

62. Frank M. Coffin, "Working with the Congress of the Future," ch. 8 of Cynthia Harrison and Russell R. Wheeler, eds., *The Federal Appellate Judiciary in the 21st Century* (Federal Judicial Center, 1989), p. 203.

63. James R. Maxeiner, "1992: High Time for American Lawyers to Learn from Europe, or Roscoe Pound's 1906 Address Revisited," 15 *Fordham International Law Journal* 1, 4 (1991–92).

64. Merryman, *supra*, note 4, at 148.

65. Griffiths, "Judicial Independence Abroad—Controlling Britian's 'Uncontrolled' Constitution," *Judges' Journal*, Summer 1989, at 37.

66. *Id.*

67. David G. T. Williams, Address, *American Law Institute—Remarks and Addresses, 67th Annual Meeting*, May 15–18, 1990, at 44.

68. For the factual statements concerning the European Court of Justice, I rely on Martin Shapiro, "The European Court of Justice," ch. 4 of Alberta M. Sbragia, ed., *Euro-Politics* (Washington, D.C.: Brookings Institution, 1992), pp. 123–56.

69. Williams, *supra*, note 67, at 46.

70. Merryman, *supra*, note 4, at 158.

71. Schwartz, *supra*, note 2, at 81.

3. THE STATE-FEDERAL COURT SYSTEM: "One Whole"

1. Julius Goebel, Jr., *Antecedents and Beginnings to 1801*, vol. 1 of *The Oliver Wendell Holmes Devise History of the Supreme Court of the United States* (New York: Macmillan, 1971), pp. 210–12.

2. *Id.* at 246–47.

3. *The Federalist*, introduction by Edward Mead Earle (New York: Modern Library, 1937), p. 528.

4. *Id.* at 537.

5. Goebel, *supra* note 1, at 502–3.

6. Act of Mar. 3, 1875, '1, 18 Stat. 470.

7. Quoted in David M. O'Brien, *Constitutional Law and Politics*, vol. 1 (New York: Norton, 1991), p. 629.

8. William J. Brennan, Jr., "The Bill of Rights and the States: The Revival of State Constitutions as Guardians of Individual Rights," in Norman Dorsen, ed., *The Evolving Constitution* (Middletown, Conn.: Wesleyan University Press, 1987), pp. 254, 269.

9. G. Alan Tarr and Mary Cornelia Aldis Porter, *State Supreme Courts in State and Nation* (New Haven, Conn.: Yale University Press, 1988), p. 6.

10. David O'Brien, *supra*, note 7, at 628.

11. Daniel J. Meador, "Concluding Remarks: National Conference on State-Federal Judicial Relationships," 78 *Virginia Law Review* 1895, 1900 (November 1992).

12. The average length of time between federal certification and federal application of the state response as reported in 1977 by Professor David Shapiro in his article "Federal Diversity Jurisdiction: A Survey and a Proposal," 91 *Harvard Law Review* 317 (1977).

13. The American Law Institute, *Complex Litigation Project*, Proposed Final Draft (April 5, 1993), pp. 208–9.

14. *Id.*, ch. 4, pp. 205–66 (Draft Proposal '4.01, Comments, and Reporter's Notes).

15. "ALI Finishes Complex Litigation Project . . .," 61 *United States Law Week* 2709 (May 25, 1993).

16. William W. Schwarzer, Nancy E. Weiss, Alan Hirsch, "Judicial Federalism in Action: Coordination of Litigation in State and Federal Courts," 78 *Virginia Law Review* 1689, 1690 (November 1992).

17. *Id.* at 1733.

18. Court Statistics Project, *State Court Caseload Statistics: Annual Report 1989*, National Center for State Courts in cooperation with the Conference of State Court Administrators: Williamsburg, Va., 1991, p. 24.

19. Court Statistics Project, *Annual Report 1990*; number of IACs is derived from cumulating state court data at pp. 185–237; Joy Chapper and Roger Hanson, *Intermediate Appellate Courts: Improving Case Processing* (Williamsburg, Va.: National Center for State Courts, 1990), p. xi.

20. Court Statistics Project, *supra* note 18, at 26–27.

21. Chapper and Hanson, *supra* note 19, at xi and 63.

22. *Id.* at xi; *see also* Court Statistics Project, *supra*, note 18, at 23–24.

23. Benjamin Kaplan, *Do Intermediate Appellate Courts Have a Lawmaking Function?* 70 *Massachusetts Law Review* No.1, at 10, 12 (March 1985).

24. Chapper and Hanson, *supra* note 19, at xiii; Court Statistics Project, *supra*, note 18, at 24–28.

25. 285 U.S. 262, 311 (1932).

26. Chapper and Hanson, *supra* note 19, at 15–22.

27. John H. Henn, "Civil Interlocutory Appeals to the Single Justice Under Massachusetts General Laws, Chapter 231, '118, First Paragraph," *Boston Bar Journal*, January–February 1989, reprinted in *Practice and Procedure Before a Single Justice of the Massachusetts Appellate Courts* (Massachusetts Continuing Legal Education, Inc., 1990), p. 139.

28. Rudolph Kass, "Reflections of a Single Justice," reprinted in *Practice and Procedure Before a Single Justice of the Massachusetts Appellate Courts, supra* note 27, at 31.

29. *Id.*

30. F. Anthony Mooney, "Single Justice Practice: The Lawyer's Perspective," reprinted in *Practice and Procedure Before a Single Justice of the Massachusetts Appellate Courts, supra* note 27, at 5, 13–15.

31. 90 *Harvard Law Review* 489 (1977).

32. Justice Shirley Abrahamson (Wisconsin), "Reincarnation of State Courts," 36 *Southwestern Law Journal* 951 (1982).

33. Justice Stewart Pollock (New Jersey), "State Constitutions as Separate Sources of Fundamental Rights," 35 *Rutgers Law Review* 707 (1983).

34. Justice Stanley Mosk (California), "State Constitutionalism After Warren: Avoiding the Potomac's Ebb and Flow," in *Developments in State Constitutional Law* (New York: McGraw-Hill, 1985), p. 201.

35. Ronald K. L. Collins, "Looking to the States," *National Law Journal*, Sept. 29, 1986, at S-2.

36. Paul Marcotte, "Federalism and the Rise of State Courts," *ABA Journal*, April 1, 1987, at 60, 62 (citing Professor Collins).

37. Barry Latzer, "The Hidden Conservatism of the State Court 'Revolution,' " 74 *Judicature* 190 (December–January 1991) (citing Professor Collins).

38. Marcotte, *supra* note 36, at 62.

39. *Id.* at 62, 64.

40. *Burbine* v. *Moran*, 753 F.2d 178 (1st Cir. 1985), *rev'd Moran* v. *Burbine*, 475 U.S. 412 (1986).

41. *State* v. *Stoddard*, 206 Conn. 157 (1988); *Haliburton* v. *State*, 514 So. 2d 1088 (Fla. 1987); *People* v. *Houston*, 724 P. 2d 1166 (Cal. 1986); *People* v. *Griggs*, Ill. Sup. Ct., No. 69790 (Sept. 24, 1992), 52 *Criminal Law Reporter* 1029–1030 (Oct. 14, 1992).

42. Latzer, *supra* note 37, at 190.

43. *Id.* at 193.

44. For a general survey of such efforts, *see* Andrew Blum, "Systems Try to Stretch Their Dollars," *National Law Journal*, July 1, 1991, at 1; and report of American Bar Association Special Committee on Funding the Justice System, *Funding the Justice System—A Call for Action*, August 1992.

45. American Bar Association Special Committee, *supra* note 44, at ii.

46. National Center for State Courts Information Service, "Special Report: Trends in the State Courts," 15 *State Court Journal* 4, 9 (Winter 1991).

47. Norman Krivosha, "In Celebration of Their 50th Anniversary of Merit Selection," 74 *Judicature* 128, 131 (October–November 1990).

48. *Chisom* v. *Roemer*, 111 S.Ct. 2354, 2367 (1991).

49. Mark Hansen, "The High Cost of Judging," 77 *American Bar Association Journal* 44 (September 1991).

50. For a recent and comprehensive analysis of this problem, the reader is referred to Larry Kramer, "Diversity Jurisdiction," *Brigham Young University Law Review* 97 (1990). *See also* my own article "Judicial Gridlock: The Case for Abolishing Diversity Jurisdiction," 10 *Brookings Review* 34 (Winter 1992).

51. Kramer, *supra* note 50, at 99–100.

4. IN CHAMBERS

1. Reginald L. Hine, *Confessions of an Un-Common Attorney* (New York: Macmillan, 1947), p. 4.

2. John Bilyeu Oakley and Robert S. Thompson, *Law Clerks and the Judicial Process* Berkeley and Los Angeles: (University of California Press, 1980), p. 11.

3. Karl Llewellyn, *The Common Law Tradition* (Boston: Little, Brown, 1960), p. 321.

4. Annual Report of the Director of the Administrative Office of the United States Courts, 1990, Table 28, p. 41.

5. Samuel Williston, *Life and Law* (Boston: Little, Brown, 1940), p. 92.

6. Oakley and Thompson, *supra* note 2, at 14.

7. *Id.* at 15.

8. Federal Judicial Center, *Judicial Writing Manual* (Washington, D.C., 1991), pp. 10–11.

9. American Bar Association, *Judicial Opinion Writing Manual* (St. Paul, Minn.: West, 1991), p. v.

10. Lewis Thomas, *The Youngest Science: Notes of a Medicine-Watcher*, (New York: Viking, 1983),

11. Irving Stone, *The Agony and the Ecstasy* (New York: Doubleday, 1961), p. 27.

5. Where Appeals Begin

1. *Coleman* v. *De Minico*, 730 F.2d 42, 47 n.4 (1st Cir. 1984).

2. *McGrath* v. *Spirito*, 733 F.2d 967, 969 (1st Cir. 1984).

3. John C. Godbold, "Twenty Pages and Twenty Minutes: Effective Advocacy on Appeal," 30 *Southwestern Law Journal* 801, 804 (1976).

4. Robert L. Stern, *Appellate Practice in the United States*, 2nd ed. (Washington, D.C.: Bureau of National Affairs, 1989), p. 71.

5. *Lisa* v. *Fournier Marine Corp.*, 866 F.2d 530, 531 (1st Cir. 1989).

6. *Id.*

7. *Id.* at 532.

6. Briefs: Reflections of an Advocates' Consumer

1. Robert L. Stern, *Appellate Practice in the United States*, 2nd ed. (Washington, D.C.: Bureau of National Affairs, 1989), p. 316.

7. Oral Argument: Conversing with the Court

1. 4 Wheaton 17 U.S.) 518 (1819).

2. Maurice G. Baxter, *One and Inseparable Daniel Webster and the Union* (Cambridge, Mass.: Belknap Press, 1984), p. 169.

3. *Id.*

4. Frank M. Coffin, *A Lexicon of Oral Advocacy* (St. Paul: National Institute for Trial Advocacy, 1984), p. 14.

5. *Id.* at 15.

6. William H. Rehnquist, *The Supreme Court: How It Was, How It Is* (New York: Morrow, 1987), p. 276.

7. Myron H. Bright, "The Ten Commandments of Oral Argument," 67 *American Bar Association Journal* 1136, 1139 (September 1981).

8. Myron H. Bright, "The Power of the Spoken Word: In Defense of Oral Argument," 72 *Iowa Law Review* 35, 40 n.34 (1986).

9. *Id.* at 40 n.32.

10. "The Argument of an Appeal," delivered as an address before the Association of the Bar of the City of New York, October 22, 1940, and printed in 26 *American Bar Association Journal* 895 (1940).

11. "John W. Davis Revisited," address to General Bench & Bar Conference, Puerto Rico, 1981.

12. Coffin, *supra* note 4.

13. John H. Wigmore, *A Panorama of the World's Legal Systems* (Washington, D.C.: Washington Law Book, 1936), p. 437.

14. The source is an article by the late Murray I. Gurfein entitled "Appellate Advocacy, Modern Style." Although I possess a printed copy, the publication is not mentioned. I have exhausted librarians' patience in pursuing computer searches for the source. Though unsuccessful in locating

a source, I insist on including the quotation, because it is so well said and sounds exactly like Judge Gurfein.

15. Myron H. Bright and Richard S. Arnold, "Oral Argument? It May Be Crucial!" 70 *American Bar Association Journal* 68, 69 (September 1984).

16. Myron H. Bright, "The Ten Commandments of Oral Argument," 67 *American Bar Association Journal* 1136, 1137 (September 1981).

17. His life is colorfully portrayed by Evan Thomas in *The Man to See* (New York: Simon & Schuster, 1991).

18. *Id.* at 441.

19. *Id.* at 442.

20. All of this account, including quotations, is derived from an article by David Lauter, "On Trial: The Tavoulareas Case," *National Law Journal*, Oct. 21, 1985, at 13.

21. Thomas, *supra* note 17, at 443.

22. *Tavoulareas* v. *Piro*, 817 F. 2d 762, 777 (D.C. Cir. 1987, en banc).

23. Thomas, *supra* note 17, at 444.

8. The Judges' Conference

1. McConkie, "Decision-Making in State Supreme Courts," 59 *Judicature* 337–43 (1976), included in Robert J. Martineau, *Cases and Materials on Appellate Practice and Procedures* (St. Paul, Minn.: West, 1987), 480–81.

2. William R. Rehnquist, *The Supreme Court: How It Was, How It Is* (New York: Morrow, 1987), p. 290.

3. *Id.* at 295.

4. Robert L. Stern, *Appellate Practice in the United States*, 2nd ed. (Washington, D.C.: Bureau of National Affairs, 1989), pp. 475–76.

9. Opinions I: Organizing the Workload
and Doing an Opinion

1. Two recent manuals have been published: the first, by a group of distinguished federal judges under the aegis of the Federal Judicial Center, *Judicial Writing Manual*, 1991; the second, by a group mainly composed of distinguished state judges under the auspices of the Appellate Judges Conference, Judicial Administration Division of the American Bar Association, *Judicial Opinion Writing Manual*, 1991. The latter, at p. 151, contains "The Art and Science of Appellate Opinion Drafting: An Annotated Bibliography, 1977–1987," by Michael J. Slinger. Notable books include Ruggero J. Aldisert, *Opinion Writing* (St. Paul, Minn.: West, 1990); B. E. Witkin, *Manual on Appellate Court Opinions* (St. Paul, Minn.: West, 1977); and Robert A. Leflar, *Appellate Judicial Opinions* (St. Paul, Minn.: West, 1974).

2. John W. Cooley, "How Decisions Are Made in the Appellate Courts," 26 *Judges' Journal* No. 2, at 2,44 (Spring 1987).

3. *Id.* at 45.

4. *The Compact Edition of the Oxford English Dictionary* (Oxford, England: Oxford University Press, 21st printing in U.S. 1981), p. 3399.

5. Federal Judicial Center, *supra* note 1, at 9, quoting R. A. Wasserstrom, *The Judicial Decision: Toward a Theory of Legal Justification* 27 (1961).

6. *Id.* at 9.

7. Frank M. Coffin, *The Ways of a Judge: Reflections from the Federal Appellate Bench* (Boston: Houghton Mifflin, 1980).

8. *Id.* at 159–60.

9. *Id.* at 155.

10. Opinions II: Working with Law Clerks

1. Ruggero J. Aldisert, *Opinion Writing*, (St. Paul, Minn.: West, 1990) pp. 8–9.

2. Federal Judicial Center, *Judicial Writing Manual*, 1991, p. 11.

11. Opinions III: The Workings of Collegiality

1. *Report of the Federal Courts Study Committee*, April 2, 1990, p. 8.

2. Robert A. Leflar, *Appellate Judicial Opinions* (St. Paul, Minn.: West, 1974), p. 210.

3. William R. Rehnquist, *The Supreme Court: How It Was, How It Is* (New York: Morrow, 1987), p. 269.

4. *Id.* at 293.

5. Walter P. Gewin, "Opinions—Dissents, Special Concurrences, Policy, Techniques," 63 *Federal Rules of Decision* 594, 595, 599 (1973).

12. On Judging Appeals I: The Quest for Legitimacy

1. Alvin B. Rubin, book reviews of *The Ways of a Judge: Reflections from the Federal Appellate Bench*, and *Courts of Appeals in the Federal Judicial System: A Study of the Second, Fifth, and District of Columbia Circuits*, 130 *University of Pennsylvania Law Review* 220, 224 (1981).

2. 5 U.S. (1 Cranch) 137 (1803).

3. Julius Goebel, Jr., *Antecedents and Beginnings to 1801*, vol. 1 of *The Oliver Wendell Holmes Devise History of the Supreme Court of the United States* (New York: Macmillan, 1971), pp. 58–59.

4. 8 Coke Rep. 107 (1610).

5. *Id.* at 118a.

6. Goeble, *supra* note 3, at 58.

7. *Id.* at 92–93.

8. *Id.* at 73–91.

9. *Id.* at 95.

10. *Id.* at 96.

11. *Id.* at 102. The states were Delaware, Georgia, Maryland, Massachusetts, New Hampshire, and Pennsylvania.

12. Louis Fisher, *Constitutional Dialogues: Interpretation as Political Process* (Princeton, N.J.: Princeton University Press, 1988), p. 47. The states were Connecticut, New Jersey, New York, North Carolina, Rhode Island, and Virginia.

13. *Bayard* v. *Singleton*, North Carolina (plaintiff, deriving title from British subject, wins suit against defendant, claiming under post-independence law confiscating land in question). Goebel, *supra* note 3, at 130. *Rutgers* v. *Waddington*, New York (patriot owner of property loses against British merchant, the court interpreting a New York statute, in light of the law of nations, to be of no help to plaintiff). *Id.* at 132–37. *Trevett* v. *Weeden*, Rhode Island (plaintiff, under new law to enforce new paper money law, sued butcher, who refused to accept his bills; court struck down the new law as unconstitutional). *Id.* at 137–40.

14. Goebel, *supra* note 3, at 131 n. 129.

15. *Id.* at 209.

16. Louis Fisher, *supra* note 12, at 49.

17. Goebel, *supra* note 3, at 239.

18. *The Federalist*, introduction by Edward Mead Earle (New York: Modern Library, 1937), pp. 505–6.

19. Goebel, *supra* note 3, at 330.

20. *Id.* at 338.

21. *Id.* at 129.

22. *Id.* at 388.

23. Louis Fisher, *supra* note 12, at 62–63.

24. Frank M. Coffin, "Working with the Congress of the Future," in C. Harrison and R. Wheeler, eds., *The Federal Appellate Judiciary in the 21st Century* (Federal Judicial Center, 1989), p. 203.

25. *Id.* at 207.

26. *Id.* at 204.

27. The Report of the National Commission on the Public Service, *Leadership for America—Rebuilding the Public Service* (Washington, D.C.: 1989), p. 17.

28. *Id.* at 41.

29. *Id.* at 44.

30. *Id.* at 3.

31. Paul C. Light, *Monitoring Government: Inspectors General and the Search for Accountability* (Washington, D.C.: Brookings Institution and Governance Institute, 1993), p. 3.

32. *Id.* at 230.

33. *Id.* at 224.

34. Stephen Breyer, *Breaking The Vicious Circle: Toward Effective Risk Regulation* (Cambridge, Mass.: Harvard University Press, 1993), p. 63.

35. Karl N. Llewellyn, *The Common Law Tradition: Deciding Appeals* (Boston: Little, Brown, 1960), p. 213 and n. 206.

36. Richard A. Posner, *The Problems of Jurisprudence* (Cambridge, Mass.: Harvard University Press, 1990), p. 23.

37. Eric Rakowski, book review of "Posner's Pragmatism," 104 *Harvard Law Review* 1681, 1686, (May 1991).

38. Ronald Dworkin, *Taking Rights Seriously* (Cambridge, Mass.: Harvard University Press, 1977), p. 105.

39. *Id.* at 107.

40. Benjamin Kaplan, book review of *The Ways of a Judge: Reflections from the Appellate Bench*, 95 *Harvard Law Review* 528, 533 (December 1981).

41. Frank M. Coffin, book review of *The Morality of Consent*, 56 *Boston University Law Review* 1029, 1039–40 (November 1976).

13. ON JUDGING APPEALS II: FAMILIAR WATERS

1. Charles P. Curtis, Jr., and Ferris Greenslet, eds., *The Practical Cogitator* (Boston: Houghton Mifflin, 1945), pp. 412–13.

2. Karl N. Llewellyn, in *The Common Law Tradition: Deciding Appeals* (Boston: Little, Brown, 1960), at pp. 521–35 in "Appendix C: Canons on Statutes," has presented a classic catalogue of opposing canons of statutory construction.

14. ON JUDGING APPEALS III: UNCHARTED DEPTHS

1. *See Duncan* v. *Louisiana*, 391 U.S. 145, 148 (1968). Professor David M. O'Brien, in vol. 2 of his *Constitutional Law and Politics* (New York: Norton, 1991), at pp. 280–81, presents a table of cases which accomplished "The Selective Nationalization of the Bill of Rights Plus Other Fundamental Rights."

2. Robert E. Heilbroner, *An Inquiry into the Human Prospect* (New York: Norton, 1975), pp. 137–38.

3. Irving Brant, *The Bill of Rights* (Indianapolis: Bobbs-Merrill, 1965), pp. 12, 15.

4. Max Farrand, *Records of the Federal Convention of 1787* (New Haven, Conn.: Yale University Press, 1966), vol. 1, pp. 400–401.

5. Brant, *supra* note 3, at 46.

6. Samuel P. Huntington, *American Politics: The Promise of Disharmony* (Cambridge, Mass.: Harvard University Press, 1981), p. 17.

7. *Bolling* v. *Sharpe*, 347 U.S. 497, 499 n. 11 (1954).

8. Benjamin N. Cardozo, *The Nature of the Judicial Process* (New Haven, Conn.: Yale University Press, 1921).

9. Frank M. Coffin, "Justice and Workability: Un Essai," 5 *Suffolk University Law Review* 565, 571 (1971).

10. *Id.* at 571.

11. *Id.* at 572.

12. *The American Heritage Dictionary of the English Language* (Boston: Houghton Mifflin, 1973), p. 1023 (discussion of synonyms of "possible").

13. Laurence H. Tribe, *American Constitutional Law*, 2nd ed. (Mineola, N.Y.: Foundation Press, 1988), p. 1445.

14. Frank M. Coffin, "Judicial Balancing: The Protean Scales of Justice," 63 *New York University Law Review* 16 (April 1988).

15. 106 S. Ct. 2841 (1986).

16. *Id.* at 2848.

17. 483 U.S. 868 (1987).

18. 1992 Annual Report of the Director, Administrative Office of the United States Courts, pp. 11, 19 (Federal Officers and Probationers).

19. 482 U.S. 78 (1987).

20. *Id.* at 89.

21. *Id.*

22. 480 U.S. 709 (1987).

23. *Id.* at 721.

24. *Id.* at 724–25.

25. 435 F.2d 1182 (1st Cir. 1970).

26. *Id.* at 1184.

27. *Id.* at 1185.

28. 408 U.S. 564 (1972).

29. *Id.* at 573.

30. *Id.* at 574 note 13.

31. 520 F.2d 374 (1st Cir. 1975).

32. *Meachum* v. *Fano*, 427 U.S. 215, 224 (1976).

33. *Id.* at 228.

34. *Id.* at 225.

35. 753 F.2d 178 (1st Cir. 1985).

36. *Id.* at 184–85.

37. 475 U.S. 412 (1986).

38. *Id.* at 422.

39. *Id.* at 423–24.

40. *Id.* at 426–27.

41. Louis Fisher, *Constitutional Dialogues: Interpretation as Political Process* (Princeton, N.J.: Princeton University Press, 1988), p. 8.

42. 347 U.S. 483 (1954).

43. Louis Fisher, "The Curious Belief in Judicial Supremacy," 25 *Suffolk University Law Review* 85, 113–14 (Spring 1991).

44. 411 U.S. 1 (1973).

45. *Id.* at 37.

46. *Id.* at 36.

47. 457 U.S. 202 (1982).

48. *Id.* at 221.

49. 478 U.S. 263, 285 (1986).

50. *Southern Burlington County NAACP* v. *Township of Mount Laurel,* 92 N.J. 158, 456 A.2d 390 (1983).

51. James S. Liebman, "Implementing *Brown* in the Nineties: Political Reconstruction, Liberal Recollection, and Litigatively Enforced Legislative Reform," 76 *Virginia Law Review* 349 (April 1990).

52. *Id.* at 368.

53. *Id.* at 372.

54. *Id.* at 378.

55. *Id.* at 423–24. *See also* Molly McUsic, "The Use of Educational Clauses in School Finance Reform Litigation," 28 *Harvard Journal on Legislation* 307 (1991); Richard J. Stark, "Education Reform: Judicial Interpretation of State Constitutions' Education Finance Provisions—Adequacy vs. Equality," 1991 *Annual Survey of American Law* 609.

56. Charles M. Haar and Daniel Wm. Fessler, *The Wrong Side of the Tracks* (New York: Simon & Schuster, 1986).

57. *Id.* at 20.

58. *Id.* at 200.

59. *Id.* at 228.

60. Tribe, *supra* note 13, at 779.

15. On the Future

1. Frank M. Coffin, "Research for Efficiency *and* Quality: Review of *Managing Appeals in Federal Courts,*" 138 *University of Pennsylvania Law Review* 1857, 1865–66 (June 1990).

2. *Id.* at 1867.

3. *Id.* at 1869.

4. *Id.* at 1870.

5. I have made my argument in detail in my article "Judicial Gridlock—The Case for Abolishing Diversity Jurisdiction," 10 *Brookings Review* 34 (Winter 1992).

6. *See* Debra Cassens Moss, "Judges Under Fire: ALJ Independence at Issue," 77 *American Bar Association Journal* 56 (November 1991).

7. The *Ohio State Law Journal* has published a series of articles, "Judges on Judging," beginning with my own article, "Grace Under Pressure: A Call for Judicial Self-Help," 50 *Ohio State Law Journal* 399 (1988). Others include Deanell Reese Tacha, "Judges and Legislators: Renewing the Relationship," 52 *Ohio St. L. J.* 279 (1991); Abner J. Mikva, "Statutory Interpretation: Getting the Law to Be Less Common," 50 *Ohio St. L. J.* 979 (1989); and James L. Oakes, "Grace Notes on 'Grace Under Pressure,' " 50 *Ohio St. L. J.* 701 (1989).

8. Jessica Copen, "Courts of the Future," 77 *American Bar Association Journal* 74 (June 1991).

9. Robert A. Katzmann, ed., *Judges and Legislators: Toward Institutional Comity* (Washington, D.C.: Brookings Institution, 1988), p. 7.

10. Remarks of Chief Justice Randall T. Shepard of Indiana in panel discussion, "Building Bridges Instead of Walls: Fostering Communication Between Judges and Legislators," 75 *Judicature* 167, 169 (October–November 1991).

11. I have reported on these forces in my chapter "Working with the Congress of the Future" in *The Federal Appellate Judiciary in the 21st Century*, Cynthia Harrison and Russell R. Wheeler, eds. (Federal Judicial Center, 1989), p. 199.

12. Much of the following information concerning state policing systems is based on a chapter by Professor Jeffrey M. Shaman, "Regulation of the Judiciary: The State Commission System," in *Ethics in the Courts: Policing Behavior in the Federal Judiciary* (National Legal Center for the Public Interest, 1990), p. 47.

13. Lisa L. Milord, "Adoption of the 1990 ABA Model Code of Judicial Conduct: A Progress Report," 14 *Judicial Conduct Reporter No. 1* 1, 6 (Spring 1992).

14. House Report No. 512 on the Judicial Improvements Act, 101st Cong. 2d Sess. 11, reprinted in 1990 U.S.C.C.A.N. 6879, 6889.

15. *Report on the National Commission on Judicial Discipline and Removal* (Washington, D.C., August 2, 1993), p. 5.

16. *Id.* at 6.

17. Malcolm M. Lucas, "Is Inadequate Funding Threatening Our System of Justice?" 74 *Judicature*, at 292 April–May 1991.

18. ABA Special Committee on Funding the Justice System, *Funding the Justice: A Call to Action*, August 1992, at 3. *See also* "Excerpts from a Report by the ABA Special Committee on Funding the Justice System," 32 *Judges' Journal* No. 1, at 7 (Winter 1993).

19. Frank M. Coffin, "The Federalist No. LXXXVI on Relations Between the Judiciary and Congress," 4 Brookings Review 27 (Winter/Spring 1986).

20. Hans A. Linde, "Observations of a State Court Judge," in Katzman, ed., *supra* note 9, at 117.

21. Shepard, *supra* note 10.

22. Besides Katzman, ed., *supra* note 9, Governance Institute work includes Robert A. Katzmann, "Building Bridges: Courts, Congress and Guidelines for Communication," *Brookings Review*, Spring 1991, at 42–50 (based on the supplementing colloquium at the Wilson Center); Robert A. Katzmann, "Bridging the Statutory Gulf Between Courts and Congress: A Challenge for Positive Political Theory," 80 *Georgetown Law Journal* 653–69 (1992) (reporting on statutory housekeeping project); Frank M. Coffin, "Communication Among the Branches: Can the Bar Serve as a Catalyst?" 75 *Judicature* 125 (October–November 1991).

23. Katzman, ed., *supra* note 9, at 176–77.

24. Frank M. Coffin, "Communication Among the Branches: Can the Bar Serve as a Catalyst?" 75 *Judicature* 125, 126, (October–November 1991).

25. ABA Special Committee, *supra* note 18, at 26–28.

26. House Report No. 512, *supra* note 14, at 6889.

APPENDIX: THE APPELLATE IDEA IN HISTORY

1. For much of the overview of history in this chapter, I am indebted to John H. Wigmore's *A Panorama of the World's Legal Systems* (Washington, D.C.: Washington Law Book Company, 1936). Where no specific reference is indicated, the source is Wigmore. Although *Panorama* is an aging work by a renowned scholar of the law of evidence, who was writing for fun rather than prestige or profit, I have not found its like for interest and stimulation.

2. Judges 4:4.

3. Edgar J. Goodspeed and J. M. Porvis Smith, eds., *The Short Bible: An American Translation* (New York: Modern Library, 1940), p. 109.

4. Will Durant, *Our Oriental Heritage* (New York: Simon & Schuster, 1954), p. 127.

5. *Id.* at 232.

6. *Id.* at 361.

7. Exodus 18:13–22.

8. This description of the ancient Hebrew judicial system, in addition to relying on Wigmore, is largely drawn from Roland de Vaux, "Ancient Israel," in *Social Institutions* (New York: McGraw-Hill, 1965), vol. 1, pp. 152–53.

9. Rene David and John E. C. Brierley, *Major Legal Systems in the World Today*, 2nd ed. (New York: Free Press, 1978), p. 480.

10. Durant, *supra* note 4, at 444.

11. Romila Thapar, *A History of India* (Harmondsworth, England: Penguin, 1966), vol. 1, pp. 87–88.

12. "Rabbinical Courts: Modern-Day Solomons," 6 *Columbia Journal of Law and Social Problems* at 52 reprinted in *Studies in Jewish Jurisprudence*, ed. Edward M. Gerschfield (New York: Hermon Press, 1971), vol. 2.

13. Plutarch, *The Lives of the Noble Grecians and Romans*, trans. John Dryden (New York: Modern Library), pp. 107–8.

14. *Id.* at 108.

15. Will Durant, *The Life of Greece* (New York: Simon & Schuster, 1939), pp. 116, 247, 257, 260.

16. Daniel J. Boorstin, *The Discoverers* (New York: Random House, 1983), p. 30.

17. Wigmore, *supra* note 1, at 313–14, citing W. S. Ferguson, *The Fall of the Athenian Empire: Law and Politics in Athens* (Cambridge Ancient History, 1927), vol. 5, p. 349.

18. The claim was taken seriously. When Paul said, "I appeal to Caesar!" the Roman governor replied, "You have appealed to Caesar: to Caesar you shall go." Shortly thereafter Paul, a superb advocate, persuaded a higher

official, King Agrippa, of his innocence, but too late. For Agrippa confided to the governor, "The fellow could have been discharged, if he had not appealed to the emperor." Acts 25:12, 26:32, *The New England Bible* (Oxford: Oxford University Press, 1970) pp. 183, 185.

19. David and Brierley, *supra* note 9, at 35–36.

20. Montesquieu, *The Spirit of Laws* (Chicago: Encyclopedia Britannica, 1952), p. 239.

21. *Id.* at 245.

22. *Id.* at 247.

23. *Id.* at 247–51.

24. *Id.* at 249–51.

25. David S. Powers, "On Judicial Review in Islamic Law," 26 *Law & Society Review* 315, 319 (1992).

26. *Id.* at 336.

Index